Also by Frank Coffee

THE SELF-SUFFICIENT HOUSE
THE COMPLETE KIT HOUSE CATALOG

by Frank Coffee

SIMON AND SCHUSTER
NEW YORK

Everything You Need to Know About Creative Home Financing

New, *Affordable* Ways to Buy
(and Sell) a Home, Condo, or Co-op

Published by Simon and Schuster
A Division of Simon & Schuster, Inc.
Simon & Schuster Building
Rockefeller Center
1230 Avenue of the Americas
New York, New York 10020
SIMON AND SCHUSTER and colophon are registered trademarks
of Simon & Schuster, Inc.
Designed by Irving Perkins Associates
Manufactured in the United States of America

4   5   6   7   8   9   10

Library of Congress Cataloging in Publication Data
Coffee, Frank.
Everything you need to know about creative home financing.

Includes index.
1. Real estate business.   2. Housing—Finance.
3. Mortgage loans.   I. Title.
HD1375.C59   1982   332.7′22   82–10544
ISBN 0-671-46169-9 pbk.

*To the
baby-boom
generation*

Contents

Introduction

We're going through one of the most difficult times in history for would-be home buyers. Never have so many wanted to buy and so few been held to be able. With double-digit inflation and high mortgage interest rates threatening to become as permanent as death and taxes, fewer than one in twenty U.S. families, present homeowners included, could, in bankers' terms, "qualify" to buy a new median-priced house as a first-time buyer today.

But that's only if you accept that the home-buying rules applied in making that assessment were brought down from the mountain by Moses, or that the number of ways that you can buy a house are as limited as were the color choices with Henry Ford's Model T. It's simply not true that only the very rich can afford homeownership under present economic conditions. Where there's sufficient will to buy a house, whether a split-level in suburbia or a condominium in town, there's usually a way. At least 33 that we'll be telling you about.

If you are facing that great quandary, *how to make home-buying affordable,* chances are you'll find a solution in this book that could work for you. In addition to discoursing on such home-buying fundamentals as How Much House Can You Afford? and The Down-Payment Dilemma, this book tells you everything you need to know about creative home financing, which minimizes reliance by buyer and seller on traditional lending sources and has become the key to affordable home-buying today. It also guides you through the maze of alternative financing plans (creative after a fashion) developed by lending institutions and banking regulators to be more in tune with today's tough economic climate.

The financing of homes is going through a revolution, not an evolution, and conventional financing—the long-term, fixed-rate mortgage on which the borrower makes monthly payments that cover both principal and interest—has been given the boot by most moneylenders. Taking the place of this heritage of the Great Depression are such conditionally useful (we'll have more to say about that later) new instruments as graduated-payment mortgages, with monthly payments starting at a relatively low level and increasing gradually, over the years, as the younger home buyer's income also (presumably) grows; variable- and renegotiable-rate mortgages, with payments adjusted periodically, up or down, to reflect the national mortgage interest rate on new loans; and shared-appreciation mortgages, with the lender charging interest at below-market rates in return for a share in the capital gain realized when the house is sold.

If you can't come up with the large down payment often called for with more traditional home financing, there are such worthknowing-about alternatives as land leases and lease-options, and some hypercreative "nothing-down" techniques possible with seller financing. There also are "interest-only" bank loans, which reduce monthly mortgage payments for the first five years by delaying repayment of the loan. Instead of building equity through amortization (gradual debt reduction), the buildup today more often comes through appreciation in the home's market value. Some of these "easy-start" plans, designed with young people with typically rising income patterns in mind, are, at least in the beginning, a lot like paying rent, only with the advantage that you have a sizable tax deduction where renters do not, and build equity as the house "inflates" in value.

If you're single, and you thought the dream of owning a home would, tantalizingly, like a carrot on a stick, remain forever just beyond your reach, with spiraling housing prices always exceeding your ability to qualify for the mortgage needed, you might want to investigate co-purchasing. That's the pooling of your resources with a co-mortgagor in a like situation for what neither of you could afford separately. If your means are more modest, but you are industrious and handy with tools, the route to take might be urban homesteading, under which, in many cities, both large and small, it is possible to acquire an older house in need of renovation for as little as one dollar.

A house *is* your best hedge against inflation. Buy whatever you can barely afford in a "starter house" and begin building equity. With appreciation and refinancing, you just might be able to trade up from that less-than-perfect first home to that dream house in a few short years. It's not an uncommon practice these days. Many families move up the housing ladder to something bigger, newer, and more luxurious every three to five years. Housing prices climbed an average of 10.3 percent a year from 1971 to 1981, and virtually any property acquired when exercising commonsense judgment today will outstrip inflation and be worth more tomorrow, possibly a lot more.

If you're the typical first-timer, you'll buy an existing, or resale, house and not a newly built one. Resales predominate in the housing market, outnumbering new-home purchases by better than three to one. And it's here that financing can be its most malleable, with buyer and seller rewriting the home-buying rules. Not surprisingly, the majority of older-home sales since 1980 have been effected via creative financing, using the existing financing on the property or having the seller help with the financing.

Don't wait for mortgage interest rates (not to be confused with the prime rate, which is short term and has no direct relationship with long-term rates) to tumble. Gradual deregulation of the banking industry, under the far-reaching Depository Institutions Deregulation and Monetary Control Act of 1980, and the necessity to pay higher interest rates to attract savings are expected to keep mortgage interest rates in double digits most of the time in the 1980s. When mortgage rates do come down even a few percentage points, housing prices are bound to surge. A buyer's market will be turned into a seller's market. There just aren't going to be that many housing units available.

With 42 million Americans entering their thirties—the prime house-buying age group—during the decade, and allowing for the usual attrition due to demolition, fire, and flood, housing-market analysts forecast an effective demand for 2.4 million* new houses and apartment units per year through the 1980s. New construction, however, has been falling below that underlying demand by nearly one million units per year. At the 1980–81 building rate, and with many home builders having quit the business or gone bankrupt, we could be facing a monumental housing shortage.

It's not just inflation and high mortgage interest rates that are contributing to the housing crisis. The old demographic that first-time buyers almost without exception were young married couples with one or more children no longer is valid. In recent surveys, "a home of one's own" was the No. 1 priority on the "must-have" list of single persons in the 24-to-29 age bracket. The singles market, with more divorces and more career-minded individuals choosing not to marry, is growing like Topsy. Today, nearly one out of every four homes sold—duplexes, town houses, and condominium apartments included—go to singles.

With the post-World War II baby-boom generation, the 72 million of us born between 1946 and 1964, moving through the nation's economy like a pig in a python, there is a deep concern that a severe shortage of rental housing and the rising costs of homeownership could trigger enormous social problems. One housing authority, Leon Weiner, a past president of the National Association of Home Builders, has warned that "unless these problems are dealt with successfully, housing may become the Vietnam of the 1980s."

All of which means that you who thought you couldn't afford to buy a home more than likely *can't afford not to buy one*. And the sooner you apply what you can learn here the better. Based on the national average of housing appreciation during the past 10 years, each day's delay in buying a $70,000 home—approximately the median price of a new single-family house in January 1982—could cost you an estimated $20 per day. That's $600 per month, $7,200 per year. What you might save by buying a house at a pos-

* The figure is an average of housing-start projections by the National Association of Home Builders, MIT-Harvard Joint Center for Urban Studies, Data Resources, Inc., and the Federal National Mortgage Association.

sibly lower interest rate in the future could be wiped out by the increased price of the house. You would also have missed out on appreciated value.

Don't be overly distressed by that $70,000 price tag. *Median* means that while 50 percent of all new-home sales were for that price or more, 50 percent were for that price or less. *Half of all the houses that go on the block sell for less than the median price.* So don't be misled by the sky-high prices of houses and condominiums being bought by recording stars, the rich-rich, and buyers from abroad with briefcases full of greenbacks. Resourceful shoppers not only can find resale homes going for a lot less than the median price of a new single-family house but can often beat the going mortgage interest rate and get around the downpayment obstacle too. You'll learn here how to do all those things.

Home-Buying Basics

Before getting into the many different ways the purchase of a home can be financed today, you should be acquainted with certain home-buying fundamentals that are likely to apply no matter how the financing is arranged. You'll be able to function with some confidence when dealing with a seller, real-estate broker, lawyer, or banker if you have at least a basic grasp of everything from how "affordability" is assayed to true costs and closing costs.

We'll begin with a short history of the mortgage, since a mortgage is going to be your "ticket" to homeownership. The pledging of property to a creditor as security for the payment of a debt, or mortgaging, while retaining beneficial ownership, goes back to ancient Greece. "Mortgage," which is not Greek but Old French, literally means "dead" (*mort*) "pledge" (*gage*). When the debt, money in this case, has been paid, the pledge becomes "dead," or void.

In some states, a document known as a "deed of trust" is used in place of the mortgage. With a deed of trust, there is some advantage to the lender should the buyer default, being more easily foreclosed upon than is the case with a mortgage. Otherwise, there's little difference between a deed of trust and a mortgage. For convenience, *mortgage* is used as a generic term throughout this book. The person who borrows the money is called the *mortgagor;* the person who lends the money is called the *mortgagee.*

In this country, through the first three decades of this century, mortgage loans seldom were written for more than half the appraised value of the property and had to be repaid in full within five years or less, but could be renewed at the lender's discretion. At various intervals, the mortgagor paid the interest due and whatever he could or chose to pay against the loan balance. Such loans were not amortized. Second mortgages could be obtained, but at much higher interest rates than on first mortgages, and were a stigma to be avoided if at all possible. When those first- and second-mortgage "balloon" payments, meaning the balance of the loan, came due during the Great Depression of the 1930s, even those homeowners fortunate enough to have jobs were unable to refinance, anywhere, at any interest rate. What equity they had vanished in the general decline in values. As delinquencies on mortgage payments and real-estate taxes began to be measured in years, thousands of families lost their mortgaged homes. There were many bank failures at the beginning of the Depression as well.

To help bring order out of chaos, the Federal Home Loan Bank Board was created in 1932 as a regulatory agency with the responsibility to correct inherent problems in the home-mortgage market. Under the Banking Act of 1933, the Board was given authorization to issue charters to newly formed savings-and-loan associations (S&Ls), and federally chartered S&Ls became the nation's principal source of mortgage loans. The fully amortized, fixed-rate, long-term mortgage introduced through the S&Ls became the standard for nearly 50 years and helped tens of millions of families achieve the dream of homeownership.

The creation of the Federal Housing Administration (FHA) in 1934 to insure home-mortgage loans and to aid lower-income home buyers and, post-World War II, the introduction of GI loan guarantees for veterans opened the door to homeownership for additional millions of Americas. Today, two out of three American families own their homes, a considerably higher rate of homeownership than prevails in England, France, Switzerland, or West Germany.

From the 1930s until well into the 1970s, there were just five commonly used methods of "financing" the purchase of a home in this country:

1. the conventional mortgage
2. government-backed loans
3. mortgage assumptions
4. land contracts
5. cash purchases

We'll get into the details of the other methods later, but for now, all you need to know is that an all-cash purchase not only is unlikely but, for almost all home buyers, would be financially foolish today. With Uncle Sam as a silent partner, and the opportunity to "write off" a portion of your interest payments against your federal income tax, virtually all financial experts advise against putting up any more cash than required to secure the mortgage commitment or manage the mortgage payments. Cash can be put to better use elsewhere.

To see why this is so, let's say you're a young married couple, both working, and have $10,000 in savings that you could add to the required 10 percent down payment on the $60,000 house you are buying. Instead of committing yourself to paying $683 per month (at an arbitrary 15 percent rate of interest) on a conventional 30-year $54,000 loan, your monthly mortgage payment would be reduced to $556 on $44,000. At tax time, you'd then have a home-mortgage interest deduction, excluding the first-year payment on principal, of $6,660 (vs. $8,180).

But let's say that instead of applying that $10,000 to reduce the monthly mortgage payments, you invest it and lock in a matching 15 percent first-year return. At tax time, you'd include an additional $1,500 in your adjusted gross income. Say that additional $1,500 brings your adjusted gross up to $35,000. Filing a joint return and taking an $8,180 deduction for interest on the $54,000 mortgage loan, you'd have to pay a federal income tax (based on 1981 tax schedules) of $4,575. That would leave you with an after-tax income of $22,245 for the year. On the other hand, applying that $10,000 to the down payment on the house, you'd have a tax bill (based on an adjusted gross income of $33,500, a home-mortgage interest deduction of $6,660) of $4,582, and an after-tax net of $22,258.

The $13 difference ($22,258 vs. $22,245) would hardly seem to be worth writing about. But there's more here than meets the eye.

down payment	$6,000	$16,000
loan amount	54,000	44,000
investment income	1,500	—
adjusted gross income	35,000	33,500
interest deduction	8,180	6,660
	26,820	26,840
federal income tax	4,575	4,582
after-tax net	$22,245	$22,258

Whether filing a single or joint return, and regardless of your tax bracket, your after-tax net *for the first year* would be virtually the same using either option. There is a clear advantage, however, in investing the $10,000. Even where the initial rate of return on the investment is *less* than the mortgage interest rate, you'd come out ahead in the long run if you invest the money. The hidden kicker here is that when you invest, you normally allow the yield to compound.

With interest compounding, money invested at 15 percent doubles in about 4.8 years. That's going by a useful, though not 100 percent accurate, rule of thumb known as "the rule of 72." Divide 72 by the interest rate and you have the number of years it takes for money to double if the interest is left to compound. Money invested at 8 percent doubles in nine years, at 6 percent it doubles in twelve.

The only situation where an all-cash or largely cash purchase might make sense would be if a retiree or other person with little taxable income (some folks do keep most of their savings in tax-free municipal bonds) were buying a house or condominium unit and had no way to take advantage of a deduction for home-mortgage interest. Most cash purchases can be credited to empty-nesters selling a large family house and retiring to smaller quarters in the Sunbelt, and to wealthy foreigners motivated by political and economic conditions to get their money to safer havens.

There are other reasons, however, why you should go after the largest mortgage, based on loan-to-value ratio, you can get. For one thing, it's almost easier to resell a house during a credit crunch if it has a large mortgage on it; coming up with the cash to buy out a big equity could be difficult for later prospective purchasers. Even more important, with continuing inflation, *any money borrowed today will be paid back tomorrow and tomorrow and tomorrow with cheaper, inflated dollars.*

If inflation continues at even a moderate rate, three years from now you could be paying back today's borrowed dollars at 75 cents on the dollar. Look at what happened from 1970 to 1980. Inflation, as measured by the Consumer Price Index, rose at an average annual rate of 7.8 percent and slashed the purchasing power of the dollar by 55 percent. Mortgagors who bought in easier times found that monthly payments that took 19 percent of their income in 1970 took only 9 percent in 1980—their mortgages, designed for stable prices, having stayed constant in cost. Money left in most passbook savings accounts, however, lost money even after allowing for the interest earned. At the same time, the median-priced existing single-family house appreciated at a compound annual rate of 10.8 percent.

Anytime housing prices outstrip inflation, you've got a "can't-miss" opportunity as a home buyer. As a debtor, with a big mortgage and sizable tax deductions, the case can be made that *you* are being paid to borrow. If your income-tax bracket reduces your mortgage-loan costs from 14 percent, say, to a true cost of 9.1 percent, as it does in the 35 percent bracket (4.9—35 percent of 14—subtracted from 14 equals 9.1), and if your home appreciates in value at a rate of 10.8 percent annually, you are being paid 1.7 percent to borrow! Inflation reduces the remaining principal of a flat-rate mortgage in terms of purchasing power. As economist Milton Friedman has explained it: "The greater part of the payments designated 'interest' have really been a repayment of principal."

The results are even more exhilarating when compounded over a longer term during periods of accelerating inflation. Applied to such housing hot spots of the late 1970s as Hawaii, Southern California, Connecticut, Washington, D.C., and South Florida, where it was not unusual for the prices of whole neighborhoods of existing homes to leap 30 percent and more a year, the financial gains reaped by both home buyers and sellers were downright embarrassing.

THE "TRUE COST" OF A MORTGAGE

Taxable Income	Tax Bracket	Interest Rate							
		11%	12%	13%	14%	15%	16%	17%	18%
$16,001	22%	8.58	9.36	10.14	10.92	11.70	12.48	13.26	14.04
20,201	25	8.25	9.00	9.75	10.50	11.25	12.00	12.75	13.50
24,601	29	7.81	8.52	9.23	9.94	10.65	11.36	12.07	12.78
29,901	33	7.37	8.04	8.71	9.38	10.05	10.72	11.39	12.06
35,201	39	6.71	7.32	7.93	8.54	9.15	9.76	10.37	10.98
45,801	44	6.16	6.72	7.28	7.84	8.40	8.96	9.52	10.08
60,001	49	5.61	6.12	6.63	7.14	7.65	8.16	8.67	9.18

Inflation and "bracket creep" aren't all bad. The higher your tax bracket, the lower the true rate of interest paid on a home-mortgage loan. To see just how big a break you might get with those interest deductions, locate the stated mortgage interest rate and read down to your tax bracket. The table shows the effective mortgage interest rate, or net cost, after allowing for itemized federal tax deductions. Figures are based on a joint return and 1982 income-tax schedules. If single, figures are .55 to 1.08 percentage points lower than shown.

Investors took advantage of the opportunity to make a killing and many pyramided modest investments in housing and other real estate into small fortunes. Buy a $100,000 property with 10 percent cash down and a $90,000 mortgage loan at 15 percent. In one year you will have paid out $13,656 in principal and interest, before taxes. But if you can sell that house for $125,000 at the end of 12 months, you will have doubled your money and then some, for you've put up only $10,000, not $100,000. That's the magic of leveraging—borrowing money to make money.

Accepting that paying any more cash for a house than you have to would be foolish, that's not to say that you're not going to find yourself in a position where you're going to *have* to come up with a large down payment. But first let's see just how much house you can afford.

HOW MUCH HOUSE CAN YOU AFFORD?

In 1970, the median price of a new single-family house was $23,400, a price that, going by a then commonly used home-buying rule of thumb (a mortgage loan should not exceed twice or at most two and a half times the borrower's income), more than half of America's families could afford. But economic conditions have changed (boy have they changed!), and the American dream of owning a single-family detached house in suburbia is not a very restful one for most young families today.

Less than a decade ago, the typical first-time home buyer was between 27 and 33 years of age, married, with one child and often another one on the way. Dad was the sole breadwinner. Mom was a housewife. Completing the picture: a pet or two and, usually, a station wagon.

That image of the American-as-apple-pie family represents only a small minority of new owner-occupied households in the 1980s. For one thing, 51 percent of all married women now work outside the home. For another, there's been a decided retreat from suburbia. Even more importantly, there's been a dramatic increase in one-person owner-occupied households, as well as in households of childless couples, one-parent (usually female) households, and nonfamily households composed of two or more unrelated persons sharing resources.

Beyond inflation and the age structure of the population, changing life-styles and the viewing of homeownership as an investment, and not primarily as shelter, accounted for the incredible surge in household formations—close to 14 million units, both rented and owner occupied—between 1970 and 1979. Another major factor was the exercising by women of their economic clout in the home-buying market.

Prior to enactment of the Equal Credit Opportunity Act in 1975, women—single or married, divorced or widowed—were treated as poor credit risks by most of those who arranged credit. For young married couples, the wife's income, even though she was regularly employed, carried little or no weight in securing a home mortgage. Unless she could convince the loan officer that she could not, as per a doctor's written assurance of infertility, or would not have a child for a specified period of time, her salary generally was not counted in calculating the amount of money the family might borrow.

Under the Equal Credit Opportunity Act and other changes in the federal credit laws covering all who regularly extend credit to individuals, an applicant for a mortgage loan today may not be refused credit on the grounds of sex, age (if of legal age), race, religion, national origin, color, or marital status. Everyone must be judged on the basis of individual credit-worthiness. A wife's income must be treated the same as the husband's, and the lender must consider all steady income of both husband and wife, including part-time income. For women applying for a mortgage loan, credit-worthiness must be judged not only on salaried income but also on alimony and child-support payments, if likely to be consistently made.

The obligatory crediting of working wives' incomes and the trend to two-career families were major factors in making 1976, 1977, and 1978 three of the biggest house-building years in U.S. history. Not surprisingly, single women also played a role in the boom; since 1975, they've been buying homes on their own, condominium apartments in particular, as never before. Where, in 1974, only one out of every thirty-five mortgage-loan applicants

HOW TO FIGURE THE MONTHLY MORTGAGE COST

Interest Rate	Payment Period				
	10 Years	15 Years	20 Years	25 Years	30 Years
10%	$13.22	$10.75	$ 9.66	$ 9.09	$ 8.78
10.5	13.50	11.06	9.99	9.45	9.15
11	13.78	11.37	10.33	9.81	9.53
11.5	14.06	11.69	10.67	10.17	9.91
12	14.35	12.01	11.02	10.54	10.29
12.5	14.64	12.33	11.37	10.91	10.68
13	14.94	12.66	11.72	11.28	11.07
13.5	15.23	12.99	12.08	11.66	11.46
14	15.53	13.32	12.44	12.04	11.85
14.5	15.83	13.66	12.80	12.43	12.25
15	16.14	14.00	13.17	12.81	12.65
15.5	16.45	14.34	13.54	13.20	13.05
16	16.76	14.69	13.92	13.59	13.45
16.5	17.07	15.04	14.29	13.99	13.86
17	17.38	15.40	14.67	14.38	14.26
17.5	17.70	15.75	15.05	14.78	14.67
18	18.02	16.11	15.44	15.18	15.08
18.5	18.35	16.47	15.82	15.58	15.48
19	18.67	16.83	16.21	15.98	15.89
19.5	19.00	17.20	16.60	16.39	16.30
20	19.33	17.57	16.99	16.79	16.72

The table shows the monthly principal-and-interest payments per $1,000 borrowed at each of the double-digit interest rates and payment periods indicated. To calculate the monthly P/I payment for any size mortgage loan, multiply the appropriate monthly-payment-per-$1,000 in the table by the number of thousands of dollars to be borrowed. Example: A $50,000 loan for 25 years at 14.5 percent interest would call for a monthly P/I payment of $12.43 x 50, or $621.50. These figures do not include property taxes and hazard insurance.

was a single woman, today, with more and more women moving into better-paying jobs, the figures are one in ten.

Essentially then, no mortgage lender taking applications from would-be home buyers can disqualify you out of hand for the extension of mortgage credit *if*, whether on a single or combined income, you can 1) establish that your credit rating is good, 2) meet the required down payment, and 3) handle the monthly mortgage payments on a house within an established price range without stretching your income beyond reason.

With long-term mortgage interest rates at around 8.25 percent in 1970, that $23,400 median-price house could be bought, after a 20 percent down payment, and going by that old home-buying rule of thumb, with a reliable gross annual income (that's before taxes) of as little as $9,400.

Applied today, that rule of thumb would mean that it would take a pre-tax income of between $24,000 and $30,000 to qualify for a house costing $60,000. With a 20 percent down payment and 15 percent interest on a conventional 30-year loan, you'd be paying $607 per month for principal and interest on that $60,000 house. Real-estate taxes and hazard insurance easily could raise your monthly payment to $750, or $9,000 per year. But just try to get a conservative financial officer to grant you a mortgage loan for that $48,000 (after a $12,000 down payment) on a gross annual income of $24,000!

The majority of lenders want borrowers to keep monthly housing payments (principal, interest, taxes, and insurance—or PITI) below 25 percent of their monthly family income in the first year of ownership. At $24,000 a year, monthly income would be $2,000. Going by the book, many mortgage lenders wouldn't qualify you for the purchase of a $60,000 house unless your income was $3,000 per month, or $36,000 per year. Not with mortgage interest rates at 15 percent or higher. Under the 25 percent rule, interest rates would have to drop to an unlikely 8 percent (and $352 per month principal and interest on that $48,000) before you could qualify.

Not all lenders are that strict, however. More than 38 percent of all home buyers today exceed the 25 percent guideline. Buyers with 33 percent of their salaries committed to PITI payments have become commonplace. At 33 percent, you'd need a minimum monthly income of $2,250, or a mortgage interest rate of 12.75 percent or less, to qualify for that $48,000 loan.

Maybe you've got a merit or cost-of-living raise coming to you in a few months. A reasonable loan officer would likely take this into account. Or you might persuade your wife, if she's able and not presently working, to take a part-time job. You need an additional $3,000 per year income. If you're forced to wait until you get a $3,000 boost in salary, the price of the house will likely have gone up too. Alternatively, if you could squeeze an additional $8,000 out of your savings, investments, life insurance, borrowings from relatives, or whatever, to boost the down payment to $20,000, you'd be within the 33 percent limit with your $2,000-per-month gross.

This loosely presented example is intended merely to register what it can take to qualify for a *conventional* mortgage loan at a traditional mortgage source. There are many alternative ways of arranging for the financing of a home, often at less than prevailing institutional mortgage interest rates, that might well work for you, and we'll be getting into them in detail in later chapters.

The rules of thumb most often used by loan officers today, then, focus on your monthly installment obligations. Happily for those on the way up, an increasing number of lending institutions are following the examples set by Mortgage Guaranty Insurance Corporation and other major insurers of home mortgages and lifting the acceptable debt ratio from 25 to 33 percent of gross income, and to 38 percent for *total* indebtedness (housing costs plus auto and other installment loans extending beyond seven months).

This liberalizing of loan limits recognizes the younger borrower's potential for increased earnings and the effect of inflation on both salaried income and housing prices. And while a home may gobble up as much as a third of a young family's income in the first few years of ownership, a gradual reduction in the percentage of income going to housing costs can be anticipated. All of which contributes to a reasonable certitude of adequate loan quality, the lender's primary concern.

Not all lenders are in touch with reality. But you can find lenders who will stretch the 25 percent rule *if* you don't have

MATCHING YOUR INCOME TO HOUSING PRICES
(In thousands of dollars, 000s omitted)

Mortgage Interest Rate	Gross Annual Income													
	$17,500	$20,000	$22,500	$25,000	$27,500	$30,000	$32,500	$35,000	$37,500	$40,000	$42,500	$45,000	$47,500	$50,000
20%	30	34	39	43	47	52	56	60	65	69	74	78	82	87
19	31	36	40	45	50	54	59	63	68	72	77	81	86	90
18	33	38	42	47	52	57	61	66	71	76	80	85	90	94
17	34	39	44	49	54	59	64	69	74	79	84	89	94	99
16	36	41	47	52	57	62	67	73	78	83	88	93	99	104
15	38	43	49	54	60	65	71	76	82	87	93	98	104	109
14	40	46	52	57	63	69	75	80	86	92	98	104	109	115

13	42	48	54	61	67	73	79	85	91	97	103	109	115	121
12	45	51	58	64	71	77	83	90	96	103	109	116	122	129
11	47	54	61	68	75	81	88	95	102	109	116	122	129	136
10	50	58	65	72	80	87	94	101	109	116	123	131	138	145

The figures shown in the table are the theoretical limits of affordability (in thousands of dollars) with a fixed-rate, 30-year, fully amortized mortgage loan, a 20 percent down payment, and mortgage payments held to 33 percent of the home buyer's gross monthly income. Allowances for property taxes and hazard insurance, which have been incorporated, are based on 2.5 percent and 0.4 percent of the home value, respectively.

Examples: With a gross annual income of $32,500, a mortgage interest rate of 14 percent, and conventional financing, you probably couldn't qualify to buy a house costing more than $75,000, including a $15,000 down payment. To extrapolate for larger incomes than are shown here: For a gross annual income of $65,000, simply double the figures given at $32,500. At 14 percent, that would give a house-hunting ceiling of $150,000. For fractional interest rates, split the difference between vertical pairs of figures. At 15.5 percent and a gross annual income of $32,500, the affordability figure would be $69,000.

other heavy debt obligations or a large family. Some will want to include heating and utility costs (don't underestimate monthly operating expenses!) within that 33 percent limit. But just as real-estate taxes can be "no problem" in some locales and reason enough to avoid others like the plague, an enlightened loan officer will be aware of how such items should be weighted; two homes with the same sales price can have *very* different total monthly costs. The lender could be more concerned about the make and model-year of the car you drive than how much it's going to cost to heat the house. Vanity wheels, or a new-car-every-other-year habit, can take a substantial bite out of your budget. If, on the other hand, as with Manhattanites (New Yorkers) and the residents of several other metropolises, owning a car can be more of an inconvenience than a convenience, you might have an additional couple of thousand dollars that could be applied annually toward mortgage payments. If single, chances are you're not carrying the life-insurance load that a family man should, or your employer may offer life-insurance policies as an employment perk. That easily could represent another 5 percent or more of your gross annual income that could be earmarked for housing costs. Conceivably, without car payments and a heavy insurance load, you might be able to apply as much as 50 percent of your gross income to housing costs. We know more than a few career-oriented city dwellers who are paying out half of their income for rent. And *they* don't get a tax break on a penny of it!

Rules of thumb, like averages, have some validity when applied to large samplings. But when you get down to cases, they fall into a category known to the scientific community as SWAG, which is an acronym for "statistical wild-ass guessing." There's only one way to determine how much *you* can comfortably afford to spend on housing, and that's with real figures, taken from your actual income and your spending habits. You're going to have to sit down and carefully work out a balance sheet, showing just what your nonhousing outlays are likely to be and then how much you can budget for housing, including the mortgage payments, property taxes, homeowner's insurance, utilities, and maintenance and repairs.

Don't shortchange yourself on your allocation for housing costs by setting down an income figure based on take-home pay. With housing-related deductibles of $700 per month and an adjusted gross annual income of $30,000, for example, the tax load, based on a joint return, is nearly $2,500 less than it would be without those deductions. Your income entry on the balance sheet should reflect gross rather than net income. The only adjustments should be for Social Security and pension-plan withholdings. Federal (and any other) income taxes should be subtracted from the difference between your gross income and nonhousing outlays, but only after adjusting for projected mortgage-interest and property-tax deductions.

With a number of methods of creative financing, you don't have any involvement with a bank or thrift institution and don't have to conform to any rules of thumb or otherwise qualify for the "loan." But you should have a pretty good fix on just how much you can afford to pay out for monthly housing costs *before* you sit down with the seller and/or his lawyer.

Unless you're set on living in a particular area, and couldn't be budged by a bulldozer, the costs of homeownership just might influence a major relocation on your part. If you have a job skill that is in demand, and you can pull up stakes without too much suffering, a move to a less expensive area could be worth considering if you've made homeownership a top priority.

Just how much difference geographical location makes was made startlingly clear by a 1981 study of home prices in major real-estate markets across the United States. Conducted by Nationwide Relocation Service, Inc., a Chicago-based subsidiary of Coldwell, Banker and Company, the study focused on a 2,000-square-foot detached house—with three bedrooms, two baths, a family room, an eat-in kitchen, and an adjacent garage—located on a standard-sized lot in a suburban community where "middle-level executives" typically live.

Nationwide's comprehensive survey of 107 metropolitan areas showed such relative bargain areas as Norfolk, Virginia; Colorado Springs, Colorado; Jacksonville, Florida; San Antonio, Texas; and Salt Lake City, Utah. These areas offered the "standard" house in the study at prices ranging from $66,000 (Norfolk) to $72,500 (Salt Lake City). Seventeen of the markets surveyed, including eight in

California, three in Connecticut, and two in Florida, wanted $125,000 or more for the same house. Just outside Buffalo, New York, the house went for $57,000. In Palo Alto, California, the identical house cost $325,000!

THE DOWN-PAYMENT DILEMMA

The how-to-get-rich-quick-in-real-estate books promote the idea that it's easy to acquire property with little or no cash down. Some of the techniques presented, however, are as specious as the suggestions that you borrow the down payment from your Uncle Jack, or, for the Beverly Hills crowd no doubt, offer your Mercedes-Benz to the seller of the property. There *are* some perfectly acceptable methods of financing the purchase of a house with no down payment, such as with a VA-guaranteed loan, which, for qualified veterans, conditionally allows 100 percent financing. By paying extra for mortgage insurance, even conventional mortgages can be obtained with as little as 5 percent down, and FHA loans for less than 5 percent. But low or no down payments are a mixed blessing for home buyers. The less you put down, the greater your monthly payments.

If you have a high monthly income but, lacking discipline, not enough savings to fatten up a piggy bank, you probably should consider a low down payment, even though you may have to pay a premium on the full amount borrowed. If, on the other hand, your monthly income doesn't otherwise qualify you for the financing needed, your only alternative with institutional lenders would be to reduce the monthly payments by putting a larger amount down. Sometimes, too, you can bargain for a better deal when you offer a larger amount of cash. With seller financing, you may have no choice but to come up with a substantial down payment in order to assume an existing mortgage at a below-market interest rate.

Families trading up are likely to have enough equity in the house they are leaving to more than cover the down payment on the new one. But for first-time buyers, the down payment can be their single biggest hurdle. Even with VA-guaranteed financing, a down payment may be demanded if your monthly income doesn't measure up to the lender's guidelines.

There's no way an income of $20,000 can be stretched to pay for a $60,000 house with conventional financing and a 15 percent interest rate unless you can come up with a whopping down payment representing nearly half the purchase price. If a 20 percent down payment ($12,000) is all you can manage, interest rates would have to plunge to below 10 percent before you'd likely find financing at traditional lending sources.

So how are so many young people making home-buying afford-able at today's prices and interest rates? For one thing, six out of ten first-time buyers are families in which both husband and wife hold jobs. For another, first-timers tend to buy older houses rather than newly built ones; in 1979, the median sales price of existing single-family houses was $55,700, or $7,200 below the median sales price of new single-family houses. Young buyers also are turning to condominium apartments and town houses, which often have more affordable price tags than do single-family de-tached houses.

There are also any number of methods of creative financing that can help first-time buyers get started. A land lease can reduce both the down payment needed and the monthly payments. A lease with an option to buy would give you a house to live in and time to save up for the down payment, with some or all of the rent you pay credited toward the purchase price. If the seller is taking back the mortgage, you can offer him a top price in return for low- or no-down-payment financing.

Without getting into the nitty-gritty of creative and other al-ternative methods of financing here, what we would like to make clear is that, for most of you, the down-payment question is not going to be a question of how much you might choose to put down but how much you're going to be *required* to put down. If you have the income, and that's the way you want to handle it, no- or low-down-payment financing is certainly within the realm of possibility. But more than likely you're going to have to come up with a stiff down payment to keep the monthly payments manageable and find acceptance with a lender. Some situations will *demand* 20 or 25 percent down; restrictions may disqualify you or the house for lower down payments.

While few home buyers are likely to continue a 30-year mortgage to maturity, if you are concerned with the total financing costs of such a loan, keep in mind that the larger the down payment, the smaller the mortgage loan—and the lower the overall interest charges you'll have to pay. With a fixed-rate 30-year loan at 15 percent continued to maturity, you'd pay out more than $35,000 in interest on every $10,000 borrowed!

But don't sweat it. We've already shown you how tax deductions for mortgage interest and escalating housing values can combine to keep you ahead in the mortgage game. If inflation continues at anywhere near 10 percent, hamburger could cost $30 a pound 30 years from now, and starting salaries for college graduates could begin at $300,000 per year.

Don't plan on committing *all* of your savings to the down payment. There are other expenses that must be taken into consideration when facing up to the down-payment question. You'll need cash for closing costs, which, depending on the size of the down payment, legal fees, and other charges, can run to several thousand dollars on a $50,000 mortgage. If you are forming your first household, you'll likely have to set money aside for furniture and, possibly, major appliances. Moving expenses may have to be considered too.

In 1980, the average down payment for first-time home buyers was 20.5 percent of the purchase price. On a $60,000 house, that's better than $12,000. About the only comforting thought we can offer here is that saving up for a down payment generally is a one-time sacrifice. Buying that first home is the biggest step many of you will ever take. It also represents the biggest—and best—investment most of you will ever make. With contractors grimly joking that it takes *two* working wives to afford a house today, sacrifices are the rule rather than the exception. Florence Glorian, one of South Florida's most successful real-estate agents, advises would-be home buyers to "make the biggest sacrifice of your lives, live on the bare necessities," so they can have a decent down payment.

You may have to postpone vacations, make your clunker of a car do for a while longer, and work your tail off at two jobs for a year or more to get the down payment together. If you're married, and the two of you are working, you might try to live on one income and put the other into savings. Most young wives who want children are postponing motherhood (the percentage of childless married women in their twenties has nearly doubled since 1960) and joining the labor force until after they're into a home of their own.

You should have a pretty good line on your assets, and probably know to within a few hundred dollars how much cash you could raise for a down payment. But here are some suggestions on where to look for down-payment cash without getting into hock with other institutional lenders. Borrowing short-term money from a bank to meet the down payment isn't a good idea. The mortgage lender is basing your ability to meet those monthly mortgage payments on a nearly debt-free position.

For most first-time buyers, the bulk of the down payment comes from savings, the typical first-timer taking nearly two years to accumulate the down payment. If you've made buying a house your No. 1 priority, you shouldn't put money you are setting aside for the down payment into speculative investments. You could lose it all, or a good portion of it. Look at what happened to those who bought gold at $850, silver at $45. At the same time, don't settle for 5.25 percent interest on passbook savings when money-market funds are returning 15 to 17 percent or better, as they did during almost all of 1981.

If you're carrying life insurance, you may have a cash-value policy on which you can borrow at well below bank rates. Whole-life policies, with borrowing rates of from 5 to 8 percent, depending on the age and provisions of the policy, often provide the cheapest loans around.

You may have some collectibles that no longer are appreciating at the rate they did in the speculative fever of the late 1970s. Maybe it's time to unload them. Chances are your investment in a home of your own will appreciate even faster through the 1980s than those Jim Beam bottles and that art-deco statuary would have.

And don't be too proud to approach your parents or in-laws for a loan. Tapping the family for at least part of the down payment is common practice these days. Most parents are well aware of the difficulties facing younger first-time home buyers. If they have a home of their own, they've likely got some "idle equity" in that house on which they could borrow to help you get a leg up on the housing ladder.

FINDING FINANCING

There are so many variables in home financing today that it really does pay, sometimes exceedingly well, to shop around for a mortgage. If the loan is to be arranged through a traditional lending source, though, you could be in for a lot of rejection. With billions of dollars in low-yielding, fixed-rate mortgages on their books, the savings and loans, historically the nation's largest suppliers of residential mortgage money, are ailing. Strapped for cash, many of them closed their doors to would-be home buyers in 1981, preferring instead to dole out their dwindling funds in the form of equity loans and other higher-yielding consumer-type loans.

Finding financing that you can live with for the next 30 years, if need be, is going to take time and more than a little effort. Shop around. Ask about alternative kinds of mortgages in your area. Compare rates, down payments, and closing costs among different types of lenders. There is no single nationwide mortgage rate; interest rates can vary according to the amount of the mortgage, the length of the loan, and from lender to lender. But look at the entire package that's being offered, including the fine print about penalties and assumptions. Where the interest rate is not fixed for the life of the loan, have the lender do the math for the "worst-case" scenario.

Check out at least four mortgage sources, without getting so involved in the early stages that you'll be required to pay for a credit report and appraisal in advance. Lenders don't like loan shoppers, but don't let financial officers intimidate you. Be persistent. It takes work to buy a home today. You might luck on to an affordable house or apartment and the financing for it in a matter of weeks, but it's not uncommon for a young family to spend four to six months looking for an acceptable home and the financing.

Creative financing presents a different order of priorities. Here, it can come down to looking only at those houses within an established price range that carry an assumable mortgage, or where the seller has indicated a willingness to "take back" a mortgage or to make other long- or short-term financing arrangements with the buyer.

"Seller-assisted" financing doesn't mean that you're going to be limited to looking at houses that are for sale by owner (FSBO), most of whom tend to overpraise and overprice their houses. The great majority of houses and condominiums that are bought using creative financing are handled by real-estate brokers. Indeed, it's usually the broker who sells the owner on the advantages of participating in the financing.

With creative financing, rather than finding a house that pleases you and then making the rounds of the lending institutions to try to arrange for financing, you'll be looking mostly at houses that come with some, it not all, of the financing and then deciding whether the house is for you. The real-estate classifieds can tip you off to the possibilities:

"Owner will hold first mortgage."

"Super financing available—or lease-option."

"Motivated owner will hold 20-year mortgage for 12 percent interest."

"Assumable 8.5 percent mortgage and owner will assist."

"Owner will consider wraparound mortgage with $20,000 cash down."

"Assume VA mortgage. No qualifying. No closing costs."

It should be noted that the ads quoted here appeared at a time when the prevailing mortgage interest rate was around 17 percent!

You'll spot similar opportunities in ads placed by both owners and real-estate firms. If you have the time and patience, you could drive around and check the "curb appeal," as it's called in the business, of every home advertised in the classifieds that halfway intrigues you (phoning for addresses where needed), and then follow up by making appointments to tour those that pass your eye exam. Or, especially if you're unfamiliar with the area, you can go to a real-estate professional, give him your financial background, tell him what your requirements are, including neighborhoods, and ask him to show you any homes on his books—or the computer—that offer financing that might be more manageable than conventional financing would be to a person in your situation. With a buyer's market, many real-estate brokers will know of more than a few anxious sellers who will finance your purchase— often at below-market interest rates. You might even find a broker (who may or may not be a Realtor, which is a trademarked name bestowed on members of the National Association of Realtors, the nation's largest realty organization) specializing in creative financing arrangements.

Buyers have long been duped into believing that the real-estate broker's commission, when you do find a property through him, is paid by the seller. In point of fact, it's the buyer who pays it, since it's almost always built into the selling price of the house. There is a development worth noting here, though. In some areas of the country, buyers are turning to discount realty brokers, who, for a fee, or for a commission of from 3 to 5 percent of the selling price, and based on their knowledge of the market, search for and negotiate for a residence at the lowest possible price to the client. Since the owner of the property doesn't have to pay the customary 6 or 7 percent (and sometimes higher) commission to a broker for selling the house for him, he can afford to lower his asking price by at least that much.

The FHA, however, has introduced a "Catch-22" ruling that comes down hard on buyer-brokering, even though the cost-cutting technique is seen as a wave of the future by Consumers Union and has been endorsed by officials at the Federal Trade Commission. The FHA ruling is that it will allow use of "the buyer's broker plan" only where it has become "customary" in a particular market area. While this applies only to FHA-insured financing, there's not much chance that buyer-brokering can become customary where conventional financing is involved without FHA endorsement, since most banking institutions take their lead from FHA. However, there's no reason why buyer-brokering

can't work with unconventional financing, with the broker negotiating with the seller for favorable financing for his client. A
buyer's broker usually represents the buyer in all phases of the
acquisition—from contract terms through settlement.

Unless you've made some special arrangement with a broker,
then, keep in mind that the broker is working principally for the
seller, whether directly, under a legally binding contract, or indirectly, as through multiple-listing services. As the seller's agent,
he'll get the highest price he can for the property, but he doesn't
want to discourage prospective buyers by setting the price *too*
high. In a slow market, with a commission at stake, some brokers
will turn an indecisive buyer every which way but loose before
they'll pass up a sale. More and more frequently, that includes
turning both buyer and seller on to creative financing.

Home builders and developers are also getting to be quite
creative when it comes to financing. They'll usually advertise the
fact, in splashy ads headlining terms that are difficult to believe.
But when you get to the fine print or footnote, you find that those
attractive rates generally apply only during the first year or two of
the mortgage. To stimulate sales, a builder may absorb closing
costs as well. Some major builders/developers have wholly owned
subsidiaries through which they fund mortgages; others may have
a forward rate commitment for home-mortgage money from an
out-of-state bank or other source, made months earlier, at an interest rate below today's rates. If you are looking to buy a new
house, rather than a resale, you might get a good deal on the financing here. On the other hand, while entry into homeownership has been made easier for you, these "builder buy-downs"
are not always the bargains they appear to be, the promotion
costs usually being built into the selling price of the house. (For
more on builder buy-downs, see page 137.)

Don't rule out institutional financing. You could be in for a
heap of rejection, as noted, but you'll find a whole smorgasbord of
mortgage-loan instruments at some lending institutions—everything from variable- and adjustable-rate mortgages to graduated-
payment and FHA or VA fixed-interest-rate loans. What any one
source offers in the way of "flexible financing," as the new institutional alternatives are collectively labeled, depends largely on

whether the source operates under a federal or a state charter. If federally chartered, the lender will generally offer financing plans or variations endorsed by the regulatory bodies in Washington. State-chartered institutions tend to be a lot more innovative. On the state level, however, what might be found acceptable in one state could be barred in another by restrictive state laws—all of which contributes to the plethora of mortgage instruments and terms.

You can't take advantage of the home-financing package that best fits your needs and expectations though without being aware of the many different financing opportunities available. You owe it to yourself to explore all the possibilities; these are not ordinary times. To make the best use of this book, it should be read in its entirety. You might have selected it for the information it contains on wraparound mortgages or co-purchasing. But if you skip a section or two, you just might miss the one method of financing that is tailor-made for your situation. It might not only get you the house you *really* want, but save you thousands of dollars in the bargain.

If you're going to be dealing with a lending institution, it's not a bad idea to "pre-qualify" for a mortgage loan before you get down to serious house-hunting. Many S&Ls, in particular, offer mortgage preview plans. By having you fill out a simple form, they can give you an accurate estimate of how much mortgage money you might expect from them. There's no point in looking at $90,000 houses when a loan officer has made it clear that you can't comfortably afford a home costing more than $75,000, assuming the interest rates hold. Try to remain relatively uncommitted at this stage of your shopping. If you're required to fill out a loan application, make sure that any fee involved is refundable if you aren't offered a loan.

By all means, look into the possibilities of arranging for financing where you regularly bank. Keep in mind though that a commercial bank is not likely to be very active in the home-mortgage market where it has stiff competition from one or more savings banks or S&Ls.

Savings and loans, by law and custom, invest the bulk of their assets in residential mortgages, and account for a majority of the loans written on private residences by the lending institutions. There are some 4,500 S&Ls (not counting branches), about evenly divided between federally chartered and state-chartered associations. They are primarily local lenders. A helpful hint: It's to your advantage to have a savings account at the S&L where you apply for a mortgage loan.

Mutual savings banks, which are state-chartered institutions, also invest heavily in residential mortgages. They tend to acquire loans over wider geographical areas than do S&Ls, but mutuals can be a lot harder to find. There are approximately 450 mutual savings banks, and they exist in only 17 states, mostly in the Northeast. Mutual savings banks and S&Ls are commonly referred to as "thrifts."

Properly, the only "banks" are commercial, or full-service, banks. They may be either federally chartered or state-chartered institutions, and there are about 14,000 of them. Their lending activities, unless the only banking facility in town, generally are targeted toward high-yielding business, construction, and personal loans. This could change though. With deregulation, S&Ls are moving heavily into checking accounts, credit cards, and consumer-type loans. They're becoming much more competitive with commercial banks. Commercial banks, in turn, could become more active in the home-mortgage market. With home mortgages, banks generally require larger down payments than do the thrifts.

If money is tight and you keep running into closed loan windows, or if you're looking for a shortcut, you might avail yourself of the services of a mortgage broker. As an independent agent, he makes it his business to know which local lenders are granting loans and at what terms. He aggressively seeks loans and works closely with real-estate agents, and may himself be a real-estate broker. In a number of states, including California, New York, Pennsylvania, New Jersey, Michigan, Illinois, and Florida, mortgage brokers are required to have a real-estate license. Mortgage brokers have good connections not only with local lending institutions but with insurance companies, pension funds, and out-of-state savings institutions. They can sometimes arrange for financing below the going local rate. For a fee averaging about 1 percent of the mortgage amount, a mortgage broker will match the borrower with a lender and save him the time and trouble of finding a lender on his own. Like Avis, mortgage brokers claim to try harder.

Mortgage brokers are often confused with mortgage companies, sometimes called mortgage bankers. A mortgage company typically is a regular business corporation, operating mainly on funds borrowed from a commercial bank on a short-term basis. A mortgage company "originates" mortgages, collects the monthly payments, and otherwise services the mortgages, but it doesn't necessarily hold them. Instead, it packages like mortgages into "portfolios" that are then sold to wholesale lenders or to one of the government-sponsored national mortgage associations. The latter, known by such sobriquets as Fannie Mae and Freddie Mac, were created by Congress to stimulate housing by establishing a "secondary market" in which investors could participate. Mortgage companies are more disposed than most lending institutions, mutual savings banks excepted, toward handling government-backed FHA and VA loans.

Mortgage companies are still fighting down a bad reputation earned by some black sheep among them who were found guilty in the early-to-mid-1970s of participating in a widespread loan-fraud scheme that cost the FHA—and U.S. taxpayers—tens of millions of dollars. As uncovered in 20 cities across the U.S., unscrupulous lenders would commit inner-city home buyers to payments they could not meet for very long on FHA-insured loans, and then quickly foreclose on the loans when the borrowers missed a payment or two. The mortgage company would then collect a fat check (based on an unrealistically high appraisal that went unchallenged by FHA) in repayment for its "loss"—and stick the government with a ghetto property that could not easily be resold. Know your limits—and your lender.

If you're a member of a large credit union, this could be the best source of all for a conventional mortgage loan. As a member of a credit union, you can generally save money on the overall mortgage costs; credit unions rarely charge extra fees of any kind when you get a loan. The mortgage interest rate might even be a quarter of a percentage point or two below the rates at local thrifts.

Federally chartered credit unions can offer home-mortgage loans for up to 30 years. The dwelling to be financed must be the borrower's principal residence (no vacation-home financing or investment properties) and priced at not more than 150 percent of the median sales price for homes in the area.

Once you've found a house or apartment that you believe to be within your means and would like to buy, you may be asked by the broker, or the seller, if acting alone, to sign a binder, purchase offer, or real-estate sales contract, and to give him a portion of the down payment, called an "earnest money deposit," as evidence that you really intend to go through with the deal.

Don't let the agent or the owner pressure you into a hasty decision. Before making any offer, signing a purchase agreement, or putting any money down, get a handle on your likely utility costs, property taxes, and any special assessments that you might be facing. If the house is one of a kind, or if the broker can't provide a "competitive market analysis" showing the asking price for the house to be fair, based on recent sales prices of comparable homes in the neighborhood, have the house evaluated by a professional appraiser.

With an independent, detailed appraisal (cost: about $2 to $3 per $1,000 of value) as a bargaining tool, the seller may be more easily persuaded that your purchase offer is a good deal fairer than his asking price. Don't be reluctant to haggle over the price. While the prices of new homes are generally less flexible, few resale houses are bought at the owner's asking price. Make sure, however, that the price you specify in the contract or offer is not subject to change (other than downward should the lender's commitment, based on *his* appraiser's evaluation of the property, come up short). Some contracts, for new houses especially, may contain an "escalator" clause, which can be a risky business for the buyer.

The contract should include a legal description of the property (a street address will not do) and spell out how much you are prepared to pay for the house, under what financing terms, whether such items as drapes, carpeting, and appliances are to be included in the purchase, your right of inspection prior to the closing, and the expected date of possession. If the seller will be financing the first or second mortgage, this should be noted in the offer. Known defects, such as a leaky roof or faulty plumbing, should be disclosed, unless the property is to be sold "as is." In many areas, a termite-inspection provision should be included as well, to protect both buyer and seller.

All purchase offers should be made conditional, with a mortgage contingency clause that releases you from any obligation and ensures the return of your earnest money deposit if the financing specified can't be arranged—or if the seller fails to meet all the terms of the contract. The most common contingency clause runs something like this: "This purchase offer is contingent upon buyer obtaining a commitment for a mortgage loan in the amount of $_____, amortized over not less than _____ years, annual interest rate not to exceed _____ percent, and with a loan fee of not more than _____ points." Should you decide to back out of the deal, other than for failure to secure the financing specified, you would stand to forfeit all or a portion of the deposit.

During these negotiations, which are a ritual of American house-buying, with offers and counteroffers that may go on for weeks, it could be a costly mistake not to have a lawyer of your own choice in your corner, since the contract is the blueprint for the closing. Do not enlist just any lawyer, but seek out one who specializes in real-estate closings.

Once you and your lawyer have put your conditions in writing, or amended the conditions as drawn up by the broker, the offer goes to the seller for his approval. He may sign the contract as is or request certain changes before returning the signed contract to you. If it is then acceptable to you, you merely initial any changes made by the seller in the now legally binding document.

The standard purchase agreement gives the prospective buyer 30 to 45 days to find financing. It would be unfair to the seller to ask him to take the property off the market for much longer than that. If you're going for conventional financing, and money is tight, you may have to negotiate a delayed closing—or accept a "kick-out" clause in the contract, which allows the seller to put the property back on the market after a certain date, even though he has signed a contract with you. If another buyer then makes a comparable offer, and is prepared for a fast closing, you would be given up to 72 hours to guarantee your deal. Without a commitment in hand from a lender, the seller has no assurance that you're going to be able to come up with the agreed-upon financing. Don't allow yourself to be drawn into a bidding contest, however. The only winner then is the seller of the property.

Unless the bulk of the financing is to be arranged with the seller, you're now ready to hit the street running for the mortgage commitment. Shop aggressively. Go back to every banker who seemed at least minimally disposed toward financing your proposed purchase with a loan that could be tailored to your financial situation. Identify the property you want to buy and state the price you propose to pay. If you haven't yet done so, fill out a formal loan application with likely lenders. Be prepared to answer personal questions you wouldn't consider answering to close friends. Be honest. If the lender later finds out, after the loan has been granted, that you lied in your application, he could call the loan and you could be subject to prosecution.

The lender will check your financial statement, credit character, and credit capacity. He'll check into your employment history, the likelihood of your continuing in your present employment, the length of time you've been at your current level of income, and your potential for increased earnings.

The loan commitment, if forthcoming, will be based on an evaluation of the property made by a professional appraiser engaged or employed by the lender. If the appraised value of the property does not coincide with the price you have agreed to pay for it, the loan will be based on the lower of the sale or appraisal figures. The commitment could be for 100 percent of the appraisal value, in the case of a GI loan; more likely it will be for 75 or 80 percent. The balance would be made up by the down payment.

In compliance with the Federal Truth in Lending Act, the lender must reveal all conditions of the loan to the borrower before the loan is made. This would include an approximation of the closing costs and what they cover, how many "points" the buyer might be required to pay, and what happens should the borrower be late with or miss a payment. Some of these items are negotiable. If you have a choice, favor a lender who does not impose burdensome penalties on the borrower for prepayments.

No prepayment penalties are permitted with FHA-insured and VA-guaranteed mortgage loans. But you could find yourself in the position with a conventional loan where it could cost you a couple of thousand dollars if, for one reason or another, you chose to pay off the loan early. Since most borrowers do pay off their mortgages well before maturity, it's not a bad idea to look for liberal conditions on prepayment.

Try for minimal penalites—or no penalty at all—on paying off the balance of the loan early. The magic words to look for are "or more" where the monthly payment is specified on the promissory note for the mortgage. Those two little words give you the right to prepay your mortgage at any time. If you're granted a long-term, fixed-rate mortgage at a high rate of interest, it could be of more than a little comfort to know that you might refinance the loan at a lower rate of interest should mortgage interest rates come down enough to make refinancing and all it entails profitable. Or, if you're faced with having to pay off the mortgage early to sell the property "free and clear of any encumbrances," it would be nice not to have to cut the lender in for a slice of the profit, if any.

You might come into some money and wish to shorten the life of the mortgage to reduce the overall interest costs. Should you be penalized for this? Lenders insist that the only way they can protect themselves against loss of future earnings on their money is with prepayment penalties (lenders would prefer that you call them "prepayment *privileges,*" pointing out that it is the borrower who is breaking the contract). But then, isn't the lender in the catbird seat when borrowers prepay on older loans written at lower rates of interest?

Your mortgage contract might have a prepayment clause that allows you to prepay a limited amount of the loan principal annually without penalty. Federal savings and loans, for example, must permit prepayment of at least 20 percent of the amount of the original mortgage loan during any 12-month period without a prepayment penalty. However, you might then be assessed six months' interest on prepayments above 20 percent of the original balance. That could run into big money if you are faced with having to pay off the loan during the first few years.

Some mortgage contracts lift all prepayment penalties after the first five years. You might also reside in one of several states where prepayment penalties are barred; it's generally those states where the "due-on-sale" clause had been held to be unenforceable that are on the side of the borrower here. A due-on-sale clause, if enforced, means that the mortgage can't be assumed by the new owner when the home is sold without the lender being given the opportunity to qualify the buyer and raise the interest rate on the loan if the prevailing rate is appreciably higher. Try to avoid a due-on-sale clause.

You should also be concerned about the length of the loan. What are the advantages, if any, of a 20-year loan, say, or a 40-year loan, as opposed to a conventional 30-year loan? Too many loan seekers with a smattering of math believe that if you double the term of a loan you cut the monthly payment in half. It doesn't work that way. Monthly principal-and-interest payments on a 15-year $50,000 loan at 15 percent would be $669.80. On a 30-year loan, the payments would be $632.23.

MONTHLY P/I PAYMENT TO PAY OFF A $50,000 LOAN AT 15% INTEREST

10 Years — $806.68
15 Years — $669.80
20 Years — $658.40
25 Years — $640.42
30 Years — $632.23
35 Years — $628.41
40 Years — $626.62

Further stretching out of the loan doesn't help much either. Take that same 30-year loan and extend the payback period to 40 years and you reduce the payments a mere $5.61 per month. At the same time, if the loan is held to maturity, you'll end up paying more than $73,000 in interest for that extra decade! The advantages in borrowing for more than 25 or 30 years are all with the lender. At high interest rates, it takes forever with longer loans to begin building equity through amortization. After 10 years of payments on a 40-year loan at 15 percent, 99.11 percent of the original loan remains unpaid; with a $50,000 loan, *only $445* would have been applied toward the reduction of principal! Because of the risks inherent in the longer commitment, lenders also charge higher interest on longer-term loans.

You might question the wisdom of a lender granting a long-term loan to an older applicant. A senior citizen with cash for the down payment and a secure income often can qualify for a loan more easily than a much younger applicant. Although there is little likelihood of a person in his seventies living to pay off a 30-year mortgage, the lender couldn't care less. One way or another, so long as the loan-to-value ratio of the property is preserved, the mortgage will be paid off.

Having submitted to the mortgage interview and completed the loan application, you must now wait anywhere from a week to a month or more until the mortgage-loan committee passes on your application (by which time interest rates may well be higher!). Even if you don't get the loan, you may be required to pay for the processing of your application. This varies. If you are offered a mortgage, even though you don't accept it, there's generally a fee.

Again, a real-estate broker can be a big help here, steering you to lending sources that are likely to find the particular property you wish to purchase a sound investment for both mortgagor and mortgagee. If you come up with more than one loan commitment, at terms you can still afford, so much the better. You can then pick and choose. Once you have the loan commitment, which is an agreement to provide financing on specified terms within a specified period, you're ready for the big day, when you close on the property and take possession.

CONDOS AND CO-OPS

Condominiums and cooperatives are neither special types of structures nor counterculture communes. They are legal plans of residential ownership that increasingly are being applied to suburban garden apartments and detached dwellings as well as to connected town houses and metropolitan high-rises. In a condominium (condo, for short), you own a particu-lar living unit and have a proportional interest in the common property (grounds, hallways, elevators, etc.) and community facilities. You also share the responsibility for management and upkeep of the condo complex. In a co-op, rather than holding legal title to an individual apartment unit, you buy shares of stock corresponding to the value of your unit in a nonprofit, tenant-run corporation that owns the building and are given a long-term "proprietary lease" on your apartment.

The attraction of both condos and co-ops is that they offer the tax and investment advantages of homeownership, but generally for less money than would be needed to buy a sin-gle-family detached house in the immediate area. Many of the newer complexes also include such amenities as swimming pools, saunas, and tennis courts, which few residents could afford to maintain as individuals.

Condos, in particular, represent one of the hottest seg-ments of the housing industry. From an estimated 85,000 ex-isting units in 1970, primarily in resort areas, there are well over two million condo units today. In such cities as Chicago, Houston, San Francisco, Atlanta, Milwaukee, Boston, and Washington, D.C., they dominate the housing market, with singles and childless young marrieds who want to be close to their jobs in booming downtown office areas the big buyers. Co-ops, on the other hand, are almost exclusively a New York City phenomenon; they first appeared there at the turn of the century. Co-ops exist in other areas, but there probably aren't more than 70,000 "independent" co-op units (as distin-guished from federally subsidized co-ops for low-income fami-lies in mostly older, inner-city apartment complexes) in the entire United States.

The fundamental differences between condos and co-ops carry over into their financing. As the buyer of a condo, you would take out a mortgage loan to finance it, essentially as you would for a single-family home. Lenders have no prob-lems with condos in general, since the individual mortgage is secured by a specific condo unit and each owner has his own deed. Where you might run into a problem is finding a lender willing to grant a loan in a development where you might be his only mortgagor; the time and expense of establishing the value of an individual apartment could prove too costly. However, with both newly built condos and conversions of apartment houses from rentals to condos, the builder or developer usually arranges for a large, long-term loan commitment and directs would-be buyers to a designated lender for individual financing. Both FHA-insured and VA-guaranteed loans can be obtained for up to 30-year condo financing.

With co-ops, there's usually one master mortgage on the entire building or complex, and buying in can be much more of a problem. Lenders tend to regard co-op loans as "unsecured." For years, the only way prospective tenant shareholders could finance co-op purchases was with high-rate, short-term personal loans. It wasn't until 1971 that thrifts in New York State were permitted to accept co-op shares as collateral. Even now, co-op loans generally aren't granted for more than 10 or 15 years and at mortgage rates at least 1.5 percentage points above the prevailing interest rate for conventional home-mortgage loans. Which is one reason why in New York City nearly two-thirds of the co-op purchases are all-cash deals.

Creative financing, with the seller participating, is the obvious recourse with both condo and co-op resales. Sellers of co-ops frequently have to take back purchase-money mortgages to facilitate the sale. Another hurdle with selling a co-op is that the co-op's board of directors (elected annually by the membership) can reject would-be buyers for no cause, a right of approval jealously guarded. One reason for the tight screening: Any defaults on the part of tenant shareholders must be borne by all the other owners. While the seller of a condo may, in a few jurisdictions, have an obligation to offer his unit to the condo association under a right of first refusal, at the price offered by an outsider, he usually can make just about any arrangement he wants with whomever he chooses, dealing with the unit as though it were a private dwelling.

Condo owners pay their own mortgage indebtedness and taxes. They also pay a monthly assessment to the association to cover their proportionate share of the common charges for management, maintenance, repairs, and energy costs. The purchaser of a co-op pays a monthly carrying charge that covers a proportionate share of the corporation's current operating expenses, mortgage payments, and property taxes. Operating costs of both condos and co-ops often exceed projections. The two biggest complaints of owners center on as-

sessments and soundproofing, with too much of one and too
little of the other.

Because they present more difficulties in financing and resale, older co-ops tend to be less expensive than comparable
condo units. Co-ops hold one advantage though. Closing
costs are minimal. The change of ownership is effected by
transferring the necessary shares of stock, a relatively simple
legal transaction. There's also this potential: When co-ops go
condo, a recent trend, they usually rise dramatically in market
value.

THE CLOSING: DON'T LET IT UNSETTLE YOU

Some call it the closing. Others call it the settlement. By whatever name, the legal transfer of title to the property is a peculiarly
American ritual. Including buyer, seller, real-estate broker, up to
three lawyers, often someone representing the title insurance
firm, the bank loan officer, and a spouse or two, there may be as
many as eight or ten people sitting stiffly at the conference table.
If you've had a good real-estate lawyer in your corner from the
beginning, however, the closing should be a piece of cake. That's
not to say it's not going to be an expensive occasion. Think of that
cake as pastry ordered from Fauchon in Paris, and flown here on
the Concorde.

Don't set yourself up for some unsettling surprises. By law, if
obtaining the loan from a conventional lending source, you will
have been provided with a "good faith estimate" of the amount or
rate of charges for specific settlement services not more than
three business days after your loan application was received. This
forewarning about costs has been required since 1975, when the
Real Estate Settlement Procedures Act (RESPA) was passed by
Congress to give needed protection to home buyers. Previous to
RESPA, buyers too often came to the table with little warning
that they were going to have to come up with a bundle of cash to
pay off a whole laundry list of settlement items.

RESPA further requires that the person who will be conducting the settlement must provide the buyer, at his request, with a full disclosure of all known actual costs payable at the closing, at least one day prior to the closing. The act additionally prohibits the referral fees and kickbacks that used to be prevalent in the mortgage industry, although many lenders, lawyers, and title companies still scratch each other's backs. Recommendations might be made to you (indeed, if a stranger in town, you might welcome them), but you are under no obligation to use any particular real-estate broker, lender, lawyer, mortgage insurer, or title firm. One of the principal aims of RESPA was to encourage home buyers to shop around for the best deal on any of the negotiable items included in the closing—and to give them time to do so.

You should bring up closing costs at your first meetings with mortgage loan officers and real-estate brokers. This would apply whether you are looking into new or resale houses, traditional or alternative financing. If you're taking over an existing mortgage, or if the seller is "financing" the sale, there can be any number of savings, but you'll still go to a closing, some charges and formalities being unavoidable. With new-home sales, closing costs are frequently included in the selling price of the house. Developers do manage to bring down closing costs with their volume operation, in much the same way they cut down on building costs. But you could end up paying for those "absorbed" costs, if included in the mortgage, several times over in additional interest.

Always find out in advance what closing costs are customary in the area in which you are house-hunting. While many of the amounts will depend on such factors as the size of the mortgage and the down payment, closing-cost tallies can vary from state to state and from lender to lender. Find out which items are likely to be negotiable; charges based on a percentage of the loan amount have shot up out of all proportion to the services rendered. And find out in particular which items might be pinned on the seller.

A resourceful lawyer could cut your closing costs substantially by negotiating for inclusion of a handful of settlement items in the contract of purchase, either making the seller fully responsible or providing that the costs be split. If the seller will be getting a good price for the house, there's a good chance he'll go along with these contract stipulations. Certain closing costs *are* made the seller's responsibility in some states; in others, they fall to the buyer. As you'll find, a lot of what's involved in the closing is based on "local custom."

Excluding the down payment, the buyer's bill for closing costs might average somewhere between $2,000 and $2,500 on a median-priced home. But don't count on it. State, county, and city transfer taxes can total next to nothing in one state and more than $1,000 in another. Private mortgage insurance for a loan with a low down payment would be another expense that you might or might not have to take into consideration. The source of your loan could be a factor too: S&Ls and mortgage companies generally charge more in closing costs than do commercial banks and mutuals.

When you do take your place at the conference table, checkbook in hand, it should be with the comfort of knowing that you and your lawyer have done the best that you could to keep the costs to a minimum. As documents and papers are shuttled back and forth in a blur for signatures, you just might risk a smile, even though the transfer of property is one of the most solemn acts in which an individual can engage.

Here's a rundown of what you might expect in the way of negotiable and nonnegotiable items at the settlement (we'll call it that since more than loan-related closing costs are involved here) and how you might best handle them.

Origination Fee. This is sometimes called the initial service fee, and is the lender's charge for arranging the loan. It's been called other things too, by critics who consider it to be a gouge when collected by the actual lender and not a middleman. A whole flock of settlement charges properly should be covered by this fee, which can run from 1 to 3 percent or more of the mortgage amount, but that's not often the practice these days. Lenders increasingly are applying it as a fee unto itself. In addition to the mortgage interest rate, this is the closing-cost item to be most concerned with when shopping for a lender. As such, it's a negotiable item.

Loan Discount. This is not a break for the buyer; the lender gets the discount. As mortgage discount "points" (one point being

1 percent of the mortgage amount), this is a one-time charge that adjusts the yield the lender receives on the loan to make up any difference between an allowable rate of interest and the general market rate. The lender may also offer a lower mortgage interest rate in exchange for charging more points. (For a fuller explanation of "points," see page 79.)

Credit-Report Fee. The lender may do some checking on his own but most likely will rely on the services of a credit-reporting company to verify the applicant's financial and credit status in his home community. Nonnegotiable. Buyer pays.

Appraisal Fee. The evaluation of the property by a professional appraiser employed or engaged by the lender sets the limit of the loan commitment. The fee varies, depending on the lender and the complexity of the property, and may be paid by either buyer or seller.

Property Survey. The lender may require a survey to define the precise location of the house and its boundaries. If a survey is required, the seller's old survey, together with a "statement of no change," signed by the seller and possibly one or more of his neighbors, might be acceptable in lieu of a new survey. Ask your lawyer about this one.

Title Search. Nearly every lender requires a title search handled by an attorney or a title company to verify that the property has no claims against it. The search is best left to a title company. Most larger title companies maintain well-indexed files of duplicated public records and can run a search in far less time than a lawyer (or the clerk employed by him) plowing through dusty courthouse archives would take—and for a lot less money. In states with Marketable Title Act statutes, a 40-year search of the "chain of title" is sufficient. Get some quotes before you commit yourself on this service. The buyer usually pays all title costs, except in some western states, where the seller may share some of the expenses. Arrange to split the costs if you can.

Title Insurance. If he requires a title search, the mortgage lender will also likely call for title insurance on the property. This is to cover any liens or ownership disputes that may crop up after the property changes hands. The required insurance, covering the decreasing balance of the loan, protects the lender only. Though title challenges are rare, you should get coverage to protect your investment as well, if advised to do so by your lawyer. If coverage for both owner and lender are acquired in the same package, there is a substantial saving over policies purchased separately. You might save still more if you can get a "reissue rate" from the seller's title insurer. Depending on how much time has elapsed since the last title search, the issuer of the seller's policy might eliminate the need (and expense) for a new search. Title insurance is covered by a one-time premium and the policy remains in effect until the property again changes ownership.

Hazard Insurance. To protect the lender in the event the mortgaged property is damaged or destroyed by fire, wind, or other natural hazard, you will be required to carry a homeowner's policy covering a specified amount and naming the lender as an additional assured. Check with your insurance agent. You may be able to buy this coverage through him for less than through the lender. The premium frequently is made part of the monthly mortgage payment and is a continuing expense.

Mortgage Insurance. There are two kinds of mortgage insurance. One protects the lender from loss if the buyer defaults on his mortgage payments. It is required with FHA and most high-ratio (low-down-payment) conventional loans. A fee may also be charged by the lender for processing the application for this insurance. The other kind of mortgage insurance is reducing-term life insurance, also called "mortgage-cancellation insurance." It is designed to protect the owner's heirs by paying off the mortgage in full in the event of his early demise. You may or may not need this insurance. It would depend on how much life insurance you already carry. If you go for a mortgage-protection policy, you might cut down on your other coverage. Look for a nonbinding policy that doesn't require that the money be used to pay off the mortgage. Your heirs might appreciate the option.

Transfer Taxes. In some localities, state and/or local taxes are levied whenever property changes ownership.

Recording Fees. These are the charges made by county and other local authorities for officially recording the new deed and other documents (usually drawn up by the seller's lawyer) formalizing the transaction. A notary fee may be included here.

Escrow Fee. The lender may require that an escrow, or "impound," account (which is one that you can't get at) be set up for the handling of property taxes and insurance premiums. With government-backed loans, lenders are required by law to collect for these items on a prorated basis each month. The settlement itself might be handled by an escrow agent, to whom an additional fee would have to be paid. He would function as the custodian of all documents (held prior to recording) and as disburser of all monies involved in the transaction.

Termite Inspection. An inspection for termites is recommended in those areas of the country where they are a threat. The fee should be split between buyer and seller, if not paid by the seller, since a clean bill would free him from any liability should termites turn up in the future.

Engineering Report. With older houses, it's wise to have the house checked for any structural defects before closing. If you're going to need a new roof, make the seller responsible for the cost of the roof and any other major repair work. The report should also include an assessment of the building's energy efficiency. Unless he's guaranteed the house against substantial defects, the seller should pay for the engineering report.

Preparation of Documents. Even though preprinted forms are used for most of the documents and other papers that are necessary to the transaction, miscellaneous service fees are charged for the filling in of the details.

Closing Fee. Depending on local custom, an independent agent or an attorney representing the lender or title company may handle the settlement transaction. The fee charged for this service should be split between buyer and seller.

Prepayments. You sometimes are given the option of making direct payments for hazard insurance and property taxes or paying through the lender. Most loans, and lenders, however, require prorated prepayments of these items, taxes in particular, into an escrow account. At the closing, you'll also have to prepay interest covering the period from the date of the closing until the first scheduled mortgage payment. Adjustments may be needed with insurance and taxes as well, to get everything on a regular basis.

Adjustments of Prepaid Items. You'll likely have to reimburse the seller for any prepaid property taxes and such other items, if substantial, as fuel oil on hand, and the unexpired portions of service and utility contracts.

Legal Fees. There's a lot of fat in most lawyer's fees and you'd do well to shop for a lawyer, preferably an expert in real-estate transactions. It's usually cheaper to engage an attorney on a time-and-effort basis than to pay him a flat fee or a percentage of the purchase price of the house. If you have to economize, it's more important to have the personal services of an attorney when you are negotiating the contract and he can save you many times his fee, rather than at the closing, which is usually cut and dried. He should also "examine" the title and verify that the search was properly done. In some states, it's customary for the seller's lawyer to represent the buyer as well in real-estate transactions. But that's like being in the position of seeking a divorce and committing yourself to using your spouse's attorney. You also have to pay half of his fee.

In sum then, as a buyer, your major negotiable items are the origination fee, the title search, and your lawyer's fee. At the closing, you'll also have to take care of the balance of the down payment. Depending on the custom, all your obligations could be covered with a single fat check, which would go to an escrow agent or your lawyer for disbursements, or you may be required to write any number of smaller checks. Come prepared. The only payment that could be postponed would be your lawyer's fee, which possibly could be spread over two or three months.

The seller too has certain obligations at the closing, including payment of the broker's commission and his attorney's fee. The seller might also bear or share the cost of the appraisal, survey, title search and insurance, termite and engineering inspections, recording fees, and some nonexclusive attorney fees.

At the closing, or earlier, ask for a copy of the seller's settlement sheet and check for any duplication of charges. Be sure that the two of you aren't being charged full fees for the same thing.

When everything has been signed, including (by you) a promissory note guaranteeing to repay the loan, the mortgage document goes to the lender, you get the deed, and the property is yours.

HOME SWEET TAX BREAK

If it weren't for the many valuable tax deductions that effectively subsidize personal housing, we'd still be largely a nation of renters. Deductions taken by homeowners for mortgage interest payments and local property taxes alone "cost" the U.S. Treasury more than $36 billion in uncollected tax revenues in 1981, up from $5.4 billion in 1970. A lot of other loopholes in the tax laws have been closed to investors, but homeownership is a tax shelter that, under inflation and progressive-income-tax rates, gets better all the time.

Tax breaks apply right from the start of the hunt for a house. If you move in connection with your job or business (even if self-employed) and your new main job location is at least 35 miles farther from your former residence than your old main job location was, you can claim, as an adjustment to income, up to $1,500 for such "indirect" moving costs as outlays for transportation, meals, and lodging for house-hunting trips, as well as the cost of temporary quarters for up to 30 days while waiting to move into your new residence. As for the move itself, there is no dollar limit on the deduction that can be taken for the *actual* cost of moving your household goods, personal effects, and family to the new address. But keep in mind that *no* deduction can be taken for moving-related expenses unless you meet that 35-miles-or-better qualifier.

Some but not all of the closing costs you pay when buying a house can be applied toward reducing your taxes. Loan origination fees or points that are paid "solely for the use of money," with the loan secured by your personal residence, are treated for tax purposes as interest. As such, they are fully deductible in the year of payment. Neither title-related expenses nor attorney fees can be claimed as itemized tax deductions, but they may be added to your home's *basis* cost to reduce the net taxable profit when the house is sold. This would apply as well to recording fees and transfer taxes. You also have the option of treating these purchase-related expenses as moving expenses. There, you'd have a $3,000 limit, other indirect moving costs included.

The big, continuing deductions, of course, are for mortgage interest payments to the lender and real-estate taxes. With amortized loans, not all of the monthly mortgage payment is deductible. Part of the payment will be applied toward reducing the loan principal. In the beginning, though, nearly 100 percent of each monthly payment represents interest. Even in the 10th year of a 30-year 12 percent loan, better than 90 percent of each payment is deductible.

If you buy a house built pre-April 20, 1977, and upgrade its energy efficiency by adding insulation, installing storm doors and windows, putting in a clock thermostat, or substituting a more efficient burner for a gas- or oil-fired heating system, you can take a tax *credit* (which is better than a deduction, since it is subtracted dollar for dollar from the tax liability) of 15 percent of the first $2,000 of qualifying energy-conserving expenditures, for a maximum tax credit of $300 during the life of the credit, which expires December 31, 1985. The credit applies to your principal residence only; making a summer or vacation home more energy efficient does not qualify for the credit.

There's an even heftier tax incentive to prod you toward installing alternate-energy systems that tap a "renewable energy source." This applies to solar, geothermal, and wind energy conversion hardware—but again, for your principal residence only. The tax credit is 40 percent of the first $10,000 spent on the equipment and its installation, for a maximum dollar-for-dollar tax write-off of $4,000. This credit applies to newly constructed houses as well as to older ones. It does not matter when the house was built. Any unused credit may be carried forward through 1987.

Deductions may also be taken for mortgage prepayment penalties and for casualty losses attributable to sudden, unexpected, or unusual causes. "Sudden" is the key word here.

The costs of repairing a wind-torn roof (beyond those costs covered by insurance, less $100) would be an allowable deduction; termite damage would not be.

When you get ready to sell the house, the costs of any capital improvements—a new roof, water heater, or furnace—can be added to the basis cost of the house. Costs for superficial fix up—painting, wallpapering, and minor repair work—are generally held to be nondeductible personal expenses. However, you *can* offset them, as an adjustment in the sales price of the old residence, when buying a replacement residence and postponing tax on the gain. But only if the work was done no more than 90 days before signing the sales contract and paid for no later than 30 days after the sale.

The biggest tax break for homeowners goes to those who have reached 55 years of age and are selling a principal residence they have occupied for at least three of the five years preceding the date of sale. If you are 55 or older, you can escape taxes on up to $125,000 of profit from the sale, as a once-in-a-lifetime exclusion. The profit on the sale is the difference between the "adjusted sales price" (gross selling price less broker's commission and other selling expenses) and the "adjusted basis" (contract price plus closing costs not deductible at time of purchase and capital-improvement costs). If you're planning to sell a house that is worth a whole lot more than you paid for it and are nearing your 55th birthday, it could be to your advantage to hold off closing the deal until after that happy day.

At any age, you can sidestep having to pay tax on the profit realized on the sale of a house if you "roll over" your gain into a replacement principal residence within 24 months of selling the old one. This could be applied to a whole series of steps up the housing ladder, trading up each house for a more expensive one, and postponing the tax reckoning until you're 55 or older.

But maybe you don't want another house. Maybe the kids have left the nest and you've moved into a rental apartment or bought a small condominium for less than you grossed on the sale of your home. You may be facing having to pay tax on a sizable capital gain. Don't despair. As of January 1, 1982, the *maximum* effective capital-gains tax you'd pay on personal property sold after holding it for at least one year would be 20 percent. You do have a tax-saving alternative though. If your taxable income, including capital gains, exceeds your average income over the past four years by 20 percent or more, it could pay you to use income averaging. What it does is spread the gain over five years at lower tax rates.

The Standard
Mortgage ▬

The home-mortgage instrument from which almost all other mortgage instruments in use today derive is the fully amortized, fixed-rate, level-payment loan. It fixes the interest rate and monthly payment for the life of the loan and has been the standard residential mortgage since the 1930s.

Before the adoption of amortization on a wide scale, the mustachioed villain who foreclosed on widows in distress was not just a fictional character. In hard times, foreclosures were all too common, as families who had paid nothing but interest on their mortgages for three to five years were pressed by unsympathetic moneylenders to pay the entire principal in one lump.

The key feature of amortizing is that while the monthly mortgage payment remains fixed throughout the life of the loan, the debt is reduced each month and the borrower pays interest only on what he still owes; the balance of the payment goes toward retiring the loan. It's a form of forced saving. The debt reduction—or equity buildup—can come slowly in the mortgage's early years, especially at high rates of interest, but at the end of the loan period the entire principal will have been repaid. As long as the borrower keeps up his payments, there's never any threat of foreclosure.

The standard mortgage actually covers three basic kinds of loan. Two of them, the FHA loan and the VA (or GI) loan, are backed by the federal government. The third (and, until recently, much more prevalent) kind is the so-called conventional loan. All three are level-payment, amortized loans, but with important differences you should know about.

CONVENTIONAL HOME LOANS

For years, a conventional mortgage loan has meant a fixed-rate, level-payment, long-term, amortized loan arranged between borrower and lender without any federal involvement. The conventional loan used to represent between 65 and 75 percent of all home-mortgage loans written, with FHA, VA, and Farmers Home Administration (FmHA) loans making up the balance. It was an ideal mortgage instrument until double-digit inflation turned it into a great giveaway and knocked the financial props out from under lenders who had billions of dollars tied up in long-term mortgages written when interest rates were single digit. The consensus among lenders today is that the fixed-rate mortgage was a mistake. But then, none of them anticipated that this country would ever fall victim to chronic inflation and unpredictable interest rates.

In inflationary periods, a fixed-rate loan that is paid off in equal monthly installments can be a bonanza for the borrower, but few authorities hold out much hope for the conventional loan becoming widely available again, even should inflation be brought under control. One exception is George G. Kaufman, professor of economics and finance at Loyola University of Chicago, and a former deputy assistant secretary of the U.S. Treasury. Professor Kaufman sees a quick return of the conventional loan in a stable market, with the borrower having the option to choose a fixed-rate mortgage "and lock in today's interest rate for the life of the loan" or to bet on a favorable interest-rate change with an adjustable-rate loan. "The market would determine the relative price of each type of mortgage based on borrower and lender preferences," says Professor Kaufman.

Oakley Hunter, retired chairman of the board of the Federal

National Mortgage Association, is somewhat less optimistic. He has suggested that "the inflation rate would have to go under 5 percent if we were to see any substantial return to 30-year fixed-rate mortgages."

Depending then on the economy and a degree of optimism, you may or may not find a lender who is writing fixed-rate, long-term loans when you shop for your financing. Where fixed-rate loans do survive, they will likely be for FHA-insured and VA-guaranteed mortgages. Conventional loans, though dying a slower death than many experts expected, by the end of 1981 were being offered by only about one in three S&Ls.

Before burying this "Model T" of mortgage loans, it might be useful to see what changes have occurred with this kind of loan since its inception.

The most obvious change has been in the extension of the payback period. From under 12 years in the late 1930s, the legal limit has been stretched out to 15, 20, 25, 30, and, in December 1980, for federally chartered S&Ls, 40 years. There's even been talk of 50-year loans. But we've already shown that there's no real benefit to the borrower with loans written for more than 25 to 30 years. Nor are longer loan lengths justified by the anticipated economic life of many of the homes built in recent years. But then, for one reason or another, most borrowers settle up the old mortgage well before maturity; we move around a lot, and the average house is turned over once every seven or eight years. So, your advantage with a mortgage loan written for 25 or 30 years, rather than for a shorter term, would be in the lower monthly principal-and-interest payment per thousand dollars borrowed.

What is less obvious is that amortization, the very foundation of the standard mortgage, becomes a negligible factor with longer-term loans and high interest rates. Take an example from the 1950s: a 10-year $15,000 loan at 5 percent interest. It was paid back in 120 monthly installments of $159.10, covering principal and interest. In the first year of the loan, $1,186.50 was applied toward reducing the loan principal. By the 61st payment, at the beginning of the sixth year of the loan, the unpaid loan principal was reduced to $8,430. In this example, amortization does everything it was designed to do.

Now let's take a more recent example: a 30-year $50,000 loan at 15 percent, to be paid off in 360 monthly installments of $632.23. The stretching out of the loan, coupled with the high rate of interest, holds amortization to an exhausted snail's pace. Even after 10 years of payments, the loan principal will have been reduced by only $1,990; after 25 years of payments, more than 50 percent of the original loan will remain unpaid. Equity buildup through amortization comes much more slowly with longer-term, higher-interest loans—and little principal will have been paid off by the time most of the homes bought since the late 1970s change hands.

For many families, the prospect of building equity through amortization was a significant inducement to buy a home. With the erosion of the equity-building character of a long-term amortizing loan, we'd have to write off the importance of amortization until mortgage interest rates return to stable, much lower levels—and we don't count on that happening in the foreseeable future.

Another strike against the conventional loan has been the inclusion in most mortgages since 1976—and in some mortgages written years earlier—of a "due-on-sale" clause that permits the lender to call the entire loan (make the balance of the debt immediately payable in full) when the property is sold. Unless given permission to do so by the lender, the borrower cannot allow the new owner to assume the existing mortgage and continue payment at the interest rate at which the loan was issued. (FHA and VA loans do not include due-on-sale clauses and are guaranteed assumable at their original rate.) Due-on-sale gives the lender the option of raising the contract rate to the prevailing market level while qualifying the new buyer and executing a written assumption agreement with him.

There were a number of states, however, where, prior to a ruling by the U.S. Supreme Court in June 1982 applicable to federally chartered S&Ls, the due-on-sale clause had been held to be unenforceable. But lenders were presented with a gimmick in 1981 that, with new conventional loans, effectively overcame this obstruction. Under a "call option," the lender reserves the right to call the loan in seven years.

The Federal National Mortgage Association (FNMA), better known as Fannie Mae, was responsible for introduction of this escape hatch, having issued a directive to approved primary lenders that unless borrowers agreed to a call option, it no longer would buy conventional loans written in the 17 states* where due-on-sale clauses could not be enforced. FNMA's move was prompted by the changing rate at which the more than two million mortgages it held were being paid off. Where, in the past, the "probable life" of most residential mortgages was 12 years, and Fannie Mae could attract market investors to its mortgage-backed securities on that basis, the turn to creative financing—and a rapid growth in loan assumptions and wraparound mortgages—threatened to prolong the life-span of the lower-yielding mortgages in its portfolio to well beyond 12 years. Already stuck with a multi-billion-dollar investment portfolio in which nine out of ten loans had been written at single-digit interest rates, Fannie Mae could see the red ink flowing for decades to come.

Critics have called the seven-year call option a time bomb waiting to go off in the pocketbooks of home buyers. The option gives the lender the right to cancel the loan or renew it at a higher interest rate, when dictated by market conditions, every seven years. There is no limit on how much the interest rate might be raised. With no long-term protection, and no equity buildup to speak of, the borrower is pretty much back to where borrowers were before the Great Depression. Unless you thrive on fear of the unknown, the call option could be reason enough to walk away from a deal should it pop up.

A major shortcoming of the conventional level-payment loan is that it makes no allowance for changes in the mortgagor's earning power. For younger home buyers especially, it calls for too much too soon. With a 20 to 25 percent down payment, and fixed monthly payments for the life of the loan, it doesn't recognize the increased earnings potential of the upwardly mobile individual or family and the effects of inflation on the payment-to-income ratio.

---

* Arizona, Arkansas, California, Colorado, Florida, Georgia, Illinois, Iowa, Michigan, Minnesota, Mississippi, New Mexico, New York, Ohio, Oklahoma, South Carolina, and Washington.

Not only does the conventional loan call for a larger down payment than do FHA and VA mortgage loans, but it's usually written at a higher rate of interest. Many lenders also are front-loading conventional mortgage loans with an inflationary-risk surcharge that effectively sets the interest rate 1 to 2 percentage points higher than on adjustable-rate loans.

It *is* possible to obtain conventional loans with smaller down payments than the customary 20 to 25 percent. Loans covering up to 90 or 95 percent of the appraised value of an owner-occupied property can be arranged, provided the higher-risk portion of the loan is insured. Many young families today have good incomes but, while otherwise qualified, not nearly enough savings to come up with the 20 or 25 percent cash down payment to start a new home. The solution to that problem is to make arrangements through the lender for private mortgage insurance (PMI) covering the top 20 or 25 percent of the loan.

The coverage, paid for by the borrower, protects the lender against financial loss should the mortgagor default on the loan. Together with the insurance protection and appreciating home values, the lender's risk of ever suffering a loss on foreclosure and resale of the property becomes next to nil. As one consequence, many lenders will make high-ratio loans with PMI where they wouldn't grant uninsured loans even with a 20 or 25 percent down payment.

Let's say you've found a neighborhood S&L still making conventional loans. You're seeking financing for a home appraised at $80,000, and have been given a loan commitment for $76,000, or 95 percent of the home's value. To nail down that loan, the lender will require you to take out PMI covering the top 25 percent of the loan, reducing the lender's risk exposure by $19,000, to an easier-to-live-with $57,000. At the same time, you will have lowered the down-payment barrier from $16,000 or $20,000 to a much more manageable $4,000.

And now for the bad news. Lowering the down payment will boost both your closing costs and your monthly P/I payment. With a 5 percent down payment, PMI first-year coverage typically costs 1 percent of the full amount of the loan (in this case, $760) and is payable at the closing; with a 90 percent loan, PMI would be one-half of 1 percent. On top of the first-year payment, you will be required to pay one-quarter of 1 percent annually on the declining balance of the loan, probably until the mortgage has been paid down to below $60,000, or 75 percent of the purchase price. So figure *that* as a bump in the mortgage interest rate. And, unless you're related to the lender, he's also going to want an additional one-half of 1 percent for the life of the loan just for opening the door to homeownership for you.

These loans are sometimes referred to as "magic" loans, after MGIC, the initials for Mortgage Guaranty Insurance Corporation, the leading insurer in this field. There are more than a dozen companies writing PMI policies today, but the rates are about the same everywhere. This insurance from commercial insurance companies serves much the same purpose as FHA insurance and the VA guaranty. Depending on eligibility, you'll have to weigh the advantages of each kind of loan if your principal concern is with the down payment. One of the pluses with conventional loans, with or without PMI, is that they usually can be obtained with a minimum of red tape, often within a week or two, where the paper work when federal agencies are involved can sometimes take months.

The primary advantage with a conventional loan remains that fixed monthly payment. Even at today's interest rates, as long as inflation continues, you'll be paying off your debt with cheaper, inflated dollars. Just make sure that you aren't locked into a high rate of interest for the next 30 years by an ironbound mortgage contract. Those interest rates *could* come down one day.

THE MAE SISTERS AND FREDDIE MAC

If we had only the thrifts and the banks to fund home-mortgage loans from consumer savings, we'd *really* be hurting for housing. A *big* chunk of all the money committed to making the housing market go comes from so-called secondary-market financing. In short, the mortgage loan that you arrange for at the neighborhood savings and loan, or a mortgage company, may only originate there. If the thrift needs funds for additional mortgage lending, and almost certainly in the case of the mortgage company, your mortgage will be sold to the secondary market. Since the originator most likely will continue to service the loan, chances are you won't even know that it has been sold.

With many of the thrifts inextricably in trouble, the secondary market is rapidly becoming the country's most important source of funds for home loans. The secondary market is already buying nearly half of all the residential mortgages being written today—and is expected to be funding two out of every three first-mortgage loans by 1990.

A large portion of the mortgage "paper" that enters the secondary market goes directly from the "primary" lender to major private investors, like an insurance company or a pension fund, which find residential mortgage loans an attractive source of income. But there's also a triad of government-created secondary-market organizations designed to provide additional liquidity to the mortgage market, during periods of tight money especially, by aggregating mortgages into marketable securities.

Created in 1938 as a subsidiary of the federally owned Reconstruction Finance Corporation, and later serving as a division of the Department of Housing and Urban Development (HUD), the quasi-governmental agency that we know today as the Federal National Mortgage Association, or by its initials, FNMA, or its sobriquet, Fannie Mae, is the nation's largest supplier of residential mortgage funds. No longer an agency of the government, FNMA was rechartered by Congress in 1968 to operate as a private, stockholder-owned corporation. Fannie Mae purchases mortgages with funds borrowed in the capital markets. Much of the money comes from large institutions seeking ways to invest assets profitably and prudently. By offering to these investors competitively priced debt obligations backed by pools of mortgages, Fannie Mae channels billions of dollars annually from the capital markets into home financing. Since 1968, the corporation has bought more than 2.5 million residential mortgages.

Fannie Mae does not deal directly with consumers. The corporation guarantees approximtely 3,500 lenders across the country a market for their mortgage loans if they choose to sell them. Under an auction program conducted biweekly by phone, Fannie Mae sells "commitments" to lenders, pledging to buy specified dollar amounts of mortgage loans within a fixed period of time (normally four months) and usually at a specified yield to the corporation.

After a lender sells a package of mortgages to Fannie Mae, he generally continues to service the loans. That is, he collects the monthly payments and forwards them to Fannie Mae, maintains accounts for the payment of property taxes and hazard insurance, and keeps the necessary records on the loans until they are repaid. The corporation pays the lender a fee for servicing each loan it has purchased. Prior to 1972, FNMA bought only government-backed FHA and VA loans, but it now purchases non-government-backed loans as well; conventional mortgage loans currently comprise about one-third of its $60 billion mortgage portfolio.

Mortgage companies originate nearly 80 percent of the loans acquired by Fannie Mae; S&Ls account for only about 10 percent. Fannie Mae would like to do more business with the thrifts, but the Federal Home Loan Mortgage Corporation (FHLMC) or Freddie Mac, established as a quasi-private corporation in 1970, with a congressional mandate to develop a nationwide backup market for conventional residential mortgage loans, gets the bulk of the S&Ls' mortgage-resale business. Freddie Mac acquires mortgages through various purchase programs and issues "pass-through" securities, principally Mortgage Participation Certificates (in $100,000 or larger denominations), backed by pools of mortgages. The securities generally are marketed to major investors through a syndicate of securities dealers. Interest-and-principal payments from the underlying mortgages are passed through monthly to the holders of the certificates.

The third member of this backup group is the Government National Mortgage Association (GNMA, or Ginnie Mae). GNMA was formed when FNMA was spun off by the government in 1968 and remains a government-owned corporation within HUD. Ginnie Mae's primary responsibility is to supply mortgage credit that supports the government's housing objectives. Funded mainly by borrowings from the U.S. Treasury, GNMA purchases mortgages not readily salable in the private market. More often than not, the mortgages are secured by federally subsidized housing serving low- and moderate-income families. Ginnie Mae's general purchase authority is limited to mortgages insured or guaranteed by the government.

There also are mortgage-backed securities called "Ginnie Maes." These bondlike securities do not originate with GNMA. They originate with FHA-approved mortgagees. The issuers of Ginnie Maes are mostly mortgage banking companies but also include larger S&Ls and commercial banks. The lender can issue securities in offerings as small as $500,000, which, when backed by a pool of loans, will be guaranteed as to timely payment of principal and interest by GNMA. These government-backed securities, with mortgage interest and payments on principal passed through to shareholders, pay a higher rate of interest than comparable U.S. Treasury bonds and have ready acceptance in the securities market. More than $110 billion in Ginnie Mae pass-throughs have been sold to date.

Fannie Mae and Freddie Mac are competitive in the conventional mortgage market, but they've also worked together on devising standard mortgage instruments, as well as standardized loan-application and appraisal forms. Virtually all lenders, whether they intend to sell their mortgages or not, use these forms today. The new challenge is to package flexible mortgage instruments to make them acceptable to secondary-market investors. Since 1981, both Freddie Mac and Fannie Mae have been buying standard types of adjustable-rate mortgages.

FNMA and FHLMC scrutinize all loans before acceptance for credit and security quality and for adequate documentation. The loan must meet precise standards. On mortgages with loan-to-value ratios that exceed 80 percent, the amount in excess of 75 percent must be insured. There's no minimum mortgage amount but there are maximums: FHA—generally $67,500, more in HUD-designated high-cost areas; VA—$110,000; conventional—$98,500 ($147,500 for Alaska and Hawaii). If the lender customarily sells his loans to one of these corporations, you could run into a problem if you're seeking a loan in a higher amount.

The most potentially troublesome condition imposed by any of the national mortgage associations is in FNMA's announcement that, where not prohibited by law, it will fully enforce the due-on-sale clause (Paragraph 17 of the FNMA/FHLMC uniform mortgage document) for all transfers of ownership. Where FNMA determines it may not be able to fully enforce the due-on-sale clause, the loan must contain a call option that may be exercised in seven years.

FHA-INSURED HOME LOANS

Since 1934, when it was created to stimulate the moribund residential-construction industry, the Federal Housing Administration (FHA) has helped more than 16 million families to buy homes. The agency, which has been under the Department of Housing and Urban Development (HUD) since 1965, is many things to many people, offering a wide range of both subsidized and unsubsidized loan programs, covering everything from urban renewal to mobile homes. The program with which we are concerned here is the basic Section 203(b) HUD/FHA home-mortgage insurance program, covering unsubsidized loans for proposed, under construction, and existing single-family homes.

The FHA does not itself make loans. Under this vintage program, which is self-supporting, FHA guarantees the repayment of loans made to home buyers under its tight guidelines by banks, thrifts, mortgage companies, and other HUD/FHA-approved lenders. The Reagan Administration, in its budget cutting, may succeed in reducing, if not ending, FHA's role in the single-family, unsubsidized loan market, but as of this writing, anyone may apply for an FHA-insured mortgage loan.

The biggest, and some say only, advantage with an FHA-insured loan is a low down payment. For an FHA-insured loan of $67,500, the down payment would be $2,875. That low down payment could be a very big attraction to a young family with good monthly income but not much in savings. The down payment of an FHA-insured loan is determined by figuring 3 percent on the first $25,000, plus 5 percent on the balance of the loan. In our example, it works out like this: $25,000 x .03 ($750), plus $42,500 x .05 ($2,125), for a total of $2,875.

Unfortunately, for many would-be home buyers, $67,500 is the present ceiling on these loans, except in Hawaii, Alaska, and a few other remote areas, like Guam and the Trust Territory of the Pacific Islands. There, the loans can go as high as $90,000. Since FHA does not allow second mortgages or other supplemental financing with a new FHA loan when buying a home, the buyer of a higher-priced house would have to come up with the difference between $67,500 and the purchase price, in cash. Unless you are considering a property selling for less than $67,500, you could be better off with a conventional loan (provided you still can get one) and private mortgage insurance to reduce the down payment.

The private mortgage-insurance companies would just as soon see FHA out of the insurance business, since they serve essentially the same market. The private insurers claim to offer everything for the unsubsidized home buyer that FHA does, and for less. Much of their case is based on the fact that the mortgagor pays one-half of 1 percent interest yearly on the average outstanding balance for FHA insurance (with one-twelfth of the annual mortgage-insurance premium included in the monthly PITI payment to the lender) while private mortgage insurance on a conventional loan, after the first year, is only one-quarter of 1 percent yearly. FHA insurance also must be continued until the loan has been paid off, while private mortgage insurance usually can be terminated when the loan has been reduced through amortization to 75 percent of its original amount.

One thing the private mortgage insurers don't tell you is that FHA's insurance program consistently runs at a profit, and the mortgagor, whose premiums go into a general insurance fund against which defaults are charged, can come into a nice little dividend, typically running from $400 to $900, when he pays off the loan. They also don't tell him that the FHA program tends to be countercyclical; it often represents "the only game in town" when money is tight. FHA-insured loans also are more important in some markets than in others. Nevertheless, it's recognized in most markets that FHA now gets to underwrite mainly those riskier loans that private insurers have avoided.

The maximum interest rate that can be charged on FHA-insured loans is set by the Secretary of HUD, who adjusts the rate from time to time, up or down, to keep it a bit below the private-market level. But just because the FHA interest ceiling is set at

15, say, when the prevailing interest rate on conventional mortgage loans is 15.75, doesn't mean that you're going to have an interest edge with a government-backed loan. A lender would be
a fool to lend out money at 15 percent when money is tight and
he can, with less work, get a 15.75 percent return. To make
the FHA-insured loan equally profitable, he'll likely charge
points (see page 79) to bring the yield up to the prevailing market
level. To compute the annual percentage rate charged on an
FHA-insured mortgage loan then, the borrower not only should
add one-half of 1 percent for the insurance but prorate the cost of
any discount points that he is required to pay, whether directly or
indirectly.

FHA-insured mortgage loans generally can't be written for
terms of more than 30 years or three-quarters of the dwelling's
remaining (FHA-estimated) economic life, whichever is less. In
special circumstances, if an FHA inspection is made during the
construction of the house, 35-year terms are possible. With FHA-
insured loans, not only the borrower but the house must pass close
inspection. Builders looking for FHA approvals must build to
HUD/FHA Minimum Property Standards or other codes acceptable to FHA for design, location, and construction. Less rigid
construction standards are permitted in rural areas.

Many lenders refuse to handle FHA-insured loans because of
the red tape and time delays involved. Even with efficiencies introduced in 1980, it still takes from four to six weeks just to push
all the required paper work through the FHA maze. It's the
lender who has to deal with FHA. The borrower deals only with
the lender.

To apply for an FHA-insured mortgage loan, you first have to
find an FHA-approved lender, and not all of *them* care to deal
with the paper work and the other hassles that these loans can
entail, such as sellers who back out when told they'll have to
pay points and fix-up costs. However, roughly one-third of all
mortgage loans written by mutual savings banks are for government-backed loans. And with the development of Ginnie Mae
pass-throughs, more S&Ls, especially the larger ones, are willing
to write FHA-insured loans than was formerly the case. It's the
mortgage companies though that are most heavily committed to

the issuing of government-backed loans; many of them prosper by specializing in FHA and VA home mortgages, and routinely grant loans on properties outside the normal geographic lending radius of other lenders.

Application for a loan is made on approved FHA forms, which call for such details as a four-year history of the applicant's residency and employment. The applicant must be able to show that his prospective housing and maintenance costs, utilities included, won't exceed 35 percent of his effective net income; the FHA may make some allowances here on a case-by-case basis, depending on the number of dependents and the other debt obligations of the applicant. The lender runs a credit check on the applicant and, if he's satisfied that the applicant can handle the loan, forwards the application and supporting documents to the HUD/FHA field office that serves the area in which the property is located.

The agency's Mortgage Credit Section then reviews the application and either rejects it or assigns an appraiser to make an evaluation of the property the applicant wishes to buy. Using a building code that is acceptable to FHA, the appraiser will make a careful assessment of the property as to its fair market value and cite any corrections that would have to be made and paid for by the seller before the sale could be finalized. If the application and the appraisal meet FHA requirements, a Commitment for Insurance is issued, specifying the amount of mortgage loan FHA will assure. The insurance protects the lender against any loss on the mortgage should the buyer default. When the lender has the commitment in hand, he can set a date for the closing and the loan can be made.

For one reason or another, up to half the commitments FHA issues are never used. The appraisal may have come in too low and called for more cash to close the deal than the buyer could raise. With the long delay between the time the prospective buyer made his purchase offer and the closing, interest rates could have climbed high enough to knock him out of the housing market. Or, while waiting for the FHA commitment to come through, the buyer and the seller may have gotten together on some method of creative financing.

Closing costs are a little different with government-backed

mortgages than they are with conventional mortgage loans. For one thing, the lender is limited to a one-point mortgage origination fee or service charge. Any additional points charged would have to be paid by the seller (who generally passes the cost on to the buyer in the purchase price). The buyer also has no option as to how he will handle his payments for real-estate taxes and hazard insurance. He's required to make payments in advance into an escrow account so that the lender is assured sufficient funds are on hand when the obligations come due. If the borrower chooses, a portion of his closing costs can be included in his loan and financed over the long term, which would further serve to cut down on the cash needed at the closing. The loan would be based on FHA's assessed value of the property plus closing costs, or the sales price plus closing costs, if lower.

With FHA-insured mortgage loans, there are no prepayment penalties. The borrower can make extra payments of principal without penalty to reduce the balance of the loan, or he can pay off his entire mortgage balance for any reason. If mortgage rates drop sufficiently, he could find it to his advantage to pay off his FHA loan and take out a new mortgage loan elsewhere, or even take out a new FHA loan at a lower rate of interest.

If the borrower runs into payment difficulties down the road, there is less pressure for a foreclosure than there might be with a conventional loan. An FHA-insured homeowner threatened with foreclosure due to circumstances beyond his control, such as a job loss, may apply for assignment of the mortgage to HUD, which, if it accepts assignment, takes over the mortgage and adjusts the mortgage payments for a period of time until the homeowner can resume his financial obligations. FHA-insured mortgages also are guaranteed assumable by a future purchaser of the property at the same long-term fixed rate you receive.

Veterans can do better with VA-guaranteed home-mortgage loans, but they can also get a good deal with an FHA-insured loan. Instead of paying 3 percent on that first $25,000 of the loan, an eligible veteran has to come up with just $200 as a down payment on that much of the loan. For those still in service and in need of private housing for themselves and/or their families, members of the services on active duty can arrange for an FHA-insured mortgage loan just as any civilian would, but with the advantage that the branch of the service under which the borrower is serving pays the mortgage-insurance premiums.

Nearly four million homes are currently being financed under Section 203(b) mortgages. If you run into a situation where the property you want has an FHA-insured mortgage in force, you have several options:

• You can pay cash, obtained from your lender, and the seller can then pay off his mortgage balance. This ends the seller's obligation.

• If you are approved by FHA, the seller's lender may release him from liability on the mortgage and name you as the mortgagor. There is no minimum down-payment requirement if the sale is from one owner-occupant to another owner-occupant.

• You can buy the property *subject to the mortgage*. FHA approval is not needed; the seller's name remains on the mortgage. The seller is at some risk since he's still liable for the mortgage. The mortgagee could look to him for the mortgage payments should you fail to make them.

SORTING OUT "POINTS"

The use of "points" (one point is 1 percent of the face value of the loan) used to be pretty much limited to government-backed loans, but now they turn up at almost every closing. Lenders have bastardized their use to such an exent that borrowers are probably more confused about points than about anything else relating to home-mortgage loans. You should know what you're paying for, and why, when points are included in the settlement costs.

With FHA-insured and VA-guaranteed mortgage loans, the lender is permitted to charge a one-point service or origination fee for making the loan. (A one-point origination fee with a $47,500 loan, for example, would be $475.) This is intended to cover those overhead expenses not included in the itemized closing-cost charges and is paid out of pocket by the borrower at closing time.

In addition to this fee, the lender will likely, especially if money is tight, charge points to increase the yield on the loan, the FHA/VA loan rate usually being pegged below prevailing private-market levels. (Lenders figure that two points are roughly the equivalent of one-quarter of 1 percent over the *anticipated* life of the loan; six points, for example, would bring the lender's "true annual yield" on a 15 percent loan up to 15.75 percent.) The borrower is forbidden to pay these points with government-backed loans and they must perforce be charged to the seller.

The interest-adjusting points must also be paid at the closing, either out of the seller's pocket or from the proceeds of the loan. Since few sellers are willing to absorb the costs, they usually are passed on to the buyer in the form of a higher purchase price (negotiated earlier during contract discussions), or an under-the-table deal is worked out between buyer and seller. One way or another, the buyer almost always winds up paying the points. The charade is to keep the interest rate that the buyer pays within the limits prescribed by the federal agency. Only when the borrower is building a house to live in or refinancing a property on which there is an outstanding mortgage can the lender ask him to pay more than one point if the loan is insured by FHA or guaranteed by the VA.

Points came into wide use with conventional mortgages as interest rates climbed during 1978 and 1979 and began to bump up against state usury ceilings. If the state usury law put a ceiling of 10 percent on home-mortgage loans, and the prevailing national interest rate was a whole point or more higher, lenders adopted the practice of making up some of the difference with "discount points," for a more lucrative yield. Instead of handing over the face amount of the loan, for $50,000, say, the lender deducted $500 for each point being charged, as a discount or loan fee. With six points, the seller would receive $47,000 as the net proceeds from a $50,000 loan. But the borrower would pay interest on $50,000 over the life of the loan.

At the end of 1979, the Monetary Control Act preempted state usury ceilings on first-mortgage loans. You may still run into discount points with conventional loans, however. When money is tight, some lenders use points as a commision for granting the loan, figuring that if you aren't willing to pay the premium, another, more desperate borrower will. In this situation, you might also be given the option of paying virtually no points and accepting a slightly higher rate of interest on the loan, or a lower rate of interest in exchange for paying more points.

Most lenders today include a one-time service fee or loan-processing charge in the closing costs. It has become the custom to state the charge in points. With conventional loans, lenders aren't limited to the number of points they may charge. But if there are early indications that the lender charges more than one or two points for originating the loan, and in addition bills item by item for everything from the credit check to recording fees, you could be the victim of a gouge. Challenge him on any costs you believe to be excessive—or find another lender.

At tax time, points paid out of pocket by the borrower that effectively raise the lender's yield on the loan, or in IRS language, for the "use or forebearance of money," are deductible as interest in the year paid if the loan is secured by that home and it is the borrower's personal residence. Points paid by the seller can't be treated as an interest expense but may be deducted as a selling cost from the gross sales price of the property to reduce a capital gain. The one-point service or origination fee paid with a government-backed loan is not deductible as interest. The buyer, however, may add this expense to his basis cost for the house.

VA-GUARANTEED HOME LOANS

More than 18 million eligible veterans have never taken advantage of one of the best deals going in home mortgages. That's the GI loan, or, as it's more formally referred to today, the VA-guaranteed loan. But it's never too late. Most veterans, whether they saw service in World War II or the 1980s, have lifetime eligibility.

Like FHA, the Veterans Administration (VA) does not itself make loans. Rather, it is authorized to guarantee loans made by private lenders to eligible veterans to purchase, construct, alter, improve, or repair a home, or to purchase a residential unit in a condominium project.

The VA program aids veterans in the financing of homes by

guaranteeing the lender against loss at a rate of up to 60 percent of the loan, with a maximum guaranty of $27,500. The guaranty, in effect, takes the place of the cash down payment that would otherwise be required in FHA or conventional home financing. Such loans can be made for up to 100 percent of the purchase price or the appraised value of the property, whichever is less, and may have a maximum term of up to 30 years.

Since most lenders use a 4-to-1 ratio with VA-guaranteed loans, an eligible home buyer with sufficient income might qualify for a loan of up to $110,000, with no down payment. Unlike FHA-insured home loans, there are no insurance premiums to pay. Keep in mind, though, that a big loan with no down payment means *big* monthly payments. For a $100,000 loan at 17.5 percent interest, the VA maximum loan rate in September 1981, you'd pay nearly $1,500 per month for principal and interest alone on a 30-year mortgage.

The fact that you may have used VA financing in the past doesn't disqualify you from using it again. The loan-guaranty entitlement has been increased substantially from the $2,000 maximum that was first allowed veterans at the end of World War II. Eligibility requirements have also been liberalized. If you have settled your earlier obligation to the VA, you may have sufficient entitlement available, under the $27,500 aggregate, to secure a loan for a costlier replacement residence.

Since the end of World War II, more than 10 million veterans have bought homes under this generous program, which is partially subsidized by all taxpayers. Since many veterans and others, including some surviving spouses, are unaware of their eligibility, here's a rundown provided by the VA as to who may obtain a VA-guaranteed loan:

a. A veteran who served at any time during the period September 16, 1940, to July 25, 1947; June 27, 1950, to January 31, 1955; or August 5, 1964, to May 7, 1975; and who was discharged under conditions other than dishonorable after at least 90 days' active service (or for a service-connected disability in less than 90 days).

b. Veterans whose active-duty service occurred during the period July 25, 1947, and prior to June 27, 1950; after January 31, 1955, and before August 5, 1964; or after May 7, 1975, and prior to September 8, 1980; and who served for a period of 181 days or more and were discharged or released under conditions other than dishonorable (or who served for a lesser period and were discharged or released for a service-connected disability).

c. Veterans whose active-duty service began after September 7, 1980, and who completed at least 24 months of their original enlistment and were discharged or released under conditions other than dishonorable, or who served for at least 181 days and were discharged for hardship or disability reasons, or who served for less than 181 days and were discharged for a service-connected disability.

d. Unmarried surviving spouses of the above-described eligible persons who died as the result of service or service-connected injuries.

e. The spouse of any member of the armed forces serving on active duty who is listed as missing in action.

The maximum interest rate on VA home-mortgage loans is the same as that permitted by the Secretary of HUD for FHA-insured loans. The loans also are obtained from much the same sources, with, by one recent count showing $165 billion in outstanding VA housing loans, more than 60 percent of the total amount borrowed supplied by mortgage companies, 16 percent by S&Ls, and 13 percent by commercial banks.

The first step in securing a VA loan is to apply to your regional VA office for a Certificate of Eligibility. The veteran must submit originals or legible copies of all discharge and separation papers, together with a completed Form 26-1880, Request for Determination for Eligibility and Available Loan Guaranty Entitlement. In addition, if the veteran is now on active duty, a statement of service must be submitted, signed by the adjutant, personnel officer, or commander of the veteran's unit or higher headquarters. Any VA Benefits Counselor in the nearest VA office will give assistance in securing proof of military service.

Many lenders will also assist veterans in applying for a Certificate of Eligibility. The lender, however, will want assurance as to the veteran's eligibility before making any sort of commitment concerning a VA loan. As with FHA-insured home loans, the lender will assist the applicant with the further paper work required with the request for a VA guaranty, or Certificate of Reasonable Value, to call it by its proper name. The property on which the loan is sought must be located in the United States, its territories or possessions. The latter consist of Puerto Rico, Guam, Virgin Islands, American Samoa, and Northern Mariana Islands. VA loans are restricted to properties that veterans intend to occupy as principal residences.

If you are applying for a loan to purchase a condominium unit, be warned that the unit must be in a project approved by the VA. In Broward County, Florida, where condos are as common as collegians during spring break, VA loans are not normally available for high-rise buildings. On the other hand, condo town houses there generally can be secured by VA loans.

A loan for the purchase of a co-op apartment can be guaranteed only under very limited conditions. All or almost all of the tenant shareholders owning the building would have to be veterans who are using their entitlement.

The amount of the loan will be set by the Certificate of Reasonable Value, following the evaluation of the property by an appraiser designated by the VA. The loan guaranteed by the VA cannot exceed the appraised value of the home or its selling price, whichever is lower. If the contract sales price does not exceed the appraisal, you have no down payment to worry about, unless the lender specifically requires one (in which case, you may want to look for another lender). If you agree to pay the seller more than the reasonable value of the property as determined by the VA, you'll have to make up the difference in cash from your own resources. The VA, like FHA, does not allow supplemental financing with new loans.

Before any VA loan can be approved, the VA is required by law to make a determination that the veteran's present and anticipated income is shown to be sufficient to meet the monthly mortgage payments and other housing costs, with enough left over to support the family.

The VA makes no charge for guaranteeing or insuring the loan. Nor may a commission or brokerage fee be charged to the veteran for securing the loan. Closing costs generally include the VA appraisal, credit report, survey, title evidence, and recording fees.

The lender, as provided in schedules issued by the VA, may also make a reasonable flat charge to cover all other origination costs. The closing costs and origination charge may not be included in the loan.

There are no prepayment penalties with VA-guaranteed home loans. Refinancing to take advantage of a lower interest rate (when such lower rate is in effect) has also been made easy. Under legislation enacted into law in October 1980, the veteran can make application for a VA loan to refinance an existing higher-interest VA loan without the use of additional entitlement. The new loan would be limited to the principal balance of the old loan plus allowable closing costs and a reasonable discount charge by a lender for refinancing the loan.

VA loans also are guaranteed assumable at the original rate of interest. The party taking over the mortgage doesn't even have to be a veteran. Just be sure to inform the VA of the impending change and obtain a "release of liability." This requires the purchaser to submit a financial statement to the VA and sign an assumption (of liability) agreement. Failure to obtain a release could lead to the same sort of financial shock that stunned K.A., who recently received a letter from the U.S. General Accounting Office informing him that he owed Uncle Sam $3,373.05 plus interest.

It was a very cryptic memo and it took several long-distance phone calls before K.A. found out why he was being dunned. It seems K.A. sold his home a while back and allowed the buyer to assume the VA mortgage. The buyer defaulted on the mortgage before 12 months were up and the house was repossessed by the mortgage company that had granted the loan. When the house was resold, the price obtained was $3,373.05 less than the outstanding mortgage debt. The VA, having guaranteed the loan, had to make up this difference. But a VA home loan is not a gift. And K.A. was required to pay off the debt.

If you are a veteran, be sure to check out any local programs offering home loans to veterans. Minnesota, for example, launched a program in January 1981 offering Vietnam-era veterans interest-free loans of up to $4,000 toward the down payment on their first home. The loan doesn't have to be repaid until the property is sold. Buyers must be VA-qualified and can't have household incomes exceeding $19,000.

The Oregon Department of Veterans' Affairs administers a state program under which bargain-rate home loans are available to veterans of World War II, Korea, and Vietnam. Financing is up to 95 percent and most home loans run to 30 years. Interest rates in mid-1981 were 7.2 percent on single-family homes for new borrowers, 4 percent on mobile homes! Loans from the program can also be used for major home improvements and weatherization.

FINANCING FACTORY-BUILTS

Old images die hard and most people still call mobile homes "trailers." But with the trend toward a bigger, better product closely resembling stick-built housing, once set up, they're getting to be about as easy to move as a circus fat lady with two broken hips. What they really are today is simply "manufactured housing"—and were officially labeled as such under the 1980 Housing and Community Development Act.

If you still think that this type of housing, built more economically off the site under controlled factory conditions, is suitable only for migrant farm workers, you owe it to yourself to take another look. The cost-cutting factory-builts of the 1980s—a meld of mobile, modular, and sectional housing, intended to be fixed in place, rather than to be moved—are coming of age with a rush. While some of the low-enders perpetuate that "early-trailer-court" stigma, and continue to be sold in a used-car-lot environment, there are also posh, code-conforming double- and tri-wides that wouldn't look out of place on a residential lot in Palm Springs or Scarsdale.

The trend in "immobiles" today is to quality homes put together at the site from two or more separately transported sections, with the structure permanently attached to a conventionally constructed foundation, never to be moved again after that first trip from the factory. It's the extra width of the multisectional (the typical three-bedroom, two-bath double-wide measures 28 by 60 feet) that permits a pitched roof with overhang and all the customary detailing (from gutters to

chimney) for a conventional, houselike appearance. With car-
ports or attached garages, shingled roofs, wood sidings, bow
and bay windows, cathedral ceilings, sunken living rooms,
Roman tubs, and large modern kitchens, there's little but
price to separate these homes from the typical suburban
ranch-style home. The larger factory-builts cost about $18 to
$25 per square foot vs. $35 to $50 for a conventional single-
family house, and are built to standards that equal or exceed
the quality of construction in new subdivision homes.

You still can go out and buy new mass-produced single-
wides at an average cost of about $17,500 for a 14-by-66-foot
unit—or approximately $19 per square foot for a two-bed-
room house that includes the major kitchen appliances, floor
and wall coverings, and a basic furniture package. With a sin-
gle-wide, you might choose to have it placed on a conventional
foundation on property you own in a rural area, or you might
move into a tidy community where utility hookups are available and you'd pay monthly rent for your ground lease. Be
forewarned though that most rental parks in preferred locations are 100 percent occupied and there are long waiting
lists.

With a multisectional, you have a far wider choice of locations. You might find a well-planned subdivision with a number of attractive model homes on display and where home-
and-lot purchases are made through the sales office. Here,
prices might start at $35,000 or $40,000, including the land-
scaped lot, with no more than six homes to the acre. There
also are lavish "horizontal-condominium" communities with
clubhouses and other recreational amenities, located mostly
in the Sunbelt, where the developer provides a model sales
center just as with conventional subdivisions, or permanently
sets up the most desirable homes on lots within the community available for immediate occupancy. You also have the option in many locales of acquiring an individual residential lot
in a suburban area and having a manufactured home, ordered through a dealer, erected at the site atop a permanent
foundation, much as you would with a house built by a contractor. The difference is that the manufactured home "goes
up" in a day or two, where it can take three to six months with
a stick-built house.

Until a few years ago, virtually all mobile homes were financed like automobiles, with short-term installment loans, usually arranged through the dealer or a finance company. But today, if you're financing a multisectional and land, you can get conventional long-term bank financing for up to 30 years and the down payment can be as low as 5 percent. The Federal Home Loan Bank Board recognizes that well-built, desirably located manufactured homes have as much inherent longevity and appreciate in the same manner as any other properly maintained house that qualifies for long-term financing. Any of the alternative mortgage instruments authorized by the Board (see Flexible Mortgages) may be used to finance the purchase of manufactured homes where the loan is made on the combined security of the home and the real estate to which it is affixed.

Several states, including California, Texas, Michigan, and Vermont, also recognize the improvements that have been made in the new generation of factory-builts and have adopted legislation that prohibits cities and counties from discriminating against code-conforming multisectionals in local zoning codes. In these and other states, an architecturally compatible manufactured home can be erected just about anywhere.

Under FHA-insured financing, you can secure fixed-rate, level-payment mortgage loans for up to $47,500 to cover the cost of a double-wide and land. FHA terms can run to 25 years on double-wides, 20 years on single-wides, if set up on permanent foundations. Cash down payments with FHA-insured manufactured-home financing are 5 percent on the first $3,000 plus 10 percent on the remainder of the loan.

The VA-guaranty program for manufactured housing closely parallels that for stick-built houses and guarantees up to 50 percent of a loan to a maximum guaranty of $20,000, with no down payment required. This applies to all units, new or used, with or without a lot, or for the lot alone.

The FHA/VA interest-rate ceiling for manufactured-home loans is somewhat higher than the maximum allowable rate with conventional single-family-home loans. In September 1981, when the FHA/VA maximum interest rate on conventional single-family houses was raised to 17.5 percent, it was raised to 19.5 percent for manufactured-home (and a developed/undeveloped lot) loans. Shop around though. Interest rates on factory-builts vary more than with other housing.

Most closing costs are eliminated with new manufactured homes. They're also proving to be more energy efficient than their conventional counterparts.

As an affordable and no-need-to-apologize-for alternative to the median-priced, newly built conventional house, manufactured homes are attracting increasing numbers of young middle-income families who believe there are better ways to spend their money than on paralyzing mortgage payments. They surely won't lack for company. Nationwide, nearly 10 million of us live in factory-builts.

Flexible Mortgages

If you go shopping for a home-mortgage loan at a savings and loan or at most any other depository institution, you're likely to encounter some strange new products, bearing such acronyms as VRM, AML, GPM, and PAM. As alternatives to the fixed-rate, level-payment home loans that nearly bled the S&Ls to death, lenders are offering a mélange of new mortgage instruments, most of which adjust to changing conditions in the money market. Banking authorities would have you believe that these new mortgage plans are for the consumer's own good. Don't you believe it.

As dizzying as they are in their diversity, virtually all of these new mortgage instruments have one thing in common: they shift the risk in long-term financial commitments from the lender to the new home buyer. The halcyon days of buying a home and having the financing underwritten by an army of small savers who never earned more than 5.5 percent on their money are over. If thrifts have to pay 14 or 15 percent to attract depositors, borrowers are going to have to pay 16 or 17 percent (allowing for the thrifts' usual two-point spread to cover expenses and show a little profit) for mortgage money.

Deregulation of the banking industry is making for a whole new ball game. Now lenders can change the rules while the ball is in play, something they could never do with a long-term, fixed-rate loan. Tied to prevailing money-market rates, some of these new

mortgages are riskier than others. Should the federal government
fail to get inflation under control, and the economic doomsayers
prove right, you should be aware that there's no "cap" on some of
these plans. If the cost of money keeps rising, the lender can keep
making adjustments in the contract interest rate until the loan is
retired. Other new mortgage instruments, though they may become harder to find, allow generous but more restrictive rate increases.

But, lenders will tell you, the interest rate on many of these
loans *decreases* if the interest-rate index to which the loan is
pegged falls. That's little compensation for the protection you're
giving up. With a standard fixed-rate loan, you could always refinance (though sometimes with a stiff penalty for prepaying) to
take advantage of a slide in interest rates. At the same time, you
never had to live in fear of having the interest rate raised to the
point where you could lose your home!

The culprit here is the Federal Home Loan Bank Board, which,
as an agency of the federal government, regulates the more than
2,000 federally chartered S&Ls. The Board started off moderately
enough when it first allowed mortgages with a variable interest
rate. It made an honest effort to balance the needs of borrowers
and lenders. But reacting to the "crisis of the moment," with a se-
quence of new mortgage instruments designed to stem the tide of
red ink engulfing the S&Ls, it has taken the wraps off, and there
are few if any remaining safeguards for the consumer. In July
1981, *Consumer Reports* was sufficiently distressed by the trend
being taken with the new mortgages to caution its readers: "Be
especially careful when dealing with federal savings-and-loan associations . . . the mortgages they offer may have very unfavorable
terms."

Federally chartered banks also offer most of the new mortgage
instruments, but national banks are regulated by the Comptroller
of the Currency, and that agency has placed limits of sorts on the
size and frequency of rate increases. Most state-chartered banks
and S&Ls have introduced their own versions of the new loans.
Under state laws, however, the majority of these lenders are
barred from offering such potentially dangerous-to-the-borrower

"privileges" as negative amortization. Endorsed by the Bank Board, this controversial financing ploy has the home buyer, in effect, going deeper into debt with each monthly payment.

If you have no choice but to accept one of these new mortgage plans, whether from a federally chartered or state-chartered lender, be thorough in your evaluations and see what terms other lenders are offering with the same type of mortgage. These loans not only are riskier but can be a lot more expensive in the long run than fixed-rate, level-payment loans. Only one of the new mortgage plans can be said to respond to the needs of borrowers. That's the graduated-payment mortgage, which offers enough advantages, even with negative amortization, to make it useful to first-time buyers having difficulty getting a leg up on the housing ladder.

Even though you might not deal with a lender whose new stock-in-trade is flexible mortgages, you should be familiar with them in case there's one on a house you'd like to buy and the seller offers it to you under some method of creative financing. There, you're most likely to encounter a variable-rate mortgage, which, as the forerunner of these alternative mortgage instruments, has been used extensively in California and New England since the mid-1970s.

Some financial writers have been mischaracterizing flexible mortgages and including them under the umbrella of creative financing. They're not truly creative, at least not from the standpoint of the home buyer, to whom this book is addressed. They are simply variations, tending toward the infinite, of the standard mortgage loan. However, most authorities are agreed that adjustable mortgage loans, or AMLs, the most flexible of all these alternative mortgage instruments, are going to become the "conventional" loan of the 1980s unless the regulators in Washington come up with something to supersede them.

VARIABLE-RATE MORTGAGES

When the Nixon Administration began cautiously encouraging a plan to tie interest rates on home mortgages to the economy in

1970, Representative Wright Patman, the Populist Texas Democrat who headed the House Banking Committee, dismissed the plan as "more or less a gambling scheme in which the home buyer is always a loser." As powerful as the banking lobby is, it took nearly 10 years to get a variable-rate mortgage through Congress, and then only as an intended lifeline to the struggling savings-and-loan industry.

Variable-rate mortgages were not a new idea. They had been used in Britain in one form or another for more than a century, and in 1970 they were already in limited use by a number of state-charted S&Ls in this country. As an alternative to the fixed-rate, level-payment mortgage, they provided that if borrowing costs declined after the mortgage was negotiated, the mortgage rate would be reduced; if borrowing costs rose, the mortgage rate would rise. Home buyers who thought that interest rates, then at around 9 percent, had peaked nibbled at the cheese.

Lenders saw another side to the mortgage. With an automatic rate reduction, customers wouldn't run to a competitor for a cheaper rate for refinancing when rates dropped, a risk with conventional mortgage loans. In turn, the customer would be spared the bother and expense of refinancing. With analysts predicting that interest rates would drop a point or two within the year, the California Savings and Loan League endorsed the move of several lenders when they began offering variable-interest-rate mortgages only.

By the mid-1970s, variable-interest mortgages, which came to be known by the acronym VIMs, and later, VRMs, for variable-rate mortgages, had caught hold in California. Not only were they being offered by five of the ten biggest S&Ls in the country, but Bank of America, the largest commercial bank in the U.S., was testing consumer reaction to the "dipsy-doodle" mortgages in many of its branches. To entice borrowers, lenders were offering the mortgages at from one-quarter to one-half of 1 percentage point below the rate for a fixed-rate loan. Most lenders would allow the loan to be assumed by a credit-worthy purchaser at the going rate when the underlying property was sold, and there were no prepayment penalties.

Lenders in California, Florida, Massachusetts, Wisconsin, and the several other states where VRMs were becoming a staple at state-chartered thrifts used a number of different indexes on which to base rate changes and also set varying limits on the amount and frequency of those changes. As a rule, however, rate changes followed those established under California law and weren't made any more frequently than every six months and for no more than one-quarter of 1 percentage point at a time. Interest rates were fairly stable during those years, and while few borrowers received rate reductions, they weren't getting "hurt" with the loans.

Someone who took out a VRM for $30,000 at 8.5 percent for 30 years started out paying $230.68 per month for principal and interest. If he got hit with two maximum increases of one-quarter of 1 percent in a year's time, his payments would have been raised by less than $11, to $241.39—representing an increase of about 4.6 percent in his total yearly payment. With the inflation rate and adjustments to income running higher than that, little damage was being done except to borrowers on fixed incomes.

After being repeatedly rebuffed by Congress, the Federal Home Loan Bank Board succeeded in getting a bill passed that allowed federally chartered S&Ls to begin offering VRMs in California on January 1, 1979, and nationwide, July 1, 1979. The VRM designed by the Board (and used by most lenders still offering VRMs today) allows rate increases of no more than one-half of 1 percentage point per year and no more than 2.5 percentage points above the original contract rate over the life of the loan. Decreases are also limited to one-half of 1 percentage point per year, but there is no limit on how far the rate can fall. Rate changes are tied to the National Cost of Funds Index, which reflects the average cost of funds (the interest paid out on everything from passbook savings accounts to large CDs) to federally insured S&Ls. Rate adjustments upward are at the lender's discretion. Downward adjustments, justified by the index, are mandatory. The borrower is allowed to pay off the loan without penalty within 90 days after notification of a rate increase (or decrease).

If you took out a VRM today at 16 percent, say, you'd pay

$672.38 per month on a 30-year $50,000 loan. If interest rates kept climbing, the most you would ever have to pay under the regulations promulgated by the Bank Board would be an 18.5 percent rate, which would call for a monthly payment of $773.98. And it would take a *minimum* of five years (at upticks of one-half of 1 percentage point per year) before you could reach that plateau. In those states that include an initial 6-to-12-month grace period during which no rate changes may be made, it would take a while longer. Even if interest rates went to 20 or 25 percent, you'd still pay no more than the 18.5 percent rate. Should Reaganomics prove effective, and money rates come down, every one-half-of-1-percentage-point decrease in the mortgage rate would translate roughly into a $20 reduction in your monthly P/I payment.

As interest rates climbed slowly but steadily, more and more lenders found VRMs to be the best thing to have come their way in 40 years. Take that same 30-year $50,000 loan at 16 percent interest. With a standard fixed-rate loan carried for the full 30 years, a borrower would pay $192,000 in interest. With the "worst-case" VRM (five consecutive one-half-of-1-percentage-point increases at the earliest they could be taken), he could pay $225,000 in interest. But then in 1980, when the cost of money nose-dived in the second quarter of the year and then blasted upward again in the third quarter, lenders found that the interest-rate cap imposed on the VRM for consumer protection was destructively restrictive to the mortgagee.

With interest rates down as much as 4 or 5 percentage points, mortgagors holding VRMs written at higher rates were hardly going to be satisfied with a drawn-out series of one-half-of-1-percentage-point reductions. Many took advantage of their prepayment clause and obtained new financing at a much lower rate. The lower mortgage rates also attracted a flock of new home-buying borrowers. When interest rates shot back up again, lenders writing VRMs found they had little more protection from gyrating interest rates with the new mortgage instrument than they had had with fixed-rate, level-payment loans.

VRMs have been out of favor with most lenders since 1980,

those dramatic rate fluctuations having demonstrated all too clearly the inadequte level of protection offered lenders with flexible mortgages that can be adjusted by no more than one-half of 1 percentage point per year.

RENEGOTIABLE-RATE MORTGAGES

In Canada, where it has been in use for about 50 years, it's called a "rollover" mortgage. The traditional rollover of our neighbor to the north is a mortgage loan written for five-year terms but with a long-term amortization schedule. (The monthly payments covering principal and interest are based on a 25- or 30-year schedule.) At the end of each five-year period, the mortgage is "rolled over" at the then current market rate, whether up or down from the original contract rate, for another five years. The mortgagor has the option of accepting the new five-year interest rate or shopping for a better deal elsewhere, with no prepayment penalty.

Since the 1960s, state-chartered lenders in scattered parts of the U.S. had been offering their own versions of the Canadian rollover. Where presented with a choice of a variable-rate mortgage or a rollover, borrowers increasingly were expressing a preference for the rollover, which, while presenting more of a gamble, relieved any anxiety about an increase in monthly payments for at least five years—by which time, the borrower might well have prepaid the loan and moved up the housing ladder. Among the major lenders, Bank of America began touting rollovers at about the same time it initiated its experimental VRM program. Even then, bank officials believed that the rollover offered more stability.

When escalating interest rates began to outstrip its maximum permissible adjustment with VRMs, the Federal Home Loan Bank Board came up with a plan under which interest rates could rise or fall up to 5 percentage points over the life of a long-term mortgage. Federally chartered S&Ls were given the green light in April 1980 to use the "renegotiable-rate mortgage" (RRM) designed by the Board.

Instead of the five-year rollover of the Canadian plan, the Board's mortgage instrument called for the borrower to receive a series of loans lasting three, four, or five years, secured by a long-term mortgage, and automatically renewable at equal intervals. Interest rates, renegotiated every three to five years, depending on the arrangement when the loan was made, would be based on the current national average interest rate for new mortgages on resale houses, according to an index kept by the Board.

Under the regulations imposed by the Board, federal S&Ls were limited to rate changes of one-half of 1 percentage point per year (or 1.5 percentage points on a three-year renewal). Rate increases were optional on the lender's part. Any decreases, as signaled by the index, had to be passed on to the borrower. The interest rate was the only provision that could be changed during the life of the mortgage. The lender was required to grant each new loan, but the borrower had the option of prepaying the loan in part or in full without penalty at any time after the first renewal notice, or at any earlier time specified in the loan contract. If the mortgagor did not elect to pay the loan in full by the due date, the loan was automatically renewed at the new rate. There were no renewal fees.

(A word of caution on the option of paying off a loan without penalty and shopping for a more favorable rate: If you do arrange for financing with another lender, you're going to have to go through a lot of the closing rigmarole again, with a title search and other closing fees. Often, you're better off staying with the original lender even though his interest rate may be a bit higher than a rate being offered elsewhere.)

With introduction of its 1980-model mortgage, the Board backed off from its earlier concern for the borrower. Lenders writing RRMs were under no obligation to offer a fixed-rate mortgage as an alternative to the RRM nor to take the would-be borrower through a cost comparison, which had been among the ground rules laid down with the VRM. By the end of 1980, the RRM had become the predominant form of new home financing in many areas, with most lenders fixing on three-year renewal periods.

Since a worst-case RRM can boost the interest rate paid by the borrower 5 percentage points in 10 years' time (monthly payments on a 30-year $50,000 mortgage at an initial 16 percent interest rate could climb from $672.38 to $876.71), the lender needs some assurance that the borrower's income is likely to rise in future years. For this reason, consumer groups such as the Consumer Federation of America lambasted the plan as discriminatory against women, the elderly, and minorities.

Even so, state-chartered lenders have been writing RRMs with fewer restraints than were imposed on federally regulated lenders. Some lenders have been setting up loans with no-limit increases, or no ceiling on the total increase allowed over the life of the loan, à la Canadian rollovers. As sweeteners, lenders may waive assumption and prepayment clauses. RRMs have also been offered at up to a full percentage point under the going rate for a long-term, fixed-rate loan.

Federally regulated thrifts must automatically renew any RRM written by them, even if the mortgagor has been late in making payments. Automatic renewal is not always provided for in the RRMs offered by other lenders. If you are offered a renegotiable-rate mortgage, insist on a written guaranty from the lender that the loan will be reissued.

Within six months of its introduction of the RRM, the Bank Board was moving to increase the permissible rate adjustment to 1 percentage point per year and to allow federal S&Ls the option of shortened rollover periods; Canadian and some state-chartered S&Ls were already offering one- and two-year rollovers. But all this has become academic insofar as federally chartered S&Ls are concerned, since the Board's 1981-model flexible mortgage, the adjustable mortgage loan, takes care of any shortcomings the thrifts may have found in either the variable- or the renegotiable-rate plans.

As an example of the risks the borrower might be taking with a renegotiable-rate loan with few if any bounds, Buffalo Savings Bank wrote a flock of such loans in 1976 at 8.5 percent, with a five-year renegotiable clause. The bank was being generous. Under the state's usury ceiling on mortgage loans, then set at 8.5 percent, few New York banks were granting mortgages. At the same time, financial institutions elsewhere were getting 10.5 to 11 percent on similar loans.

When the Buffalo bank's renewable five-year loans started coming due in 1981, the bank's loan rates ranged from 17 to 18.5 percent on conventional mortgages. The bank, however, offered to bite the bullet and renew some 900 RRMs for another five years at 14 percent. Under a $30,000 mortgage at 8.5 percent, the monthly P/I payment was $230.68. At 14 percent, the payment would jump to $335.47, a 54 percent increase. At 17 percent, the bank's lowest rate for new mortgages, the monthly payment could have gone to $427.71.

Mortgagors set up such a howl of protest against having their rates raised at all—with plans for picketing the bank's branches and urging depositors to withdraw their savings—that the bank decided to make the grand gesture and swallow the bullet. For the good of its image, the bank, the area's largest mortgage lender, renewed those loans at 8.5 percent.

You should be so lucky!

ADJUSTABLE MORTGAGE LOANS

If you are offered an adjustable mortgage loan (AML), proceed as cautiously as you would when handling a porcupine. Lenders pretty much have a free hand with these loans. They can write loans that allow them to raise (or lower) the interest rate monthly, extend the length of the loan, or even increase the borrower's indebtedness while maintaining the original monthly payment schedule. With some loan variations, you could make payments for years, only to discover that, instead of building equity, you would owe more than you did at the start.

The Federal Home Loan Bank Board authorized use of AMLs—also known as ARMs, for adjustable-rate mortgages—by federally chartered savings and loans in April 1981. Most banking authorities are agreed that the Board reached the outer limits with these loans, which likely will become the predominant mortgage instruments of a difficult housing decade.

Laying it on the line, an applicant for an AML at a federal S&L must be given, at the time of receipt of application or upon request, a disclosure notice in the following form:

IMPORTANT INFORMATION ABOUT THE ADJUSTABLE MORTGAGE LOAN—PLEASE READ CAREFULLY

The adjustable mortgage loan is a flexible loan instrument. Its interest rate may be adjusted by the lender from time to time. Such adjustments will result in increases or decreases in your payment amount, in the outstanding principal loan balance, in the loan term, or in all three. Federal regulations place no limit on the amount by which the interest rate may be adjusted either at any one time or over the life of the loan, or on the frequency with which it may be adjusted. Adjustments to the interest rate must reflect the movement of a single, specified index. This does not mean that the particular loan agreement you sign must, by law, permit unlimited interest-rate changes. It merely means that, if you desire to have certain rate-adjustment limitations placed in your loan agreement, that is a matter you should negotiate with the lender. You may also want to make inquiries concerning the loan terms offered by other lenders on AMLs to compare the terms and conditions.

Another flexible feature of the AML is that the regular payment amount may be increased or decreased by the lender from time to time to reflect changes in the interest rate. Again, federal regulations place no limitations on the amount by which the lender may adjust payments at any one time, or on the frequency of payment adjustments. If you wish to have particular provisions in your loan agreement regarding adjustments to the payment amount, you should negotiate such terms with the lender.

A third flexible feature of the AML is that the outstanding principal loan balance (the total amount you owe) may be increased or decreased from time to time when, because of adjustments to the interest rate, the payment amount is either too small to cover interest due on the loan, or larger than necessary to pay off the loan over the remaining term of the loan.

The final flexible feature of the AML is that the loan term may be lengthened or shortened from time to time, corresponding to an increase or decrease in the interest rate. When the term is extended in connection with a rate increase, the payment amount does not have to be increased at the same extent as if the term had not been lengthened. In no case may the total term of the loan exceed 40 years.

The combination of these four basic features allows an [S&L] association to offer a variety of mortgage loans. For example, one type of loan could permit rate adjustments with corresponding changes in the payment amount. Alternatively, a loan could permit rate adjustments to occur more frequently than payment adjustments, limit the amount by which the payment could be adjusted, and/or provide for corresponding adjustments to the principal loan balance.

Adjustments to the interest rate of an AML must correspond directly to the movement of an index, subject to such rate-adjusting limitations as may be contained in the loan contract. If the index has moved down, the lender must reduce the interest rate by at least the decrease in the index. If the index has moved up, the lender has the right to increase the interest rate by that amount.

There's no question but that the consumer is at a real disadvantage here. Ellen Broadman, a lawyer for Consumers Union, accused the Board of "turning owning a home into a game of chance." Unlike with fixed-rate, fixed-payment loans, where you know to the penny how much your monthly P/I payment is going to be for the life of the loan, and can set up your budget accordingly, you're entering a "Tunnel of Fear" with many AMLs.

Just take the situation that developed in 1980, when money rates performed like a Yo-Yo. The weekly average auction (interest) rates on Treasury bills with three- and six-month maturities plunged from around 15 (percent) in mid-March to below 7 in mid-June. By the first week in December, they were back up to 15 and above. A new homeowner who had taken out an "uncapped" AML in June 1980, with interest-rate adjustments pegged to fluctuations in the six-month T-bill rate, could have had his monthly mortgage payment increased by nearly 50 percent within a matter of months.

Hopefully, we won't see *those* wild gyrations in interest rates again. But lenders, even without waiting to do so at the request of individual borrowers, are going to have to set some self-imposed limits on AMLs to protect borrowers against extraordinary increases in their monthly mortgage payments, or the public isn't even going to come through the doors. With some adjustable loans introduced around the country in 1981, it wouldn't take much of a jump in interest rates to send a lot of new homeowners into foreclosure.

It's still early in the game, but the trend with AMLs at this writing seems to be toward putting at least a yearly cap on rate or percentage-of-payment increases (or decreases), and adjusting payment amounts no more frequently than once a year. The Comptroller of the Currency, the government bureau that oversees national (as opposed to state-chartered) banks, has issued regulations limiting interest-rate changes on adjustable-rate mortgages written by national banks at regular intervals of not less than six months, and interest-rate increases to 1 percentage point per 6-month period. In effect, that's a 2-percentage-points-per-year adjustment cap. There is no limitation on the amount by which the rate may be increased (or decreased) over the life of the loan.

The table that follows would apply to an adjustable-rate loan with rate adjustments occurring every six months and an initial contract rate of 12 percent. It demonstrates the effects on the installment payments of the most rapid possible increases in the interest rate allowed national banks on a 30-year $50,000 loan, carried through five years:

Payments No.	Interest Rate	Amount of Payment
1–6	12%	$514.31
7–12	13	553.10
13–18	14	592.44
19–24	15	632.23
25–30	16	672.38
31–36	17	712.84
37–42	18	753.55
43–48	19	794.45
49–54	20	835.51
55–60	21	876.71

Changes in the interest rate of AMLs written by the national banks must be tied to one of three indexes: the six-month T-bill rate, the three-year Treasury securities rate, or the FHLBB's index of the national average interest rate on new mortgage loans for the purchase of existing homes. No single rate adjustment may exceed 5 percentage points. Which means that if the bank offers a loan subject to adjustments in the payment amount every three years, it could raise the interest rate by only 5 percentage points, even if a larger adjustment is indicated at that date by the index to which the loan is tied. Interest-rate decreases are subject to the same limitations.

Secondary-market investors, as represented by Freddie Mac and Fannie Mae, are also influencing the design of AMLs. For the corporations to sell these mortgages to private investors, they must be packaged in bundles of similar mortgages. Under a "pilot" program launched in 1981, the Federal Home Loan Mortgage Corporation (Freddie Mac) announced that it would purchase mortgages that:

1. adjust the mortgage interest rate according to the FHLBB's national average mortgage-rate index on new loans;
2. adjust the mortgage-rate index once a year;
3. adjust the mortgage interest rate without limit, to correspond to the movement of the index, or limit the maximum annual adjustment (up or down) to 2 percentage points;
4. do *not* adjust the term of the loan; and
5. do *not* adjust the outstanding principal balance.

Lenders may make loans every bit as flexible as FHLBB regulations permit if they wish to hold those mortgages themselves. Freddie Mac's purchase program limits acceptance to those mortgages that provide for adjustments in the interest rate only. A Freddie Mac spokesman pointed out that capital-market investors have expressed "substantial discomfort" with the idea of a mortgage in which the borrower can either a) end up owing more money than when he started out, or b) end up owing the money longer than originally anticipated. In either case, it was noted, the hidden expense to the borrower may increase substantially.

Nevertheless, Freddie Mac's parameters on adjustable loans are a good deal more restrictive than those subsequently announced by the Federal National Mortgage Association. Fannie Mae is prepared to purchase, on a regular basis, at least eight different varieties of AMLs, with adjustment periods ranging from six months to five years, and using five different indexes on which to base interest-rate changes.

Three of Fannie Mae's plans offer payment caps, which limit increases in monthly payments to 7.5 percent per year for mortgages indexed to one- and three-year Treasury securities, and 7.5 percent every six months for loans based on the index for six-month T-bills. These plans provide that whenever the index calls for a payment increase greater than 7.5 percent, the borrower must be given the option of either accepting a higher monthly payment or having the amount above the cap added to the out-standing principal. This is negative amortization. For example, if the borrower has been making monthly mortgage payments of $500, and the applicable index calls for a $50 increase in the payment, the borrower has the option of paying $550 per month, or of paying $537.50—the 7.5 percent increase—and having the balance of $12.50 per month added to the unpaid principal of the loan. At each five-year anniversary date of these plans, monthly payments will be adjusted, with no cap, so that the new payments fully amortize the balance of the loan over the remaining term.

The table below, showing the effects of a percentage limitation on the amount by which the monthly payment on a 30-year $50,000 mortgage could be increased from year to year, demonstrates negative amortization in greater detail. In this example, monthly payments are adjusted annually, and the loan interest rate increases substantially, from 12 percent to 18 percent in the first five years of the loan, and then stabilizes. In actual practice, the interest rate would more likely fluctuate. In general, for any given payment cap and any given change in the interest rate, additions to principal will be larger—in proportion to the amount of the monthly payment and the outstanding principal-loan balance—at lower interest-rate levels than at higher interest-rate levels.

Another of Fannie Mae's plans provides for level payments by

Year	Rate	Monthly Payment		Remaining Balance	
		7.5% Cap	No Cap	7.5% Cap	No Cap
1	12%	$514	$514	$49,818	$49,818
2	13.5	552	572	49,915	49,669
3	15	594	630	50,295	49,544
4	16.5	638	689	50,977	49,437
5	18	686	748	51,992	49,344
6	18	738	748	52,534	49,231
10	18	800	748	51,838	48,516
15	18	800	748	49,678	48,494
20	18	800	748	44,400	41,555
25	18	800	748	31,505	29,486
29	18	800	748	8,726	8,167

the mortgagor over three-year periods and uses the sensitive six-month T-bill rate for its index. A loan using this plan would be originated at an interest rate reflecting the lender's projection of the average level of interest rates over the next three years. (When it is assumed that interest rates are headed down, the loan would be originated at a below-market rate.) Whenever the actual interest rate is higher or lower than the projected rate, the loan balance is increased or decreased accordingly; payments remain constant. At the end of each three-year period, the payment is reset to reflect both the outstanding loan balance and the projected average interest rate for the next three-year period.

The selection of the index to which any adjustable mortgage loan will be linked is as critical as the selection of the loan instrument. It could have a major impact on the monthly payment. While the choice of index must be restricted to indexes based on nationwide interest rates and out of the lender's control, some, such as the three- and six-month T-bill indexes, can be much more volatile than others.

When the FHLBB loosed these free-swinging mortgage instruments, the Consumer Federation of America determined that if uncapped AMLs had been in effect in 1976, the monthly payment on a 30-year $60,000 mortgage would have soared from $483 (based on an initial interest rate of 9 percent) to $871 by April 1981, using the highly volatile three-month T-bill index and adjusting the loan rate every six months. Using the six-month T-bill index, the payment would have risen to $859. With the FHLBB's national average mortgage-rate index, the monthly P/I payment would have reached $694. The smallest increase, to $599, came with the so-called cost-of-funds index (the average rate paid by S&Ls to depositors to obtain money).

The cost-of-funds index (used, as you may recall, by federal S&Ls with variable-rate mortgages) is a good deal less active than the Board's other recommended indexes, but it's stacked against the consumer and doesn't accurately reflect changes in market rates. Experience with the index indicates that it tends to move steadily upward. As ceilings on the interest rates that S&Ls can pay depositors are phased out over the next few years, the cost-of-funds index may rise even if interest rates on loans are stable or declining.

Your best choice would likely be an index keyed to longer rather than short-term changes. Unless, of course, you've got "inside information" that interest rates are going to go down at a fairly brisk pace and then stabilize, and you want to be able to take advantage of those rate changes at the earliest possible adjustment dates. (A 1981 survey of federal S&Ls offering AMLs showed two out of three pegging rate changes to the FHLBB index of national average mortgage rates for existing homes.)

The least useful option with these new loans, given the mathematics of the amortization process, is to extend the term of the loan to reduce the amount of the increase in the monthly payment. A 10-year extension (the maximum permitted) of a 30-year loan can at best absorb a rate change of half a percentage point, and reduces the monthly mortgage payment only very slightly. At the same time, it calls for a much larger total interest payment over the life of the loan. In the lexicon of the gambler, it would be a "sucker play."

Many of the adjustable-rate plans offered by the lending institutions are very much like VRMs and RRMs, only with higher limits on rate adjustments. For example, instead of the Federal Home Loan Bank Board's prescribed limit with the VRM of no more than one-half of 1 percentage point per year and no more than 2.5 percentage points above the original contract rate over the life of the loan, a lender might set up an AML with a rate-adjustment cap of 1.5 percentage points per year (up or down) and no more than 7.5 percentage points above or below the origination rate over the term of the loan. But, again, if the index to which the loan is linked is that same cost-of-funds index, don't hold your breath waiting for a downside movement in the interest rate.

One of the most widely adopted AMLs has been a plan first introduced by AmeriFirst Federal Savings and Loan, the largest lender in Florida. A pace setter in the South, AmeriFirst was ready with its plan the day federal S&Ls became eligible to offer these loans. The plan, offered at a starting rate (in May 1981) of 14.75 percent (when AmeriFirst's rate on RRMs was 16 percent), allows the lender to hike the mortgage payment by up to 10 percent annually (if justified by the FHLBB's measuring of the average mortgage rate, the index to which it is linked), with an extra kick if need be every five years. There's no limit on the amount by which the loan may decrease. (AMLs issued by federal S&Ls may be prepaid in full or in part without penalty at any time during the term of the loan, so downside limits tend to be meaningless.)

With a 10 percent cap on the amount of the payment adjustment every year, a borrower who took out a 30-year $50,000 loan at 14.75 percent would pay $622.24 per month for the first year. At the beginning of the second year, the maximum amount by which the monthly mortgage payment could be increased to reflect a change in the index over the preceding 12 months would be $66.22; the third year, $68.45; the fourth year, $75.29; the fifth year, $82.82. At the beginning of the sixth year, the cap would be lifted so that the payment could be reset to fully amortize the balance of the loan over the remaining term if the interest rate were to remain constant. The cap would then go back on to regulate the adjustments for the next five years, and so on. According to the lender, the mortgagor would need about a 2.5 percent increase in income yearly to support the maximum annual increase permitted with this loan.

On the one hand, home-buying borrowers could find it easier to qualify for these loans because the initial interest rates (and monthly mortgage payments) are likely to be lower than for fixed-rate mortgages. With no need to include an inflationary-risk surcharge, as many lenders do when issuing fixed-rate loans, spreads as wide as 2 percentage points are offered in some areas. But then, a lender may also want some guarantee that the borrower's income will rise sufficiently to keep pace with possibly sizable increases in the monthly mortgage payment, should money rates take off. Not knowing how much they will be required to pay, either each month or over the life of the loan, borrowers perceived as marginal risks could be at a disadvantage. Depending on their probability of increased earnings, home buyers may need to allow themselves more budgetary leeway with a mortgage under which payments are subject to change than with a traditional fixed-rate loan.

Loans with caps usually translate into higher initial interest rates for borrowers than loans with which the interest rate can rise or fall without limit. Generally, lenders are inclined to make their largest rate concessions with AMLs that are the riskiest to the consumer. So don't take the bait without being fully aware of the danger posed by the hook. Make the lender take you through a 10-year chart of the index to which the loan will be linked. Look also for a no-penalty prepayment option. As a concession to giving lenders broad flexibility in shaping rate-sensitive mortgage-loan instruments, the Bank Board believes borrowers should be given maximum flexibility in locating alternative sources of financing should a particular interest-rate or monthly payment adjustment prove excessively burdensome.

Adjustable-rate mortgages are by no means restricted to federally chartered banks and S&Ls. Unless barred from doing so by state law, mortgage companies, credit unions, and state-chartered lenders also can offer these loans. However, there are some 30 states in which negative amortization, or the charging of interest on interest, is illegal, and at least three states in which *no* adjustments may be made in a mortgage's origination rate. (This could change, though; until recently, there were six states that effectively barred adjustable-rate loans.) Federal regulations, as promulgated by the Federal Home Loan Bank Board and the Comptroller of the Currency, preempt state banking laws, but only as regards federally regulated lenders.

If adjustable mortgage loans are all that's being offered, and it already has come down to that in many areas, you're going to have to do some very *serious* shopping, among a variety of lending institutions, for a plan with which you can feel comfortable—if you're going for traditional rather than creative financing in the 1980s.

GRADUATED-PAYMENT MORTGAGES

The graduated-payment mortgage (GPM) was the first new concept in home financing to directly address the problem of housing prices that don't hold still long enough to enable those on their way up to qualify for that first home. It is designed to permit a borrower to qualify for a larger loan than current income would normally support. Until the advent of the GPM, a lot of would-be home buyers were "making good time" in their careers, but were fighting a losing battle when it came to matching cash flow to escalating housing costs.

With a GPM, you don't need to settle for less than you can afford. During the early years of the loan, monthly payments are lower than they would be with a standard mortgage and don't fully cover the interest being charged on the loan. As a result, the outstanding principal actually increases during these years. To make up for the initial deficit financing, monthly payments are increased gradually each year during a period of up to 10 years (the "graduation period"), until they reach a level sufficient to pay all interest and principal by the end of the loan term.

In essence, a GPM is a fixed-rate mortgage, but the first year's payments can be a good 20 to 25 percent lower than they would be with a standard level-payment loan with the same maturity and interest rate. Which means that young professionals and others with good expectations of rising earnings can qualify for a GPM with significantly less income than would be required for the same loan amount with conventional fixed-rate financing. You qualify with income ratios at that low first-year interest.

The GPM was adopted by the Department of Housing and Urban Development to facilitate early homeownership for upwardly mobile families not quite eligible for standard FHA-insured loans because of insufficient income in the early years of the loan. There are no income limitations with these loans today. Anyone with reasonably bright economic prospects—and able to make the cash investment and the mortgage payments—can apply for a GPM. Larger than usual (for FHA) down payments are required with the FHA plans to prevent the total amount of the loan from exceeding statutory loan-to-value ratios. In all other aspects, the GPM is subject to the same rules governing ordinary FHA-insured loans. GPMs also are offered by federally chartered S&Ls, and other lenders where state law permits, under conventional-type (non-FHA) financing.

HUD launched GPMs under an experimental program limited to 3,000 middle-income home buyers back in 1976. The program has since been made permanent and has been opened up to all potential borrowers. Reaction to the program was so positive that, in 1979, the Federal Home Loan Bank Board authorized federally chartered S&Ls to offer conventional GPMs as well. There was some delay in getting both programs started since graduated loans involve periods of negative amortization. These "shortfalls" in interest payments are added to the outstanding balance of the loan, and from then on are treated as principal. A majority of the 50 states have banking laws that forbid the charging of interest on interest, which is the effect of negative amortization. Both FHA and the Bank Board had to go to Congress for authority to preempt state banking laws where they were in conflict with the GPM.

As per the FHA-sponsored program, most lenders issuing GPMs offer a choice of five different payment plans, varying in duration and rate of increase. Three of the plans have five-year graduation periods, with the first year's monthly payments rising 2.5, 5, or 7.5 percent at the beginning of each succeeding year, and then remaining fixed from the beginning of the sixth year through the remainder of the loan. The other two plans provide for a 10-year graduation period, with the monthly payments rising either 2 or 3 percent at the beginning of each loan anniversary, until the eleventh year, when the payments are fixed for the remaining term of the loan. With both five- and ten-year graduation series, the fixed-payment plateau that is reached after the graduation period is higher than monthly payments would be with a conventional fixed-rate, level-payment loan at the same rate of interest.

The most popular of these plans is the one calling for annual increases of 7.5 percent for five years. It allows the lowest initial monthly payments. For an example of the operation of a GPM, we'll take one of several versions of the GPM concept packaged by Mortgage Guaranty Insurance Corporation and sold to savings banks and S&Ls. Let's say you're buying a $70,000 house and have secured a 90 percent GPM loan ($63,000) for 30 years at 13 percent. Instead of paying $697 per month for 30 years under conventional level-payment financing, you would have a much lower starting monthly payment, of $522, and the following graduation:

year 1	$522 per month
2	561
3	603
4	648
5	697
6	750

From the beginning of the sixth year, the monthly mortgage payment would be fixed at $750. The interest rate on the loan never changes, only the amount of the monthly payment, and there, only through the first five years of the loan.

For the privilege of securing financing that will allow you to buy a home with monthly first-year payments $175 less than would be required with conventional financing, you will pay $53 per month more after the first five years than you would with the conventional loan. But by then, inflation and increased real income should make the loan a lot easier to handle.

Total interest with the GPM used as an example would come to $198,372; with conventional financing, the total would be $187,920. But the difference is not terribly important, since it's unlikely that the loan would be carried to maturity. The important difference is that $175—the difference between what you'd pay monthly with fixed-rate, level-payment financing and what you'd start out paying with the graduated-payment loan. If you can convince the lender that your prospects for increased earnings are as good as guaranteed, you thus can qualify for a much higher loan than would be the case when applying for a loan where no consideration is given to any income but current earnings.

As good as the GPM looks at first glance, it's not without its defects. Because of negative amortization, the balance of the loan will rise for five years. In effect, you are borrowing additional money from the lender to pay the "balance" of the interest due monthly on the note. At the end of the fifth year of the $63,000 loan, your indebtedness will be above $68,000. It will be another eight years before it's brought back down to $63,000—and you can begin building equity through amortization. If you sell the house anytime before the beginning of the fifteenth year, you're not only going to have less equity available for the next home than you would with conventional financing, but, to retire the loan, you're going to have to pay the lender more than you originally borrowed.

Many lenders have some reluctance when it comes to issuing GPMs in this still-young program. There's increased risk that the mortgagor may just walk away from the loan if he gets into difficulty with the financing; the increasing monthly payments could be a problem if anticipated wage gains do not materialize. Lenders are reasonably well protected if the loan is insured and the borrower has been required to come up with a good down payment. But, for the lender, it's not as "comfortable" a loan as a similarly covered conventional loan would represent. For this reason, private lenders may set a higher interest rate on non-FHA GPMs than on other types of fixed-rate loans. (FHA used to allow a half-percentage-point premium on its GPMs. Since November 1981, however, the FHA's ceiling interest rate on GPMs has been the same as for level-payment, single-family home loans insured by FHA or the VA.)

The mathematics of these loans is such that higher interest rates also call for substantial increases in down-payment requirements with given rates of payment graduation.

GRADUATED-PAYMENT ADJUSTABLE MORTGAGE LOANS

Do you remember the child's challenge of patting your head and rubbing your stomach at the same time? In a way, that's what graduated-payment adjustable mortgage loans (GPAMLs) succeed in doing. By combining features of the graduated-payment mortgage and the adjustable mortgage loan, lenders can offer a mortgage plan that lets the home buyer in at a lower rate while at the same time giving the mortgagee the protection of an interest rate that can be adjusted (subject to such rate-adjustment limitations as may be contained in the loan contract) to reflect the movement of a single specified index.

The GPAML is the newest loan on the books, having been authorized by the Federal Home Loan Bank Board for use by federally chartered S&Ls in July 1981. As with the GPM, the GPAML enables individuals who otherwise could not qualify for financing—but whose incomes are in a satisfactorily rising pattern—to secure home-mortgage loans.

The GPAML presents two potential concerns for both borrowers and lenders in an inflationary environment: the possibility of significant amounts of negative amortization and the possibility of large payment increases. To reduce the inherent risks, the Bank Board limits the period during which negative amortization may occur to 10 years. The Board also requires that the payment amount be adjusted every five years thereafter to a level that will fully amortize the loan over the remaining term.

While virtually the same hands-off policy applies here as with adjustable mortgage loans, the Board is of the opinion that GPAMLs can be written so that payment increases are not unduly burdensome to borrowers and negative amortization is not excessive. Only time will tell. But those potential concerns, being essentially underwriting problems, are something for the lender and the borrower to address in negotiating the provisions of the loan.

The Board is relying here to some extent on the expectation

that inflation in home prices and borrower income will ensure adequate loan quality. Although the loan balance will increase as a result of negative amortization, appreciation in the market value of the property should tend to offset the increase in the loan balance. Establishment of limitations on payment increases and on the period between payment adjustments would be the principal factors open to negotiation.

If you're looking, then, for a loan tailor-made for your particular situation, you probably couldn't find a loan with any more potentials for adjustment than a GPAML. Personally, we feel the unfettered GPAML has about as much appeal as a month's vacation in Philadelphia. We would be very, very careful in settling for a long-term financing agreement based on the GPAML without the lender having taken us through it step by step and shown us the worse-case situation.

The Bank Board's initial design for a GPAML (then simply the GPAM) combined the major features of the renegotiable-rate mortgage and the GPM, and imposed a 15 percent limit on the amount by which the monthly payment could increase from any one year to the next during the graduation period. The effect of the payment limitation is shown in the following table, which illustrates the maximum payment increases possible with a 30-year $50,000 mortgage that has an initial interest rate of 13 percent, a graduation period of five years, and permits adjustment of the interest rate every three years. In the early years, the payment changes are due only to the graduation schedule, which calls for annual increases of 7.5 percent for five years. The "RRM" limit is 1.5 percentage points on a three-year renewal.

The GPAML is still too new to have been shaped into "basic" mortgage instruments by major lending institutions and the secondary-market mortgage associations. Whatever its shape, a GPAML is not for the buyer on fixed income. Nor, with the additional element of uncertainty, and as one of the most potentially expensive of the new mortgages, is it for the faint of heart to whom buying a home is a frightening enough affair. But just consider the possibilities with a GPAML if interest rates turn down and stay down. There's also an escape clause: You may prepay a

Year	Year-End Balance	Interest Rate	Monthly Payment	Payment Increase
1	$51,362.90	13%	$428.09	0%
2	52,517.69	13	460.20	7.5
3	53,408.42	13	494.71	7.5
4	54,325.58	14.5	568.92	15
5	54,863.70	14.5	611.59	7.5
6	54,929.41	14.5	657.46	7.5
7	54,672.70	16	753.78	14.65
8	54,374.92	16	753.78	0
9	54,029.50	16	753.78	0
10	53,698.51	17.5	815.51	8.19

GPAML in whole or part without penalty at any time during the term of the loan.

FLEXIBLE-PAYMENT MORTGAGES

The flexible-payment mortgage, an earlier version of the graduated-payment mortgage, was approved by the Federal Home Loan Bank Board in 1974. It calls for the borrower to pay only interest on the loan, with no payments toward principal, for the first five years of the loan. You play catch-up later, but with inflation-cheapened dollars. This "easy-start" plan authorized by the Board worked well enough at single-digit interest rates. At double-digit rates, it doesn't reduce payments enough to excite the most desperate of would-be home buyers.

Interest-only loans are not uncommon today. They are used frequently in creative financing. Financial institutions may offer them too. But there, they are generally short-fuse, balloon-type loans. You pay only interest (no principal) for a few years—and then, *boom!*, you have to find new financing.

Unlike unamortized balloon-type loans, flexible-payment mortgages were designed for the long term. There's no refinancing to worry about at the end of the interest-only years. Payments are stepped up at the beginning of the sixth year sufficiently to amor-

tize the loan over the remaining term. There is no negative amortization, which makes the mortgage instruments acceptable to
state-chartered as well as to federally chartered lenders.

When flexible-payment mortgages were first offered, the typical 25-year $40,000 mortgage carried 8 percent interest. A con-
ventional loan required a monthly payment covering principal
and interest of $309 for 25 years. With a flexible-payment mort-
gage, you paid $267 per month for the first five years of the loan.
At the beginning of the sixth year, you had, in effect, a conventional 20-year $40,000 mortgage to pay off, at the same 8 percent
rate. That called for level payments of $335 for the next 20 years.
In the mid-1970s, the difference between paying $309 per month
and $267 per month at the start of the loan qualified a good many
first-time home buyers who wouldn't otherwise have made it.

Today, with much higher interest rates, so little of each payment goes toward paying off the principal of the loan during the
early years that flexible-payment mortgages aren't worth the
bother to the lender. With a 30-year $60,000 loan at 16 percent
interest, you'd pay $806.86 per month to fully amortize the loan
with conventional fixed-rate, level-payment financing. As an interest-only loan for the first five years, the monthly payment
would be $800, a reduction of less than 1 percent! The next time
you see the headline "PAY INTEREST-ONLY FOR FIVE
YEARS!" in a developer's ad for new subdivision homes, you'll
know that that's no big deal.

We don't see any widespread return to long-term flexible-payment mortgages unless interest rates take a real tumble. However,
a flexible-payment mortgage *can* be effective at double-digit interest rates if the loan is written for a shorter term. A 15-year
$30,000 loan at 14 percent, for example, would call for monthly
payments of $400 under conventional financing. With interest-
only payments for the first five years, the monthly payment would
be $350. At the beginning of the sixth year, presumably when you
can better afford it, those payments would jump to $465.

PLEDGED-ACCOUNT MORTGAGES

Like the basic GPM, the pledged-account mortgage (PAM) should hold a special appeal for the young, upwardly mobile, would-be home buyer who cannot now afford the payments on the usual conventional mortgage loan, but who has saved enough for a down payment. PAMs are designed to give the borrower some leverage in an inflationary economy, making it possible to buy and maintain the home he or she wants today, instead of waiting several years—and then discovering that the same house costs thousands more. Unlike the basic GPM, PAMs do not result in negative amortization.

Under a PAM, all or part of the borrower's down payment is deposited in an interest-bearing escrow account that is pledged to the lender as additional collateral and committed under the loan contract to subsidizing the mortgage payments over the first few years. In accordance with a prearranged schedule, part of the borrower's monthly payment is withdrawn by the lender from this account and the balance is paid directly by the borrower. The initial year's payments out of the mortgagor's cash flow can be as much as 30 percent lower than would be called for with a conventional mortgage loan.

Thus, while the payments received by the lender each month are equal throughout the life of the loan, the portion of the payment made directly by the borrower increases annually in the early years of the loan—just as his or her income is expected to increase. When the pledged account is depleted, all payments are made directly by the borrower for the remaining life of the loan. For up to five years, and for as little as 10 percent down, the borrower has been provided with the breathing room needed to build up his or her monthly income.

Federal S&Ls have been offering a version of the pledged-account mortgage since 1979, but the mortgages really got their start with a former real-estate agent named Allan Smith. He came up with the idea several years earlier and dubbed it the FLIP loan. FLIP is an acronym for flexible loan insurance program.

Smith now heads the FLIP Mortgage Corporation of Newton, Pennsylvania.

With a PAM (or FLIP), the borrower is, in effect, receiving more mortgage funds than he might be qualified for under conventional financing. Here's how a pledged-account mortgage could help a young couple hoping to purchase a $62,000 townhouse condominium. While they have saved up $10,000 for a down payment, they cannot qualify for the needed financing under the common rules of thumb, considering their combined gross annual income of $27,500 and a current mortgage interest rate, for illustration, of 16 percent. At that interest and with that income, about the best they could hope to qualify for with a generous lender would be a commitment on a house costing less than $55,000.

But with a 5 percent cash down payment on the $62,000 town house, they will have nearly $7,000 that can be pledged to an interest-bearing escrow account. With monthly disbursements from that account over the next five years, until the account is exhausted, they can comfortably manage the combined $700-per-month mortgage payment. The first year's monthly disbursements from the escrow account will run close to $200, leaving a little more than $500 per month to be met out of current income.

To date, PAMs have not been widely available. To the lender, they're as potentially deleterious to his fiscal health as any long-term, fixed-rate, level-payment loan. Builders have been making more use of the loan plans than banks and thrifts. But that could change. The Federal Home Loan Mortgage Corporation hopes to spur interest in pledged-account mortgages and has completed the groundwork on a secondary-market purchase program, an action that could encourage lenders to make more such mortgages available.

Shared-Appreciation Mortgages ■

In the financing of commercial and rental properties, it's not unusual for the lender to take "a piece of the action." In exchange for giving the buyer of the property a below-market interest rate on the loan, the lender gets a cut of the profits of the operation or a percentage share of the subsequent appreciation of the property that secures the loan. It's a way for a businessman to get started in a venture he couldn't otherwise afford. It can also be a way for first-time buyers to acquire a house or condominium.

Shared-appreciation mortgages (SAMs), or appreciation-participation mortgages, as they're known in some areas, have attracted swarms of would-be home buyers wherever they've been offered. They came to national attention in September 1980, when the New York investment firm of Oppenheimer & Company, through its Detroit-based subsidiary, Advance Mortgage Corporation, and Coast Federal Savings and Loan, of Sarasota, Florida, got together on a shared-equity-mortgage package under which Sarasota-area home buyers got an interest rate one-third lower than the prevailing rate for conventional loans in return for agreeing to give the lenders one-third of the appreciation in the value of the property when the home eventually is sold or the mortgage comes due, whichever occurs first. Prospective home buyers lined up outside the Sarasota bank and the $2.5 million commitment was exhausted the first day.

Advance Mortgage Corporation extended its market test to a number of other cities, including Atlanta, Denver, Phoenix, and Washington, and was swamped again and again with applications from families and individuals looking for an affordable way to acquire a home. Other lenders, and private investors too, have found that equity-sharing home-buying plans hold a lot of consumer appeal. Even the Federal Home Loan Bank Board has found more than a little merit in the mortgages. There still may be a few bugs to be worked out, but the Bank Board, at this writing, has a regulation pending that would allow federally chartered savings and loans to issue home-mortgage loans at below-market rates in return for a share in the future appreciation (limited to the first 10 years of ownership) in the home's value.

Our first look at a share-the-profit financing plan involved a condominium project in South Florida. In the winter of 1980–81, a winter of discontent for sure, with interest rates having climbed back up to around 15 percent after taking a midyear tumble, the developers of The Gardens of Sabal Palm, an adult condominium community in Tamarac, Florida, created a separate company to underwrite SAMs on 34 unsold units in Phase I of the project.

The initial response to the developer's announcement of mortgages at 9.75 percent (when the prevailing interest rate on conventional loans was 14.5 to 15 percent) was tremendous. The project was overrun with visitors. But even at that comparatively low interest rate, very few sales were made. There were many more questioners who wanted to find out more about the buying program than there were prospects interested in buying at Sabal Palm.

Several lessons could be learned from the initial response at this development. SAMs aren't for everyone. They aren't for retirees with enough savings to pay all cash for a condo, and who aren't inclined to share with others the profits of any investment they might make. They also aren't for young working couples when the plan calls for a 30 percent down payment, as it did here. But the most important lesson learned was that the public, while very curious, was still leery of innovations in home financing. Having had the homily that the best hedge against inflation is the appreciated value of your home hammered into their heads for years, not everyone, in the final analysis, was ready to share some of that appreciated value with a lender.

The developers of Sabal Palm were ready to abandon SAMs when interest in the project, with reservations being accepted for Phase II, picked up significantly at midyear. That's about the time, according to Dan Van Leeuwen, president of Vanbots of Sabal Palm, the developer (a subsidiary of Vanbots of Canada), that the home-buying public, at least in South Florida, reluctantly accepted that the days of conventional financing were all too likely a thing of the past and took another look at this new way to buy a home.

The SAM plan at Sabal Palm is amortized over 20 years with a "balloon note" due after 10 years. Typically, with 30 percent down and a 15 percent interest rate, the monthly P/I payment on a conventionally financed $60,000 Sabal Palm unit would come to $553. With a SAM—and the same 30 percent down—the buyer would pay only $405 per month.

Owners of Sabal Palm condos purchased under the share-the-profits scheme will be required to refinance their mortgages in 10 years, unless, of course, they sell their unit and move elsewhere before then. Under the SAM contract, when the unit is either sold or refinanced, Vanbots must be paid one-third of any appreciation in the value of the property. If a unit purchased in 1981 for $60,000 is sold in 1986 for $90,000, the share due Vanbots will be $10,000—the lender's one-third share of $30,000 profit. In those intervening years, the condo buyer will have saved $148 per month on his mortgage payments—or a five-year total of $8,880. For a home he might not otherwise have been able to afford, it's not a bad trade-off.

But take another look before you leap at a SAM. The buyer's obligation to refinance or sell at the end of a specified period could cause serious problems if money is tight or if interest rates have risen. Come hell or high water, you've got to come up with the cash to pay the lender his share of the appreciation in the value of the property. If you have no desire to sell, and can't raise the cash from other sources, you'll have no option but to refinance.

Say the property was originally purchased for $60,000, with $18,000 down, and 10 years later it's appraised at $120,000. At the 10-year mark, regardless of whether or not the property is sold, you've got to come up with $20,000 to cover the lender's share of the appreciated value. If the initial $42,000 mortgage carries a 10 percent interest rate, and the loan is written for 20 years, you'll still owe $30,668 on the loan at the end of 10 years. All of which means you're probably going to have to refinance for $50,000, to cover the outstanding balance on the loan and the $20,000 owed the lender as his participation share. If the prevailing mortgage interest rate is 15 percent, your monthly mortgage payment is going to jump from $405 to $632 on a 30-year loan. If interest rates are higher, it could be a lot worse. If you're living on a fixed income, well, lots of luck.

Now let's take another look at the SAM developed by Advance Mortgage Corporation and Coast Federal. The terms imposed with that first offering in Sarasota were a lot easier to live with. There was a minimum of $50,000 and a maximum of $150,000 on the loans. Only existing homes or condominiums that were to be owner-occupied qualified. Minimum down payment was 20 percent. The term of the loan was for 30 years and there were no prepayment penalties. Closing costs were the same as for conventional financing.

The Sarasota mortgagor got in for less than buyers did at Sabal Palm (20 percent down vs. 30 percent) and could hold the property for the entire 30-year term of the loan without having to refinance. Payment of the lender's share came due only when the property was sold or the fixed-rate loan was paid off. On a $50,000 SAM at 10 percent, the monthly payment would be $438.79. Compare that with $623.23 on a conventional loan at 15 percent.

Home buyers like the SAM plans. They find that cutting the lender in for a distant share in the appreciation is a small price to pay if the alternative is not being able to afford a home. As more than one home buyer has pointed out: "Two-thirds of something is better than one hundred percent of nothing." But bankers aren't all that sold on the concept. In 1981, housing values in many areas registered their smallest gains in years. Wary lenders questioned whether they could count on the rapid housing appreciation of the 1970s continuing through the 1980s. While some mortgage companies and state-chartered S&Ls were originating SAMs similar to those outlined under the Federal Home Loan Bank Board's proposed regulation, most institutional lenders were holding off until the Bank Board either released its plan or killed the concept so far as federal S&Ls were concerned.

There are several areas of controversy with the shared-appreciation plans. Does the lender get to share in the added value from any major improvements the homeowner makes? How about the homeowner's labor if he does the work himself? Does he get "paid" for his time? How will the IRS treat the share of the appreciated value that the homeowner pays to the lender? Will the homeowner have to pay capital-gains tax on money he doesn't get to keep? Or is the appreciation payment to the lender deductible as an interest expense?

Public-interest groups have been especially critical of the mandatory "sell-or-refinance" rules written into SAMs. They could force moderate-income families to sell their homes even though they had no desire to move elsewhere; refinancing could burden them with monthly mortgage payments far higher than their budgets could handle.

In its proposed regulation, the Bank Board noted that the SAM "would be most attractive to buyers ordinarily priced out of the market," with first-time home buyers and moderate-income borrowers those most likely to be interested in the SAM. The Board also suggested that "the SAM may be useful to elderly homeowners refinancing existing homes or buying down to smaller homes as a means of avoiding large monthly payments." We don't agree with the Board here. Elderly home buyers on fixed incomes could get into a real bind if forced to refinance at high interest rates.

Under the Board's proposed regulation, a lender's share would be limited to a maximum of 40 percent of net appreciated value, to be paid as "contingent interest." The maximum term of the SAM would be 10 years, with guaranteed long-term refinancing of the outstanding indebtedness on the loan, including contingent interest. The refinancing would be at the rates for new residential mortgages at the time of refinancing, using a choice of mortgage instruments offered by the lender. There would be no extension of the low-rate SAM, however.

If the borrower sells the house and the lender does not choose to accept the net sales price as fair market value, or if the loan is paid off in full prior to sale or transfer, the market value would be determined by appraisal. The appraisal would be performed by an appraiser selected by the borrower and the lender from a list of appraisers. If the borrower and the lender can't agree on an appraiser, each would choose an appraiser, and the market value would be determined by an average of the two appraisals.

While it would be sound business practice for a lender to seek to concentrate SAMs in areas or types of housing it believes will appreciate rapidly, federal S&Ls would not be able to limit the availability of these instruments to certain neighborhoods and would be prevented from introducing other limitations that are discriminating in effect. Rather than offer SAMs on which the chances of making a good return on the investment are the other side of zip, many S&Ls, even if the proposed regulation is adopted, may not offer the loans.

Equal-opportunity statutes notwithstanding, the trend to date with SAMs has been either to set high minimums, as with the $50,000-to-$150,000 range with loans made available by Advance Mortgage Corporation and its partner, high down payments, as with The Gardens of Sabal Palm, or for discretionary lenders to take a piece of the action.

Discretionary lenders are private investors. In California and other states, real-estate brokers are bringing would-be home buyers and investors together in home-grown versions of the SAM. Generally, the "partner" comes up with the down payment or as much as 20 percent of the purchase price. For his participation, he typically gets half of the appreciation in the home's value, as determined by a professional appraiser, at the end of five years. For the "cash-out," the homeowner would likely have to refinance the mortgage or sell the house, since he would be required to pay the investor not only his share of the appreciation at the end of five years, but would have to pay back the cash advanced by the investor as well. For our money, it's an expensive way to buy a home.

Just look at the payout! Say you're buying an $80,000 house and an investor puts up $16,000 for the down payment. Unlike with a bank-arranged reduced-rate SAM, you're going to have to shop for conventional financing on a $64,000 mortgage at current market rates. For illustration, we'll make that a 30-year fixed-rate loan at 16 percent. In five years, if the property appreciates an average of 10 percent a year, the house should have a market value of $120,000. You now have an outstanding balance of $63,334 on your mortgage—and you owe your partner $36,000 ($20,000 as his share of the appreciation, plus the $16,000 he put up for your down payment).

If you sell the house for $120,000 and pay off all your debts (including a broker's fee for selling the house), you're going to have only about $13,500 to put into a replacement residence. That's not an awful lot to show for five years of homeownership in an inflationary climate. If you refinance for $100,000 (to cover the remaining balance on the loan and to pay off your partner) at the same 16 percent rate, your monthly mortgage payment will jump from $860.66 to $1,344.76. That $16,000 put up by your partner is going to cost you far more than you ever bargained for!

A more equitable arrangement, it seems to us, would be in the "real-estate futures" concept originated by Robert Flower, a real-estate broker, in Rye, New York. A typical Flower arrangement is to have an investor put up $10,000, say, for a home buyer who is short of cash for a down payment. In exchange, the investor would get 20 percent of any increase in the appreciation at the end of five years. The borrower would pay no interest or principal on the $10,000.

Variations of the SAM are being spawned all across the country. Some of the terms in the plans cooked up by nonbanking sources are pretty outrageous. These plans should be examined very, very closely, not only by the prospective home buyer, but by his lawyer or accountant, and probably by the state attorney general, as well. Frankly, we would avoid any shared-equity plan that called for paying out more than 20 percent of the appreciation without offering long-term, below-market-rate financing on the full amount of the loan.

Co-purchasing

Until well into the 1970s, it was almost impossible for an unrelated couple to obtain conventional financing as co-mortgagors for the purchase of a home through the traditional lending sources. Today, the more signatures there are on the mortgage note, the happier they are at the bank. Co-purchasing has become the new phenomenon on the housing scene. Not only do the lending institutions welcome two or more credit-worthy people buying property jointly, but developers are building condominium apartments, town houses, and detached suburban homes expressly for this burgeoning market. In many cities, two-or-more-sharing is seen as the wave of the future.

Two certainly can't live as cheaply as one, but two pooling their resources can often afford to buy where one cannot. In 1979, Judy Mason, 27, and Bob Dressler, 30, who had worked together in the same lower Manhattan brokerage house for six years, co-purchased a three-story brownstone in Hoboken, New Jersey, for $87,500. They've since put close to $25,000 into improvements, but now have a property easily worth $140,000. Judy and Bob are not lovers; they each date others. They each have their "private" floor and share the living room, kitchen, and dining area of the bottom floor. Had they remained in the New York East Side apartments each of them rented before they moved into their house in Hoboken, their combined rent in early 1982 would have been $1,350 monthly. They now pay less than that on their PITI

127

payments and other housing costs, utilities included—and, being just across the Hudson River from lower Manhattan, are only 20 minutes from their place of work.

For young professionals hungry for the tax advantages and satisfaction that can come with owning a home, co-ownership can represent an equity-building halfway house between paying ever-rising apartment rents and owning the home of one's dreams. However, there unquestionably are still more co-mortgagors for whom the arrangement is more pleasure than business, with the ownership shared by an unrelated male and female; in bureaucratic language, they're known as POSSLQs (poss-el-cues)—Persons of Opposite Sexes Sharing Living Quarters.

The building trend tells what's happening today, though. Where in the past, co-purchasing for most buyers represented a practical, love-in arrangement, the units being built for occupancy by two or more unrelated owners typically feature two master bedroom suites, each with its own full bath. For privacy, bedroom suites are separated by the shared living room and kitchen. These units are being designed for occupancy by two or more individuals—or even two married couples—with a compatible investment philosophy.

In South Florida, condominiums away from the expensive beachfront strips are being put up with an increasing share of the units designed for occupancy by "mingles," the new marketing buzz word applied to shared buying by two or more singles. At the Lakes at Deer Creek, in North Broward, "courtyard homes" and "town villas" are being built with an upstairs master bedroom plus a downstairs master bedroom. Split two ways, the starting price of $97,000 makes "luxury living" affordable for two buyers at $48,500 each.

Departing from the duplexes of old, the "tandem houses" of California architect Barry Berkus feature two master bedrooms and separate dens, but provide a shared kitchen—eliminating duplication of the most expensive room of a house. Berkus' kitchens feature dual pantries and even two refrigerators, so a single kitchen is no great sacrifice for mingles who rarely are together except at breakfast. As Berkus has pointed out, the bedrooms are like two separate apartments.

Tandems are popping up not only in California, which is rife with co-purchasers, but in such booming areas as Houston and Washington, D.C. In a suburban Washington-area development, Wingate of Arlington, double-master-bedroom town houses, planned with co-purchasers in mind, could be bought for as little as $66,000 in 1980. In the spring of 1981, Berkus-designed tandem houses in the Arlington area were selling for $100,000 and up.

In California, there even are brokers who run "matchmaking bureaus" to team up buyers looking for an entry into real estate without ravaging their budgets. At the Everett East condo in the Los Angeles suburb of Glendale, where half of the units have been designed especially for unrelated individuals and couples, many of the deals with the designated lender have had three and four co-mortgagors.

With rentals becoming scare and frighteningly expensive in such cities as New York, Washington, Chicago, and San Francisco, there is increasing pressure on young professionals to own property in a good neighborhood close to their jobs. A good many sharers—whether close friends, casual friends, or just-mets—simply get together out of desperation and then shop for a large enough apartment or house suitable to their common needs and do whatever retrofitting is necessary to give each of the co-mortgagors his or her own space. It's not at all unusual for four or five young careerists to team up and buy a large house, local zoning ordinances permitting, and convert it into something not unlike an old-fashioned boardinghouse.

In the San Francisco Bay Area, where housing prices are in the stratosphere, Mark Anderson and three friends bought a six-bedroom house in the Berkeley Hills in December 1980. It was where they wanted to live and, at $265,000, it was something they could collectively afford. Anderson, a 32-year-old optometrist, joined with another optometrist, a computer analyst, and an auto-repair-shop owner to buy the Berkeley Hills house, the mortgage payments on which run to nearly $3,000 per month. Anderson had been house-hunting for some time but he didn't want to go above $70,000. For that kind of money, he couldn't live within 50 miles of where he's now living. As he explained his decision: "Instead of a $70,000 house, I bought one-fourth of a $265,000 house."

Anyone contemplating a co-purchase should be aware that, like marriages, these things don't always work out. Sharing a house can be demanding and difficult. There also are legal pitfalls for the unwary. To protect your investment, a detailed agreement, drawn up by a lawyer, spelling out each owner's rights and responsibilities, is a must.

When a married couple, or an as-good-as-married couple, own property together, it's usually held in "joint tenancy," which carries with it the right of survivorship. They take title with the understanding (confirmed in the deed) that in the event of the death of either, the other will automatically become the sole owner. As an individual, you'd undoubtedly want to be able to pass your interest in the property on to your next of kin, rather than to the surviving owner or owners. You might also want to have the option to sell your share at some time in the future. That's allowed under "tenancy in common," which makes more sense than joint tenancy for these essentially business arrangements.

As tenants in common, each owner has legal title to "the whole of an undivided part" and reports income gain or claims tax deductions according to his or her share of ownership. When contracts are drawn up, it is up to the co-purchasers to divide the house (there may be unequal shares of ownership) and assign each party a legal share of the property. Both the sales contract and the deed should specify the co-owners' relationship as tenants in common. Each owner then has a legal title to the property that can be willed to others or sold. The option to sell, however, should be made subject to a "first-right-of-refusal" clause, requiring that the share be offered to the other co-owner(s) before it is offered for sale outside the "family."

All this should be spelled out in a carefully drawn up legal agreement covering every contingency. What happens, for instance, if one co-mortgagor fails to come up with his or her share of the monthly mortgage payment? Who is responsible for repairs and improvements? What happens in the event one of the co-owners is transferred out of the area by an employer? What if one co-owner marries and wishes to expand the ménage? What about a forced sale caused by incompatibility? For mutual protection, the agreement should cover every worst-case scenario.

The most frequent breakdown with these arrangements comes with POSSLQs who pool their resources without any thought having been given to the possibility of an eventual breakup. But then there's "the big fight," and one party wants the other party out. If one wants to sell and the other doesn't, the one who wants to sell can go to court and, as a tenant in common, petition the court to "partition" the property. Since the property could not be physically divided fairly and equitably, the court can order a sale of the property and divide the proceeds between the owners.

In one case that was in the courts for months, an unmarried California couple had bought a house in suburban Walnut Creek. Love died and the girl wanted her share of the money she had contributed for the purchase of the house. The money she had put up for her share of the down payment was in cash. Or so she claimed. The down payment, however, had been fully covered by a single check written by her boy friend. Nowhere in the agreement was there any reference to her cash contribution.

In Houston, Texas, two young bachelors, one a geologist, the other a high-school science teacher, purchased a development town house with an upstairs bedroom suite connected to a loft overlooking the combination dining/living room and a downstairs suite that opened onto a walled patio. Things were peaceful enough until the upstairs bachelor's stewardess girl friend moved in with him. Her odd hours frayed the nerves of the downstairs bachelor (the teacher), and since their co-purchasing agreement specifically barred "permanent guests," he asked the geologist either to get rid of the girl or to buy him out. The upstairs bachelor was reluctant to do the former and couldn't afford the latter. The downstairs bachelor consulted a lawyer who went over the paper work and determined that the only way the girl could stay on in the house without putting the geologist in financial jeopardy would be if she were to purchase a one-third share in the house. The whole thing got to be pretty testy and the house has since been sold. With the loss taken on the forced sale, each bachelor is out more than $4,000 for the 11-month experience in community living.

Cover every eventuality you can before you settle in—but don't ever lose sight of the benefits of a successful arrangement with a co-owner or two. When it comes to buying, all income of all who are involved in the purchase counts toward qualifying for the loan. When co-owners eventually sell to go their separate ways, the taxes on any profit can be deferred under the "residence replacement rule." But instead of being required to buy replacement residences of equal or greater cost than the dwelling they are leaving, the replacement rule would apply only to each owner's share of the net proceeds. If the house was originally purchased for $80,000 and is sold for $130,000, say, each former co-owner (assuming two) could defer taxes on his or her $25,000 profit by buying a replacement residence, within 24 months after the sale, costing $65,000 or more.

When selling a property with a large appreciation, unrelated owners get a bigger tax break than married ones. Where a married couple gets only the one $125,000 exemption on profits, at age 55 or over, each co-owner could claim up to $125,000 as tax-free profit. It's something to look forward to.

Where a veteran (with eligibility) is involved in a co-purchase, a nonveteran can join in obtaining a VA-guaranteed loan, but the amount of the loan on which the guaranty is based is in proportion to the veteran's interest in the loan. The guaranty cannot extend to any portion of the loan which may constitute all or part of the nonveteran's contribution to the purchase.

It should be noted, too, that a co-mortgagor doesn't have to be an equal partner or even live there. For example, you might want to buy a house you can't yet afford. There's no reason why a member of your family, or a close friend, can't chip in part of the down payment and agree to pay, say, one-fourth of the monthly mortgage payment. This is perfectly legal and acceptable to most lenders. Your co-mortgagor would be entitled to a tax break on his share of the monthly payments. Depending on how fast the property appreciates or your income rises, you might be able to refinance in a couple of years and buy out your co-mortgagor. You might then perform the same service for him.

Taking the shared-equity concept one step further, a real-estate broker can often find a local investor who would like to put some cash to work where housing is appreciating at a rapid rate, in return for tax benefits and a share of that appreciation at some future date. In California and Texas, it's referred to as "bringing in a rich uncle." The third-party investor contributes the down payment and then collects a small monthly "rent" payment from the owner-occupant. This makes the investor eligible (unless he gets shot down by IRS) to claim depreciation on the property at tax time. He also shares in the appreciation when the property is sold.

Another interesting third-party arrangement is the Home Ownership for Beginners (H.O.B.) program designed by Skufca & Shelton, of Littleton, Colorado. Skufca & Shelton are builders of town houses and condominiums in the Denver area. Under their H.O.B. shared-equity program, an investor puts up half the down payment and half the monthly payments for three years. There's also an interest-rate reduction of approximately 4 percentage points. So the buyer gets an $80,000 town house, say, with payments based on a $40,000 home, and at an interest rate 4 percentage points below the market at closing. The buyer and the nonresident investor are tenants in common. The investor gets continuing tax benefits on his share of the interest payments as well as 50 percent of the appreciated value of the home when it is sold or refinanced. For the first three years, at least, the carrying costs to the buyer aren't much more than they would be for a good rental apartment.

Co-signing

Most young homeowners are in debt up to their armpits and it's obvious that few of us pay much heed to that oft-quoted bit of advice given by the voluble Polonius to his son, Laertes, in *Hamlet:* "Neither a borrower nor a lender be." If we obeyed the first half of that dictum the way we accept the admonishment to *never co-sign a loan,* the majority of us would still be living with our parents, if not our grandparents.

There's nothing immoral about co-signing for a mortgage loan. First-time buyers without a credit record often bring in a parental co-signer. It's also another way to handle the purchase of a home by two unrelated buyers. There may be a tax advantage in having one "owner," who could claim all the deductions relating to the house, with the other purchaser taking the standard (or "zero bracket") deduction. In effect, this gives the co-owners an additional deduction worth as much as $2,300. One becomes the owner listed on the warranty deed; the other adds his or her signature to the promissory note only.

Co-signing for a mortgage loan should not be equated with co-signing a short-term note for someone living on MasterCard and having difficulty persuading a finance company to advance him a few hundred dollars to clear up some other pressing debts. Most young would-be home buyers, however, don't even consider getting a co-signature on a home loan, primarily because they want to shoulder their own debts and don't understand the mechanics of co-signing for a mortgage. If you're frustrated by your inability to show sufficient credit to qualify for a mortgage loan, find yourself a co-signer. With mortgage insurance and even a minimal rate of appreciation in the value of the property, the co-signer's obligations become pro forma today.

First-time buyers are entering the ailing housing market in surprisingly large numbers. From 21 percent in 1979, the percentage of sales attributable to first-time buyers had increased to 40 percent by the end of 1981. Without the benefit of a co-signer, and often some financial help in meeting the down payment, the percentage would be much, much lower. Hidebound loan officers can be such sticklers for "rules" that they make no distinction between qualifying a young professional with a bright future and a tied-down family man with six kids with bad teeth. If you have a short employment history, a limited credit background, or are new to the area, many lenders are going to want a second signature.

It's becoming so common for a parent to put up at least part of the down payment and co-sign the note that George Sternlieb, professor of urban and regional planning at Rutgers University, refers to the trend as "the new GI bill—Generous In-laws." Industry estimates are that three out of four young buyers require financial help from a parent to get into that first home.

Fred Turner typifies what's happending today. In September 1981, Fred had been out of college a little more than two years and was working for a major oil company in Denver. At the rate he was progressing, he could expect to be making a minimum of $30,000 a year within three years. At his then $20,500 salary, however, he couldn't qualify for the $58,000 condominium he wanted to buy near trendy Tamarac Square. With a wood-burning fireplace, a den, and a balcony facing the front range of the Rockies, he knew that the one-bedroom, one-and-a-half-bath apartment had excellent value, even with the area's then housing glut.

The developer of the new Denver high-rise was offering buyers 14 percent mortgages for the first three years. At the end of three years, the mortgage rate would be pegged at prevailing market rates. Fred talked things over with his dad, who lives in Fort Collins, Colorado. Fred, Sr., agreed to come up with $7,500 toward a 25 percent down payment (the other $7,000 was to come out of Fred's savings) and to co-sign the mortgage note. Now Fred's in his apartment and paying $515 per month in principal and interest—and managing at the same time to put aside $140 a month to pay back his dad, though Fred, Sr., gave his son the $7,500 with no strings.

We're not advocating that you take on more mortgage than you can handle. But as is the situation with so many young people today, trying to qualify to buy at least a "starter house" is like running after a train that is leaving the station. With a slight concession from a lender, you might have swung the deal for that house a couple of years ago—and been ahead thousands of dollars in net worth today to boot. You need that extra "kick" to catch up to the train and get on board. A co-signer can provide that extra kick.

There are additional advantages in having a co-signer. You not only can qualify for a bigger mortgage but for a higher loan-to-value ratio (less money down). And you're not limited to just one co-signer. With many lenders, an applicant who might not otherwise qualify for a loan may bring in an unlimited number of co-signers.

Don't confuse co-signers with co-purchasers who are going to share the house or apartment, or with investors looking for a share in the future value of the property. In most cases, a co-signer is simply a relative, employer, or close friend who is being asked to make a bet on you that a conservative professional, the lender, who knows next to nothing about you, is reluctant to make. The co-signer is legally bound to pay the loan should you default. We must assume, however, that the co-signer has every confidence in your ability to manage those payments. If the worst happens, the property would have to be sold and the loan paid off. But with 90 and 95 percent financing, which would automatically require mortgage insurance, the co-signer's obligations would be alleviated. With continuing inflation, even at the single-digit level, there's little risk that anyone would ever have to take a loss on that co-signed note.

Builder Buy-Downs

At a time in 1981 when the national average mortgage rate ranged between 17 and 18.5 percent on new loans, Centex Homes was advertising 30-year "no-gimmick" mortgages at 14 percent on new single-family homes and town houses in South Florida. In addition to offering "the good old-fashioned kind of mortgage," on medium-priced homes in Boca Raton and the Palm Beaches, Centex absorbed closing costs as well, saving the buyer hundreds, if not thousands, of dollars more.

In Texas, U.S. Home, the nation's largest residential home builder, was offering two-story homes on Lake Ray Hubbard, in the Dallas area, for 12 percent fixed-rate financing and a $1 total move-in cost to qualified veterans. Also near Dallas, in the mid-cities Arlington area, Merrill Lynch Realty was offering one- and two-bedroom condominiums overlooking Great Southwest Golf Course for 5 percent down and with 12.25 percent fixed-rate financing, mortgage insurance included.

These financing deals were not all that unique. Nor were the properties all that expensive, being priced from the mid-$40s at Fairway Manor, in Arlington, Texas, and from the high-$60s at Saddlebrook, in Boca Raton, Florida. Similar buying opportunities were being offered—and exist today—on new single-family homes, town houses, and condo apartments everywhere from the suburbs of the nation's capital to Orange County, California.

The lending institutions aren't in any position to undercut each other's mortgage rates. But in a sluggish housing market brought on by continued high interest rates, builders and developers have little recourse but to engage in "price wars" to move their products out of inventory. Construction money costs even more than mortgage money, and builders can't afford to sit around waiting for the prevailing interest rates to come down to a level that would make their unsold houses and condominium units affordable to buyers waiting in the wings. They either have to build and sell properties or get out of the business.

There are several ways a builder or developer can make the financing on finished houses attractive enough to bring out buyers without going belly up, or even taking a loss at all. Recognizing that the move-in costs and the amount of the monthly mortgage payment are more important to most purchasers today than what the eventual cost of the home might be—especially if the buyer intends to move up to something better in a few years—a builder might ease the financial burden of home buying by picking up the tab for closing costs, including prorated interest, taxes, and insurance escrows. He might offer a plan that relieves the new homeowner of the monthly mortgage-payment burden for anywhere from three months to a full year, offer a sizable cash rebate, or buy down the mortgage to provide the buyer with a lower interest rate and make qualifying easier. In effect, any and all of these credit arrangements are "buy-downs," the counterpart of creative financing in the resale-housing market.

Some builders, as noted, may offer financing at a permanently reduced rate. This practice is usually limited to major builders/developers who have the resources to do their own mortgage lending and are in a position to regulate their own interest rates. Without that advantage, a builder might effectively lower the interest rate the home-buying borrower pays in one of two ways: with a monthly cash rebate, which the buyer could apply toward the monthly P/I payments, or by providing money to the designated lender in a lump sum to be used to lower the buyer's monthly payments in the early years of the loan.

To offer these subsidies, the seller may bite the bullet and forgo a healthy cut of his profit, but he's more likely to add a good share of the cost to the purchase price of the house, if the traffic will bear it. Instead of asking $64,000 for a house, he might raise the price several thousand and hand the equivalent of the increase and a little more over to the lender to make the effective interest rate 13 percent, say, instead of 16 percent for the first three years of the loan. The buyer thus gets in at a more comfortable rate and can qualify for financing on the basis of the lower early payments. For example, with rates at 16 percent and a 20 percent down payment, it would take a family income of at least $32,500 to qualify for a mortgage loan on a $67,000 house. If the payments are bought down to 13 percent during the first years of the mortgage, a family might qualify with as little as $27,500 in income.

To buy down a $53,600 mortgage ($67,000 less 20 percent) by 3 percentage points for three years would cost the seller approximately $4,500. Even if he has to sacrifice some of his profit on the sale to arrange the buy-down, it's a whole lot better than taking a big cut in the selling price or paying 21 or 22 percent interest on the construction loan while the house sits empty and unsold.

Here, the builder has absorbed a $1,500 reduction in profit. Had he reduced the selling price of the house by that much—from $64,000 to $62,500—it would not have been nearly as effective as the buy-down. At $62,500, and with a 20 percent down payment, the purchaser of the house would have a monthly P/I payment of $672.38, at 16 percent. With the house priced at $67,000 and the mortgage rate bought down to 13 percent, those payments would be $592.93 per month. The buy-down thus provides the extra leverage needed by the new home buyer to enter the housing market.

Builders who had resisted the selling tool in 1980 when it first gained acceptance have been increasingly turning to buy-downs to produce needed cash flow. Weekend real-estate sections of major newspapers are filled with display ads seeking to lure would-be home buyers by promising them not the moon but the next best thing—lower interest rates. With dozens of builders fighting for the reader's attention, there's a need to be different, and increased sales are determined by the developer's ingenuity.

On that score, Oriole Homes Corporation, a major builder/developer based in Pompano Beach, Florida, would be deserving of at least a blue ribbon.

Among the innovative buy-down programs devised or employed by Oriole to assist prospective purchasers:

• **M.A.G.I.C. "Plus."** The initials, M.A.G.I.C., stand for mortgage-assistance-guaranteed interest checks. The buyer gets a check for $200 from the builder every month for a year after closing. Applied to his monthly mortgage payment, this will effectively reduce the interest rate on the average mortgage loan by from 4.5 to 5 percentage points. In addition—the "Plus"—should prevailing interest rates fall during the first two years of the mortgage, the buyer would be able to refinance the loan at a lower interest rate at nominal cost.

• **F.A.M.E. Plan.** Under the financing-assistance-made-easy plan, the builder agrees to send the buyer a check every month for three years that will effectively reduce his monthly P/I payment by approximately 5 percentage points. For example, the builder might pay the difference between the payment on a $70,000 mortgage at 15 percent and 9.75 percent, or $284 per month. Over the three-year term of the plan, this would represent a saving of $10,244 to the home buyer.

• **No-Payment Mortgage.** When a purchaser closes on a selected residence after having been approved for a mortgage by the designated lender, the builder sends the purchaser a check equal to the P/I payment on his mortgage, up to the maximum amount that would apply, say, on a $65,000 loan. The buyer receives a check for the same amount every month for a full year. At 15 percent, the monthly payment on a $65,000 loan is $821.89. For 12 months, that comes to nearly $10,000.

Oriole also attracted considerable attention when it advertised mortgages at 8 percent, for a limited number of residences at various developments. The plan calls for 10 percent down at contract and an additional 20 percent at closing. On a $75,000 purchase, the buyer then pays only 8 percent interest on a $52,500 loan, obtained through Oriole's wholly owned mortgage subsidiary, for five years. At the end of five years, the purchaser is required to re-finance his mortgage with another lender (or, he may be ready to sell, since the average South Florida home is turned over once every six years). Instead of paying $738 at 16.75 percent, the pre-vailing rate when the plan was first announced, the buyer pays only $385 per month for five years, for a total saving of more than $21,000.

As a prospective purchaser, a perusal of the weekend real-es-tate section of a newspaper serving the major market area in which you are planning to buy will likely disclose any number of display ads for new houses and condominiums, quoting interest rates that haven't been available for years. Reading beyond the eye-catching headlines though, you'll usually find what you were hoping not to find: the low-low interest rate is good only for a short term. How long are you permitted to benefit from the artifi-cially low rate? The trend is to three-year buy-downs. There are many builders, however, who buy down the interest rate for one year only. The unalloyed truth is generally disclosed in a small-type footnote at the very bottom of the ad. For example, the headline reads: *"12%* Financing!"* But then there's the barely discernible footnote: *"*The developer shall contribute sufficient funds to the lender to reduce the effective interest rate to 12% for the first year of the mortgage."*

Interest rates that are anywhere from 6 to 8 percentage points below the market *are* too good to be believed in many cases. They sometimes apply to homes and apartments that other buyers have been passing up for months for good reason, and are priced for a close-out. You may note that the buy-down applies to "selected residences." Or the hook may be a 30 percent or larger cash down payment. Or a nonrefundable 10 percent down and 20 percent more at the closing. There, the builder may be gambling on enough buyers putting down that 10 percent deposit, and then failing to get the needed financing from a lender, to keep him afloat until the housing market turns around.

Buy-downs *can* produce legitimate bargains, particularly when a developer has a wholly owned mortgage subsidiary through which it can fund its own mortgages. U.S. Home, for example, sold $100 million in mortgage-backed bonds in 1980 and used the funds for low-down-payment and graduated-payment mortgages to sell its homes in 16 states. On new homes, builders usually have the financing arranged before they begin to build. Depending on when the forward commitment for funds was made, the builder may be able to offer a mortgage rate significantly below the current market rate without punishing himself.

But get all the details where rates that seem too good to be believed are involved. Examine the short-term promotional financing offers carefully. At the end of the buy-down, to whom do you turn for financing? What sort of rate might you be facing when the buy-down period ends? Will you have to pay added charges for refinancing? Are prepayment penalties involved? Will the mortgage loan be renegotiated or will it revert to the market rate that prevailed at the closing?

What works in one locale might not work nearly as well in another, and at the end of 1981 there were some interesting trends developing with buy-downs across the country. In the Dallas area, for example, many builders were offering 30-year fixed-rate mortgages at around 13 percent (5 percentage points below the prevailing market level!). Others were offering a buy-down with a graduated-payment plan that began at around the 12 percent level for the first year and then went up a full percentage point per year for three years, with the final rate below the prevailing interest rate on conventional mortgage loans. Fox & Jacobs, Dallas' largest home builders, with 23 separate subdivisions under way at the time in and around the city, offered an FHA-insured GPM at most locations with the first-year interest rate set at 11.5

SAMPLE BREAKDOWN

Cash price of home	$56,000
Cash down payment	2,300
Mortgage loan amount	53,700
Monthly payments (P/I):	
Year 1 (11.5%)	532
Year 2 (12.5%)	573
Year 3 (13.5%)	615
Years 4–30 (14.5%)	658

percent; second year, 12.5 percent; third year, 13.5 percent; and fourth through thirtieth years, 14.5 percent—with no negative amortization involved.

The "step-rate" mortgages were popular in the Denver area too. But there, there was also a lot of financing that began at around 11 percent for the first year, jumped a couple of percentage points at the beginning of the second year, and then was reset at the current market rate for the third and subsequent years.

In the Washington, D.C., area, the builders of The Oglethorpe House at College Park, in suburban Maryland, were offering one-, two-, and three-bedroom condominium apartments, priced from under $35,000, at 12.875 percent for 10 years, with the interest rate to be renegotiated at the beginning of the eleventh year. The developers of The Townes of Lake d'Evereux in close-in Alexandria, Virginia, were offering town-house units priced from $105,000 at 10.75 percent for the first three years, escalating to 13.5 percent for years four and five, and then subject to readjustment at the beginning of the sixth year.

The newest twist in builder buy-downs has the builder "taking back" a second mortgage that is interest-free and not due and payable for a period of up to three years. With a 10 percent down payment on an $85,000 house, and an interest-free $20,000 second mortgage, the buyer, for example, would only have to qualify with the lender for a $56,500 first mortgage. And even here he may get a little help from the builder, with a bought-down renegotiable first mortgage. In three years, if the dust has settled on mortgage interest rates, the buyer might then "wrap" the first mortgage around the second, combining both into one. Or, if he can come up with enough cash through refinancing and from other resources, he could retire the second mortgage.

If you're thinking that the financing on some of these deals might get just a little bit complicated, check this footnote for Alpert Homes ("*10% 'Move-in-Now' Plan**"), in the Denver area: *"**Based on a first mortgage with a fixed rate of 10% simple interest and monthly loan payments for a term of five years calculated on the basis of a 30-year amortization. In addition there is a second mortgage with a variable interest rate which is adjusted each cal-*

endar quarter and which is based on the difference between a) the interest rate of 10% under the first mortgage and b) the 180-day U.S. Treasury bill rate in effect on the last day of the preceding calendar quarter plus 4 percentage points. The annual percentage rate of the second mortgage in effect on the date of closing may thereafter increase or decrease in accordance with adjustments in the 180-day U.S. Treasury bill rate, but such annual percentage rate may not exceed the maximum rate permitted by law. The interest charged on the second mortgage is not due and payable monthly; instead, it is accrued and becomes due and payable on resale of the property, refinancing of the mortgage, or in five years, whichever occurs first."

Oh, for the days of simple fixed-rate, level-payment loans!

There have been some significant developments that should encourage many more local lenders to cooperate with builders and others and make the buying-down of mortgages a continuing, common practice. For one, the FHA has authorized buy-downs with FHA-insured mortgage loans. Interest-payment reductions are limited to 3 percentage points with the FHA-insured loans and the buy-down must be for a minimum of three years. With the FHA program, the builder (or other seller) puts a sufficient amount of cash into an escrow account to reduce the monthly mortgage payments by a fixed amount. For another, Fannie Mae is now making a secondary market in mortgages with buy-down features. Loans of up to $98,500 are accepted with subsidy periods of from one to ten years; the interest-rate reduction is limited to 3 percentage points in any one year. Fannie Mae accepts "graduated" buy-downs provided the payments remain constant for 12-month periods.

Of particular interest here, Fannie Mae is not only making a secondary market for buy-down mortgages involving builders/developers but also for individual home sellers—and buyers. If a young couple are having trouble getting their financing act together and can't afford market-rate interest, there's nothing to prevent a parent or other relative from subsidizing the mortgage rate for a period of three years, say, when cash flow is essential to the new home buyers.

Buy-downs have also been discovered by the "Fortune 500"

and other major employers. The cost of a buy-down can be deducted from corporate income taxes and they're being used more and more in connection with executive transfers. Accountants have found it's a lot cheaper to buy down a transferred employee's new mortgage than to increase his salary to make up for the additional expenses of relocating in a new city.

Life Estates and Other Gambles

The elderly widow was moving to Phoenix to live with her sister and was asking $40,000, with $10,000 down and the balance payable over five years, for a suburban Chicago home easily worth $100,000. Was it a good deal? Probably not. When she dies, the buyer would no longer own the house. It would revert to the widow's late husband's estate and be passed down to his children by an earlier marriage. Under dower rights, the widow holds a life estate to the property. If she lives another 10, 15, or 20 years, the buyer will have done better than he would paying rent for a comparable dwelling. But if Arizona's climate doesn't prove to be all that salubrious, and the widow pops off in the next few years, the buyer will have made an expensive investment.

The purchase of a life estate (even if you take out an insurance policy on the seller) is always a risky business for someone looking for a place to call home. There are some new twists to "buy-and-die" plans, however, that are attacting attention, particularly in retirement areas. A plan gaining favor in Florida is an adaptation of an age-old French real-estate plan called *"en viager"*—from the Latin *viage*, meaning during one's lifetime. In France, real-estate transactions *en viager* involve sales by elderly persons who, quite simply, are trading the accumulated equity in their homes for a lump-sum down payment and a guaranteed income for life. More often than not, they continue living in the house or apartment until their death—be it for two months or 20 years. The late French President Charles de Gaulle acquired his 14-room country manor, La Boisserie, at Colombey-les-Deux-Eglises, *en viager* from an elderly widow when he was still a colonel in the army. Ex-President Valery Giscard d'Estaing bought the château of an elderly aunt the same way.

Translated to real-estate practices in this country, the owner sells the property for a price that is dependent on how long he or she is expected to live, based on the life-expectancy tables used by insurance companies. There's a substantial cash down payment, and then monthly payments, usually indexed to relieve the seller of any inflationary pressures. If the seller lives longer than projected in the tables, the buyer continues the payments, losing some of his investment edge with each additional payment. If the seller dies earlier than expected (and let's hope it's not as a victim of foul play at the hands of you-know-who), the buyer will have made that much better an investment.

For an example of just how this works, Bess Cohen, a widow with no children, recently sold her Hallandale, Florida, condominium for $20,000 down and a monthly payment that began at $358 per month but was indexed to offset any rise in the cost of living. As long as she lives (insurance charts give her about 10 more years), Mrs. Cohen will continue to occupy the apartment. It's a good deal for her. She's still living in a home and neighborhood where she feels comfortable. She has a nice cash cushion and should have no future financial worries.

It's also a good deal for the investor. He pays toward the principal only; there's no interest involved here. Going by the actuarial tables, his total investment isn't likely to exceed the market value of the condominium at the time of the agreement. That value, of course, is expected to keep rising with continuing inflation. When Mrs. Cohen goes to her reward, no matter how many payments have been made, the buyer gets the condo.

A plan favored in the West originated with Fouratt Corporation of Carmel, California, and could be described as a sale/lease-back. Here's how it works: Fouratt, a mortgage banking company, brings together homeowners over age 65 with younger investors seeking tax shelters or real-estate bargains. The investor arranges to buy the house, which should be free and clear, for 15 to 30 percent less than its appraised value. He generally puts down 10 percent, with the rest scheduled to be paid in monthly installments over 10 or 15 years, depending on the age of the seller. He also pays the property taxes, hazard insurance, and most maintenance costs on the home. In return, the seller, who continues in residency, pays him a small monthly rent (guaranteed to rise more slowly than his retirement income). The investor thus gets a tax shelter as a landlord. Should the seller of the house live beyond his life expectancy, the investor still has an attractive deal—he knows that his property is in good hands and increasing in value.

En viager and sale/leaseback agreements come under the general heading of split-equity contracts. Unlike most other purchasing agreements, they entail actual sale of the property but no mortgage loan. Numerous split-equity schemes are conceivable, and the more elaborate contracts provide for contingencies such as a seller with rent-free life tenure who subsequently wishes to change residences. Sellers also frequently use the proceeds from the sale to purchase an annuity contract to supplement their income.

There's still another way for the owner of a house to create a life estate and at the same time guarantee himself an adequate income through his remaining years. That's by giving the house away. It shouldn't be done without the advice of a tax attorney, but a property with good value given to certain tax-exempt charities or foundations (progressive universities, churches, and the like) can create a charitable gift annuity. The donor would get a guaranteed monthly income while retaining the right to rent-free occupancy for a fixed term of years or life.

These really aren't ways for a young buyer to acquire that first home. They're presented here more to satisfy the curiosity of those among you who may have heard something about life estates and the like and were hoping for some commentary on the viability of these methods of acquiring a home.

REVERSE MORTGAGES: UNFREEZING YOUR ASSETS

While reverse mortgages have nothing to do with buying a home, they too could be something to look forward to in your later years. They're designed to allow elderly persons to use the equity in their homes as additional monthly income during the remainder of their lifetime without having to sell their homes.

A reverse mortgage is just like a regular mortgage—only instead of you paying the bank each month, the bank pays you. The basic idea had been gaining adherents for a number of years, but it took hard lobbying by the United States League of Savings Associations to get the concept through the Federal Home Loan Bank Board and the Congress and into the S&Ls' inventory of mortgage instruments in 1979.

The majority of this country's senior citizens own their homes free and clear. By the time they enter their retirement years, most of their net worth is represented by the accumulated equity in that property. But, as retirees, there's little they can do to tap that equity short of selling their home. With little income beyond Social Security and maybe a modest pension, not many can even qualify for a home equity loan; the additonal interest expense would prove too much of a burden for those on an already tight budget. As a result, a great many of the elderly are "house rich, cash poor." Unless they sell and move, they can't cash in on their largest single asset.

Thus, the birth of the reverse mortgage, which is a loan that becomes payable upon sale of the property, death of the borrower, or at some other agreed-upon date. The intent is not for the lender to own the home. If you borrowed $35,000 on your home, you owe $35,000 plus accrued interest. And if you die, your estate owes the money—a debt it would have to pay (unless it forfeits the house) either by selling the property or out of other resources. It reduces the size of the estate that you could be leaving to your children. But then, any "kids" would likely be in their thirties or forties, if not older, and should be capable of fending for themselves.

Among the many home-financing alternatives proposed in the 1970s, it was the reverse mortgage, also known as the reverse-annuity mortgage, or RAM, that drew the most interest from consumers and the news media. It was anticipated that such plans, once approved for use by the federally chartered lending institutions, would attract elderly borrowers in droves. That has not been the case.

A rising-debt reverse mortgage, the simplest of the reverse-mortgage instruments that have been introduced to date, typically works like this: A couple in their early seventies have a paid-for house with an appraised value of $80,000. They're living on Social Security and a small pension. Having exhausted their other savings, they apply at an S&L for a reverse-mortgage loan that will return them $400 per month for the next five years, with no payment due the lender until the maturity date of the mortgage or the death of the surviving spouse, whichever comes first.

The limits on the total amount that can be borrowed by the homeowner are based on a percentage of the equity, the number of payments to be made (usually over a five-, seven-, or ten-year period), and the prevailing mortgage interest rate at the signing. In this case, the requested $24,000 over five years falls well within the lender's guidelines. Our couple will owe that plus interest accrued on the loan and added to the loan principal over the five years. On payment No. 1, there will have been five years' accrued interest; on payment No. 59, only one month's interest.

For this example, let's say the accumulated interest comes to $10,000. Our couple, if still alive, will owe the lender $34,000 at the due date of the loan. However, if the property has appreciated an average of 10 percent a year, it would then be worth $125,000. They could sell the house, pay off their indebtedness, and use the income from the net proceeds of the sale to make other living arrangements. Or, if they want to continue living in the house for as long as they can, they could negotiate for a new reverse mortgage. However, the equity in their home would then be liquidated at a faster rate, since they would also be paying interest on the initial mortgage. The major drawback with the rising-debt plan, of course, is that it does not guarantee life tenure. Mortgagors who "live too long" could be in real trouble.

The proponents of the reverse mortgage thought they had the solution to that in a lifetime-annuity plan, but that was before interest rates went up like a helium-filled balloon. That

$400-per-month payment to our elderly couple might be described as an "annuity," but a reverse-annuity mortgage is really a mortgage of a different color, since it would necessarily involve a life-insurance company. There are many options available with RAMs, up to and including lifetime annuities. The plans are structured to convert up to 80 percent of the market value of the property into one or more annuity contracts that, while doling out a little something to the homeowner each month, at the same time pay off the interest owed on the loan. High mortgage interest rates and the insurance company's profit margin on these loans, however, leave so little for the homeowner as to make them a bad bet for anyone much under 75. They just don't generate enough cash flow for borrowers at high interest rates to be practicable.

For all the talk about reverse mortgages—and doing something to relieve the burden that inflation has placed on those on fixed income—only a handful of lenders have offered any form of reverse-mortgage loan to date. Instead of setting up guidelines as to how such mortgages should be structured, the Federal Home Loan Bank Board, in authorizing such loans, asked the savings and loans to come up with some designs of their own. Most lenders, who don't see much profit in the mortgages, adopted a wait-and-see attitude to see how others might handle the mortgages. Their wariness paid off when sky-high interest rates showed up the deficiencies in the RAM plans being tested.

Reverse mortgages, RAMs included, might one day open up an enormous new source of demand for mortgage loans. But at high interest rates, lenders who have tested the loans found that they don't hold all that much appeal to the elderly, who tend to grow more cautious with advanced years and have a great reluctance to liquidate their wealth. It's going to take trial-and-error with a number of loan variations to see what works well for both borrowers and lenders and becomes standardized, and then cash-poor homeowners are going to have to be shown that here's a safe way they can live more comfortably the rest of their days without having to sell the homestead.

Seller
Financing

More than half the houses changing hands today involve some form of seller financing. A phenomenon of the 1980s, seller financing provides the most frequent solution to the problem of tight money and high interest rates where existing houses are for sale. Utilizing purchase-money mortgages, land contracts, mortgage assumptions, wraparound mortgages, lease-options, and land leases to expedite sales, this is home financing at its most creative.

Seller financing doesn't necessarily mean that the seller provides all of the financing. In many cases, the home seller's participation is limited to "taking back" a short-term second mortgage to fill the gap between the buyer's down payment (if any) and the amount a conventional money source will agree to provide in a first-mortgage loan. More often, though, seller financing is based on an existing low-rate mortgage that is either assumed by the buyer or "wrapped" to combine elements of assumption and second mortgages.

It's not difficult to find sellers who are willing to help with the financing in order to make the sale. You'll spot the key phrases—"owner will hold mortgage," "assumable mortgage," "owner will take back second mortgage," "lease with option to buy"—in ads placed by both individual sellers and real-estate firms in the weekend classified section of any major newspaper. In some areas of the country, real-estate brokers won't even take a listing unless the seller will carry at least part of the financing.

While often you can literally write your own terms, it is not a good idea to go into one of these "do-it-yourself" deals without having a real-estate professional involved. It is also strongly recommended that you *not* make a purchase offer or sign anything that could be legally binding without consulting an attorney well versed in real-estate procedures. There are many more pitfalls to be avoided when using creative financing than there are with conventional financing.

Unfamiliarity with applicable federal and state laws could expose buyers and sellers to later legal imbroglios with lenders or to suits and countersuits against each other. Varying state and local laws could also affect whether or not certain methods of creative financing may be used at all for the transaction. For example, although Congress has preempted state interest ceilings as they apply to first-mortgage loans made by institutional lenders, some states still have usury ceilings in force for individuals making real-estate loans.

Not every real-estate broker is worth his shingle when it comes to creative financing. However, there's an easy way to meet agents who understand today's new realty finance methods. Visit weekend "open houses" and talk to the agent or agents on the scene. When you find one who really knows his business, simply take it from there. Most agents use open houses to meet prospective buyers for their other properties anyway, and have little expectation of making a sale on the home being shown that day.

Creative techniques accounted for barely 5 percent of home sales in the United States as recently as 1979. They've since been used by hundreds of thousands of resourceful individuals to buy and sell homes that might otherwise still be overhanging the market. Where both parties are well informed, or well advised, each acting in what he considers his own best interest, most of the techniques represent safe, sound answers to the needs of buyers and sellers. Serious abuses have been cropping up, however. In California, land of razzle-dazzle, buyers have been making deals that not only avoid a down payment but sometimes have the seller turning back cash (from bank-loan proceeds) to the buyer, as a sort of reverse down payment.

Many creative arrangements, in California and elsewhere, call for a "balloon" payment in three years or less, and there is growing concern for the tens of thousands of mortgagors who are going to have to come up with large sums of money one, two, or three years down the road. What if interest rates are as high as if not higher than they are today—or if money's not there for the borrowing? Housing-industry analysts are predicting that foreclosures and legal battles will escalate in direct proportion to the "tightness" of money.

The Federal Reserve Board was sufficiently alarmed by the potential problems ahead for inexperienced home buyers who acquire their properties with seller financing to propose a regulation that would require that real-estate brokers who help arrange more than five seller-financed transactions a year observe the same "truth-in-lending" regulations that apply to banks, savings and loans, and mortgage companies when apprising borrowers of the costs and conditions of a loan. Those agents would be required to spell out key differences of creatively financed mortgages to prospective home buyers in a one-page disclosure statement before the buyer signs a binding sales contract.

Many buyers turn to seller financing because they can't qualify for a large enough bank loan to swing the deal. And yet, few sellers bother to ask their real-estate agent to order a credit report on the prospective purchaser. Wouldn't you want to know to whom you were extending credit? With seller financing, the property being sold should be security enough for the loan; if the buyer doesn't pay, the seller forecloses and gets the property back. But still, without a check of the buyer's past credit history, the seller could be letting himself in for endless collection problems.

As a buyer, you should have no more objection to a credit check being made than you would when borrowing from a bank or thrift. This doesn't mean that the seller is going to be as conservative as a banker who won't qualify a buyer who would be paying out better than 25 or 33 percent of his gross income for housing. Most sellers can afford to be more generous than that. If the seller wants to ensure his investment, all he really needs to do is have the buyer come up with a good down payment. The down payment, representing "protective equity" in the house, would give the buyer incentive to keep payments current and avoid foreclosure in the first place.

The buyer would seem to have most of the advantages where the seller carries back all or part of the financing. But there also are benefits to the seller. It can mean a quick, easy sale, often at top dollar if he'll accept a small down payment or a below-market interest rate. There's that steady stream of interest earnings on the buyer's unpaid balance. And an installment sale allows him to spread out his profit over a number of years, reducing the tax bite.

The reason most houses won't sell isn't the pricing. It's the financing. But don't expect the seller to cut his price to the point where you can qualify for bank financing. Sellers will make almost any concession as long as they don't have to touch the price. Which is why some buyers are able to get financing at 12 percent when the prevailing market rate is closer to 18 percent. In effect, sellers do cut their prices, substantially, when they accept below-market interest rates.

As a buyer obtaining property without resorting to traditional financing, you won't have any loan origination fees or points to pay, and you can avoid those delays, sometimes running to several months, while a lender processes your loan application. You'll also have fewer closing costs, but that doesn't mean that you can afford to ignore procedures that are now elective. A title search and a survey of the property are no less important with seller financing than they are with bank financing. The services of an expert appraiser to establish the value of the property and point out deficiencies are also well worth the cost.

If the seller is offering financing, you should know exactly what is involved. It's also important to know *why* the seller is selling. Is he an investor looking to get as much cash as he can out of the property? Is he a retiree interested in dependable monthly income? Or is he being transferred to another city by his employer and anxious for a quick sale? Depending on the seller's motivation, you may be able to suggest different methods of financing. Often the seller doesn't know what he will accept until the buyer lays it out for him. It's usually up to the buyer to convince the seller that holding the mortgage and offering an affordable interest rate are not only practicable but profitable options.

Don't let the real-estate agent dissuade you from involving the seller in the financing. Make conditional offers to buy every house you inspect and would like to own, on terms *you* want. Agents are legally bound to present all purchase offers to their clients. Will the seller agree to those terms? You'll never know unless you ask.

PURCHASE-MONEY MORTGAGES

When mortgage money is hard to get from other sources, a motivated seller may agree to "loan" the prospective buyer a large portion of the money needed to purchase his, the seller's, property. The practice is commonly referred to as "taking back the mortgage," and the instrument used is known as a purchase-money mortgage. The mortgage is as binding as one issued by a bank or thrift. Foreclosure action can be taken if the buyer defaults. The seller can even include a due-on-sale clause in the contract to keep the buyer from assigning the property without first settling his debt with him.

Take-back mortgages generally provide for short- rather than long-term financing, no more than five or ten years, but with payments based on a 25- or 30-year amortization schedule. The buyer makes a cash down payment and signs a promissory note for the balance of the contract price. At the end of the loan term, the buyer negotiates a new loan with the seller, or finds new financing elsewhere. By then, however, he should have enough equity in the property (the difference between its market value and the existing mortgage) to make refinancing relatively painless.

This do-it-yourself sort of financing is becoming popular with home sellers for a number of reasons, not the least of which is that a purchase-money mortgage can be a highly lucrative investment. The interest the seller earns often gives him a better return on his money than he could get elsewhere, and the interest rate doesn't fluctuate as it can with a money-market fund or T-bill rollovers. Besides representing a safe investment, a purchase-money mortgage allows the seller to spread his tax-favored capital gains under the installment method of reporting.

Purchase-money mortgages (and we're talking here about first mortgages; purchase-money seconds are covered under "Secondary Financing") save the loan origination fee and most of the other closing costs that a lending institution would charge the buyer-borrower. So, right from the start, the buyer could be a couple of thousand dollars ahead. And, since the seller doesn't have any of the overhead costs of a conventional loan source, he can afford to accept a lower interest rate. The interest rate charged on take-backs typically runs 2 to 3 percentage points below prevailing first-mortgage rates.

Taking the place of the bank, however, the seller does need to observe a few precautions, even though he won't actually be handing out any cash. If he's smart, he will have a credit check run on the prospective buyer. He may also insist on a loan provision that protects him against inflation—say, an interest-rate increase of 1 percentage point per year after the third year, if justified by market conditions. He's also going to have to be a part-time bookkeeper, and this is the role that sellers enjoy the least. He will have the responsibility of seeing to it that property-tax and hazard-insurance payments are met on time, and he may also find that his buyer needs frequent reminders to get those monthly mortgage payments to him by the first of the month.

As a prospective buyer, you have nothing to lose by providing in your purchase offer that the seller is to take back the mortgage, even though there has been no discussion of this (you may not even have met the seller) as a possible arrangement. Ask the broker to explain to the seller all the advantages in taking back the mortgage. You might then avoid the traditional moneylenders and work out a contract with terms that both you and the seller can handle. For example, it could be to your advantage to accept an increase in the selling price, provided the seller will accept a lower rate of interest (this could be the solution, too, to complying with state usury laws). If he gets a higher price for the property, he can then better afford to sell the mortgage at a discount if he needs to cash-out. He also will have a larger capital gain, which can net him more after taxes than increased interest payments, which are taxed as ordinary income.

Three basic payment arrangements are used with take-backs:

• **Interest and principal.** With the monthly payments calculated to amortize the loan, this works just like any conventional long-term mortgage.

• **Interest only.** The monthly mortgage payments all go toward interest, with no reduction of principal. Sometimes called a standing mortgage, this arrangement can work to the advantage of both buyer and seller. The seller delays receiving any capital gain and keeps all of his principal working. For the buyer, the monthly mortgage payments are fully tax deductible. Having a big mortgage balance can also make the home easier to resell in future years.

• **Balloon note.** At the end of a specified term, whether two years or ten, the buyer is required to pay off the loan balance. Short-fuse (two-to-three-year) balloon notes are dangerous for the buyer. There also are those additional closing costs when required to refinance with another lender. Where a life-disrupting balloon note is to be included in the mortgage, hold out for at least a five-year delay before it comes due.

For an example of how one young couple acquired a home with a purchase-money mortgage, take the experience of Bill and Virginia Miller. In the spring of 1981, Bill and Virginia made a purchase offer for a house in Tenafly, New Jersey. The price they agreed to pay was $105,000, but the offer was made contingent on their obtaining bank financing for an $84,000 mortgage at 13 percent or less. They had earlier made the rounds of the local lending institutions and had succeeded in securing a tentative commitment from an S&L at the 13 percent rate. But by the time the Millers got an acceptance from the seller and the thrift had completed processing their formal application for the loan, the mortgage interest rate had soared to 16 percent and was threatening to climb still higher before they could close on the property. Instead of paying $929 or less per month on the mortgage, they would now have to pay at least $1,129 per month. That is, if they could find a lender. The S&L they had been counting on would no longer qualify them unless the market rate dropped to 14 percent or less. Having been turned down by other loan officers when pre-shopping for money at 13 percent or less, the Millers knew there was no way they could get a lending institution to agree to their paying $1,129 or more per month based on their mid-1981 income.

To save the sale, the real-estate broker recommended to the home seller that he take back a purchase-money mortgage for $84,000 at the original 13 percent rate, with payments based on a 30-year amortization schedule. At the end of five years, the mortgage interest rate would be subject to renegotiaton, and at the end of 10 years, the Millers would have to find financing from another source and pay off the remaining loan balance to the home seller.

When the Millers found that they would save more than $2,500 in loan points and other closing costs, and still get their needed financing at 13 percent, there was little hesitation on their part to close the deal. The seller, who had better than $80,000 of equity in the property, warmed to the idea of becoming a banker when he was shown how he would get additional tax breaks with the installment sale. The broker told him to think of his home as a long-term annuity; he didn't make his money all at once and shouldn't expect to get it out all at once.

The seller, who was winterizing a bed-and-breakfast guesthouse in the Poconos for year-round business, needed more than the $21,000 cash represented by the down payment. As a "concession" for the 13 percent interest, the Millers were required to prepay the first 12 installments on the mortgage. Bill and Virginia held on to their Aspen time-shares and Morgan dollars but had to borrow on Bill's life insurance and go into hock down to their socks to come up with the nearly $33,000 in cash needed to close the deal. They made it, however, and all parties have been more than satisfied to date with the financing arrangement.

The investment is secured by the property. Should the Millers default, the seller would get to keep the money paid in, repossess the house, and could then sell it again. As a purchaser, however, it was important that the Millers record the deed to the property *before* the seller recorded the purchase-money mortgage. If done in the reverse order, it would appear from the records that the Millers were mortgaging property that is recorded in the seller's name.

If the seller becomes a reluctant mortgagee and finds he later needs to raise some additional cash, he can hypothecate the mortgage—pledge it to a local lender as security for a loan without transferring possession. Most banks will lend about 50 percent of the unpaid balance of a seller-held first mortgage.

The Federal National Mortgage Association will do even more for a seller-financier. Under Fannie Mae's Home Seller Loan Program, launched in 1980, sellers can turn over all of the administrative headaches associated with originating and "servicing" the mortgage to a professional mortgage lender. The program also enables them, under certain conditions, to arrange for sale of the loan to FNMA, should they wish to liquidate the mortgage at some future date.

Here's how the program works. A home seller, having agreed to provide financing for the buyer, contracts for an FNMA-approved bank, S&L, or mortgage company to perform all the services associated with originating the loan and collecting the monthly payments. At this point, the seller may also request that the loan be submitted to Fannie Mae for review prior to the closing. This provides assurance that the loan is currently acceptable for subsequent sale to Fannie Mae.

Fannie Mae will buy only mortgages that are fully amortized over the term of the loan (not to exceed 30 years) by level installments of principal and interest payable on the first day of each month. The maximum loan amount accepted by Fannie Mae for a single-family conventional mortgage under the program is $98,500. Private mortgage insurance must be obtained on mortgages with loan-to-value ratios above 80 percent.

To sell the loan, the home seller notifies the lender servicing the loan that he wishes to convert the loan to cash. The lender informs the home seller of the rate required by FNMA and handles the transaction. Fannie Mae's purchase price generally is based on mortgage-market rates. If the interest rate on the loan is the same as or higher than prevailing mortgage interest rates at the

time of the sale to Fannie Mae, the home seller receives the full
remaining principal balance of the loan.

If the interest rate on the mortgage is lower than the prevailing
mortgage interest rate, the seller receives a discounted amount.
For example: The outstanding mortgage balance is $80,000 and
the interest rate on the mortgage is 13 percent. At the time of
sale, Fannie Mae requires 15 percent. The home seller receives
$71,288.

There are a number of fees involved with this program. Home
sellers can expect to pay the lender a fee for the loan origination,
the monthly servicing (which includes collection of monthly payments, escrowing and payments of taxes and insurance, pass-
through of principal and interest to the home seller, accounting
records), and probably for selling the loan to Fannie Mae (if the
home seller wants to convert the loan to cash). These fees are negotiable, and some may be paid by the buyer.

LAND CONTRACTS

When a house is purchased under a land contract, also known
as a contract for deed or an installment land contract, the buyer
occupies the property, but the seller continues to hold legal title
to it until all or an agreed-upon number of installments have been
paid. The buyer, under this arrangement, is known as the "equitable owner." He pays the taxes and assessments on the property,
and has the tax and equity benefits of homeownership, without
the property having actually been deeded over to him. If there is
an underlying mortgage on the property, the seller continues to
pay on it, out of the installment payments made to him by the
buyer.

Land contracts are frequently used when the buyer makes no or
a very small down payment on a house, and/or where the buyer's
credit-worthiness is in question. Denying title until the buyer has
built some equity in the property reduces the seller's risk. Should
the deal turn sour, the seller does not have to go through the ar-
duous, costly, and time-consuming process of foreclosing and
wresting the title away from the buyer. Land contracts are also

used during periods of tight money to buy time until interest rates come down and the buyer can turn to a lending institution for conventional long-term financing. They may be used too prior to issuance of purchase-money mortgages. Among the advantages to the seller: installment-sale tax benefits, the remedy of "strict fore-closure" (the calling off of the contract) should the buyer default, and, in many cases, a higher price than if he had held out for a cash sale.

All the terms of the land contract are negotiated between buyer and seller: the size of the down payment, the length of the con-tract, the interest rate, and the size and frequency of the pay-ments. Generally, land contracts are written for from five to ten years, with extensions sometimes provided for in the contract, or for such time until local mortgage rates drop to an agreed-upon level. The buyer is usually required to pay simple interest only; amortization is left to subsequent long-term financing.

In some states, the maximum interest rate that can be charged by the seller on a land contract will be less than can be charged by a bank or thrift on a first-mortgage note. The federal preemption of state usury laws applies only to first-mortgage loans from tradi-tional sources. In Michigan, for example, where the housing mar-ket is a real disaster due to the deep three-year slump in car sales, the most that a homeowner can charge on a land contract is 11 percent. What's worse, for all those would-be sellers of mortgage-encumbered homes who would like to quit the state and seek work in Texas and the Sunbelt, about the only way a southeastern Michigan owner *can* sell a house today is with a land contract.

Laws governing land contracts vary from state to state, and the buyer should never enter into an agreement that leaves his prop-erty legally in the seller's hands without first consulting an attor-ney who is expert in these matters. In some states, should the buyer of the property miss one or more payments, the seller can summarily dispossess the buyer and recover possession of the property.

Land contracts usually contain a clause stating that if the owner has reasonable cause to repossess the property, all of the payments made by the buyer shall be considered rent for the buyer's time of occupancy. In many states, as a consequence of the repossession, the buyer forfeits all the money he has paid to date. Under California law, it's not quite that bad. The buyer, if he's to be evicted, can recover the difference between what he has paid and what he might have been required to pay as a renter.

Other pitfalls that a good lawyer might help the buyer to avoid would be possible problems that could arise with the death or incapacity of the seller. Without the proper wording in the contract, the buyer's rights could be tied up in probate for a good many months. Some understanding needs to be reached, too, on the buyer's right to make alterations in the house, with or without the seller's written consent. But this should not be thought of as a unilateral contract. The seller needs to defend himself too, and will probably wish to include a clause prohibiting the buyer from assigning the contract or subletting the property without the written consent of the seller.

On the other hand, the contract should prohibit the seller from entering into any transactions that could affect the title (an inherent danger in the land contract from the standpoint of the buyer). As sometimes happens, the buyer makes all the scheduled payments, becomes entitled to receive the deed, and then discovers that the seller is unable to deliver a marketable title. One possible way to avoid having a clear title become clouded is to have the deed placed in an escrow trust until it comes time for the buyer to acquire it.

Where there's an existing low-rate mortgage on the property, buyers and sellers in some states have been resorting to land contracts to avoid a legally enforceable due-on-sale clause (which allows the lender to demand immediate payment of the balance of the loan if the borrower sells or "transfers" any of his interest in the property to someone else). In effect, with the land contract, the purchaser is taking out an option to apply to assume the mortgage at some later date, gambling that interest rates will drop in the meantime. Technically, until the buyer assumes the mortgage, it's not a sale. The courts have been ruling both ways on this, however. There was a recent case in northern Virginia where a court upheld an S&L's foreclosure against a husband and wife who had sold their suburban town house under a land contract and permitted the buyer to "effectively assume" their existing 9.5 percent mortgage, despite a clause in the mortgage contract prohibiting an assumption without the lender's approval of the new buyer and an adjustment of the contract interest rate to the current market level.

In the Virginia episode, the S&L might never have found out about the assumption had not the new buyer's name appeared as the beneficiary on the property hazard-insurance policy in the loan file. When the purchaser of the property resisted the bank's move to raise the loan rate to the prevailing market level, the lender put the property up for foreclosure sale and the case went to court.

Lenders in some parts of the country accept that legal title under a land contract doesn't pass immediately to the new buyer. But Virginia is one of a number of states where lenders are on the lookout for private arrangements between buyers and sellers that seek to avoid having the rate on an existing mortgage "accelerated." You now know how to avoid detection. It's a good idea, anyway, under a land contract, for the purchaser, who would be responsible for any damage to the house, to maintain his own insurance policy with the seller as a coinsured. To satisfy the lender, the seller would continue carrying hazard insurance in his own name until the mortgage is either assumed or retired.

Land contracts are also used as junior financing instruments where the terms of an existing mortgage forbid the placing of a second lien on the property. A typical scenario might have a prospective purchaser without enough cash to buy out the seller's equity in the property. The seller takes back a land contract for the difference between the selling price and the down payment plus the balance owing on the mortgage. The purchaser then assumes the mortgage (many mortgages *are* fully assumable) and makes the monthly payments to the lending institution. Payments on the land contract are made to the seller of the property. This does not constitute a second mortgage on the property and is generally accepted as not being in violation of the first mortgage. The owner, if he wishes to cash-out, can sell the land contract.

Before executing a contract sale, the potential limitations in *any* underlying mortgage should be reviewed by an expert. If the purchase arrangement could be found to be in violation of the mortgage, and foreclosure action is taken, the buyer could be left with nothing to show for his payments but a worthless contract.

INSTALLMENT-SALE TAX TACTICS

The market value of the average single-family house has nearly tripled since 1970, and most homeowners, when they put the house they've been living in for more than a few years on the block, are looking for ways to preserve as much of that equity as possible. If the seller isn't going to be able to defer his profit under the residence-replacement rule, and hasn't reached age 55, which means he's not eligible to claim that once-in-a-lifetime exclusion of $125,000, an installment sale may be just what the tax accountant ordered.

Tax-law changes effective January 1, 1982, reduce the bite on long-term capital gains (assets held more than one year) to a maximum effective rate of 20 percent. This takes some of the pain out of a seller's taking all of his profit in one year, but at the same time, the reporting could subject his other income for the year to a much higher tax rate. The most satisfactory compromise for sellers who don't require a lot of immediate cash out of the sale, or no more than would be represented by the down payment, is an installment sale. This option allows the taxpayer to level off his income and, at the same time, pay the tax in the tax year in which payments are received.

Installment sales have become increasingly popular since the Installment Sales Revision Act of 1980 liberalized and simplified many of the complex rules for selling property on the installment plan and for reporting the taxable gain on the sale. The biggest change involved elimination of a provision in the old law stating that the property seller, to reap installment-sale tax benefits, could not receive more than 30 percent of the property's gross sales price, including the down payment and payment on principal, in the year of sale. Also eliminated was the "two-payment rule," which required that a deferred-payment sale be for two or more payments, in at least two different tax years. Now, every sale of a personal residence by a person other than a dealer can be structured so that the seller is not boosted into a punishingly higher tax bracket during the year of sale, as might be the consequence with an all-cash sale or traditional mortgage financing.

These provisions work for the buyer too. By bringing tax-deferral advantages to the attention of a seller who might previously have been reluctant to take back the mortgage or agree to a land contract, you may be able to arrange for seller financing that better suits your financial condition.

Let's look at a typical installment sale. Twice, sales of George Odom's house in Springfield, Massachusetts, had fallen through due to failure of the would-be buyers to obtain the necessary bank financing. Odom, 51, and a recent widower, had a bronchial problem and was moving to Arizona at the recommendation of his doctor. He was holding out for $90,000 for the house, which would net him $55,000 as a long-term capital gain.

Since he would be a renter in Phoenix, and unable to defer taxes on any part of the $55,000 under the residence-replacement rule, Odom had looked into ways of possibly postponing the sale or payment for another four years, so that he wouldn't have to pay *any* tax on that $55,000. But the tax code clearly states that to be eligible to claim that $125,000 exclusion, the profit must be on the sale of a residence in which the taxpayer has lived as his principal home for at least three years out of the five-year period ending on the date of sale. He'd looked into lease-options and land contracts, but there was always that other qualifier: *The earliest date on which you may sell your house and still qualify for the exclusion is your 55th birthday.*

Then along came Bob and Dottie Hartman, who fell in love with the house. The Hartmans knew they couldn't qualify at a lending institution for 80 percent financing on a $90,000 property, so they proposed to buy it on an installment plan they were confident they could handle even without extraordinary future increases in their earnings. In their purchase offer, they proposed to pay $10,000 down and 12.5 percent simple interest on the balance of the contract price, with the mortgage to be held by the seller. This purchase-money mortgage was to be paid off at the rate of $1,000 per month for 10 years. The balance of the loan would be due and payable at the end of the 10th year.

The $10,000 down payment, $12,000 per year for 10 years, and the $44,042 payment at the end of the 10th year

Year	Annual Payment	Payment to Interest	Payment to Principal	Remaining Balance
1	$12,000	$10,000	$2,000	$78,000
2	12,000	9,750	2,250	75,750
3	12,000	9,469	2,531	73,219
4	12,000	9,152	2,848	70,371
5	12,000	8,796	3,204	67,167
6	12,000	8,396	3,604	63,563
7	12,000	7,945	4,055	59,508
8	12,000	7,439	4,561	54,947
9	12,000	6,868	5,132	49,815
10	12,000	6,227	5,773	44,042

would give Odom a total of $174,042 for his house. Odom's broker, in line for a $5,400 commission, liked the purchase offer, but thought, with 12.5 percent interest (at a time of 16 percent interest) on appreciating property, it needed a little sweetening. So the Hartmans were persuaded to make that a $15,000 down payment and the selling price was bumped to $95,000.

The broker improved his commission. George Odom is comfortable with the interest he's earning on the sale of his house. And the Hartmans also got a good deal. Had they secured a 30-year $80,000 mortgage loan at 16 percent from a conventional source, they would be paying $1,076 per month—almost $1,000 more per year in financing—and, at the end of 10 years, instead of having reduced the outstanding balance to $44,042, they would have a remaining unpaid balance of $77,328.

Looking at the tax aspects, had George Odom received all $90,000, as originally sought, during the year of sale, he would have been pushed into the highest tax bracket and would have been required to pay $11,000 in taxes on the $55,000 netted on the sale. This way, out of the first-year payments by the Hartmans ($15,000 down, plus $1,000 per month), he will have received $10,000 in interest, which is taxed as ordinary income, plus $17,000 in payments on the principal. Since Odom's gross-profit percentage is 63 percent ($60,000 taxable profit from the sale divided by $95,000 contract price), only 63 percent of the payment to principal he receives each year is included in his income. On that $17,000, the *maximum* he would have to pay, under long-term capital-gains treatment, would be $2,142. Best of all, since the gain from the installment sale qualifies for long-term capital-gains treatment in the year of the sale, the profit portion of all subsequent payments to principal benefit from the same treatment.

The seller can receive any amount of down payment—or none at all—and the sale will still be treated as an installment sale. Installment sales also can be combined to produce additional tax breaks with that $125,000 exclusion, if the net profit on the sale exceeds $125,000, and with the residence-replacement rule too.

Here's an example of how an installment sale might yield additional tax breaks when purchasing a replacement residence that costs less than the property being sold: Jones sells his house at a contract price of $125,000, under terms that permit him to use the installment method of reporting. He has a capital gain of $65,000 on the sale. He buys another, smaller house, postponing the tax on $30,000 of the gain. Jones's gross-profit percentage is 28 percent ($35,000 taxable profit divided by $125,000 contract price). Twenty-eight percent of the principal payment he receives each year is included in his income and taxed as a capital gain.

MORTGAGE ASSUMPTIONS

Once upon a time, when mortgage rates were in stable single digits, you could sometimes buy a house merely by assuming responsibility for the unpaid balance on the mortgage, just as you might take over from a financially strapped owner the payment book and a car on the verge of repossession. While mortgage assumptions have been called the keystone of creative financing, the mechanics of transferring a mortgage aren't quite that simple anymore. The procedure isn't seller financing as such, but it is based on the previous owner's mortgage, and can go a long way toward overseeing the problem of affordability.

A low-interest-rate mortgage that is "freely assumable" can

make this the best of all ways to buy a home. You not only acquire a portion of the needed financing at a below-market rate, you also save the origination fee and other costs of arranging for a first mortgage with an institutional lender. Where additional financing is needed, home sellers today frequently can be persuaded to take back a short-term second mortgage to fill the gap between the contract price of the property and the sum of the down payment and the mortgage debt.

The disadvantage of assuming a mortgage with a low rate of interest is that it was probably issued at a time when housing prices were from one-half to one-third of what they are now. The seller not only has built up equity in the mortgage but also substantial appreciation in the market value of the property. To take advantage of that low-rate mortgage, the buyer is going to have to come up with a sizable "cash-over" payment. Most assumptors find it necessary to obtain additional financing in the form of a second mortgage, either from the seller or a lending institution.

It is estimated that as many as one million assumable fixed-rate mortgages are available each year. Not all are assumed, of course. For one reason or another, many are paid off by the original mortgagor. But it doesn't take much house-hunting to find any number of sellers with existing mortgages that could be assumed by a new owner. Prior to June 28, 1982, when the U.S. Supreme Court effectively quashed state laws and lower court decisions that interfered with a Federal Home Loan Bank Board regulation that permits federally chartered S&Ls to enforce due-on-sale clauses, finding owners with existing mortgages that could be assumed had been even easier.

Since the mid-1970s, most conventional mortgages have included a binding due-on-sale clause, which reserves for the lender the right to declare the loan due and payable if the property securing the loan is sold or otherwise transferred without the lender's consent. The original intent of the due-on-sale clause, antecedents of which have been included in some lenders' mortgage contracts since the 1960s, was to protect lenders against assumptions by strangers who might impair the security of the loan. The clause was seldom enforced until interest rates crossed the double-digit threshold in the late 1970s. Lenders have since been using the clause to call in old low-rate mortgages and jack up the interest rate when the underlying property changes hands.

Due-on-sale led to court fights between borrowers and lenders in more than 200 jurisdictions, as federal S&Ls, in particular, waged a battle royal to prevent mortgages issued earlier at low interest rates from being assumed by new owner-mortgagors without an adjustment in the loan rate. By early 1982, the right of the lender to raise interest rates on an existing older mortgage under due-on-sale had been held to be unenforceable in some 17 states. In another dozen states, legal challenges had clouded the issue. In its 6 to 2 ruling, however, the high court upheld the Bank Board's contention that its regulation preempts state law.

While the Supreme Court's ruling applies specifically to the FHLBB and those S&Ls and mutual savings banks that operate under its authority, a number of states have parity laws that automatically give state-chartered thrifts any new powers granted to federal S&Ls. Other state-chartered S&Ls may simply convert to a federal charter unless given authority by their state legislature to enforce due-on-sale.

This will mean fewer freely assumable mortgages. But look on the bright side. *All FHA-insured and VA-guaranteed mortgages are guaranteed assumable at the same long-term fixed rate that the original mortgagor received.* And many conventional mortgages issued pre-1976, when the due-on-sale clause became part of the standard mortgage document, can be passed along to the next qualified buyer whether the lender likes it or not. Generally, loans written before 1973 don't contain any provision that the loans cannot be assumed. It is estimated that some $200 billion worth of residential mortgages are assumable. The number of assumable FHA and VA mortgages alone is placed at close to three million. These mortgages, with from 16 to 25 years remaining on the loan, are at interest rates ranging from 7 percent to 9.5 percent.

The houses most easy to sell today are those with FHA- or VA-backed mortgages. You don't have to be a veteran to assume a GI loan, and with either type of mortgage, the loan assumption fee is only about $50. Since both FHA and VA loans can be obtained with minimal down payments, the seller would be likely to have a larger remaining balance on his mortgage than would another owner with a conventional loan taken out at the same time on a similarly priced dwelling. This means you wouldn't have to come up with as much cash to cover the difference between the loan balance and the asking price.

For example, a veteran and his neighbor bought their peas-in-a-pod subdivision homes at the same time. The veteran obtained a $60,000 mortgage with no down payment—for 100 percent financing. The neighbor took out a conventional $48,000 mortgage after making a $12,000 down payment. Both loans are at the same rate of interest, both mortgages are assumable, and both owners are asking $100,000 for their homes today.

Let's say the mortgage rate on both loans is 9 percent and the houses were bought six years ago. The remaining balance on the veteran's loan is nearly $57,000. The balance on the neighbor's loan is closer to $45,000. Obviously, you're better off here buying the house with the VA-guaranteed mortgage. You'd have $12,000 less to finance at today's interest rates. The transfer would not require VA approval. You could purchase the property subject to or by assumption of the existing GI mortgage debt.

The sale or transfer of property *subject to* an existing mortgage means that the purchaser does not become personally liable for the repayment of the mortgage debt. The seller remains liable for the debt. The sale or transfer of property where the purchaser *assumes* the debt secured by the existing mortgage means that the purchaser becomes personally liable for repayment of the loan. (With VA loan assumptions, the holder of the mortgage may release the seller from all personal liability for repayment of the loan if the VA does. However, the VA has no authority to require the holder to do so. For the seller to obtain a release of liability from the VA, the assumption agreement would have to be approved by the VA and the purchaser would have to satisfy the VA that he or she is a good credit risk.)

In the above example, although an appraiser might set the same value on both houses, the veteran's house is worth more. The larger assumable mortgage would not be reflected in the appraised value, but it does make the property more valuable than the neighboring property. The house could also be more valuable than higher-priced properties without assumable mortgages.

These days, it's the resale house without an assumable mortgage that is the hardest to sell.

Buying a house subject to the mortgage is not the same as a simple assumption. The buyer acquires title to the property and normally makes the payments to the mortgagee, but, as noted, the seller remains personally liable for the mortgage. Under some arrangements, the buyer makes the monthly mortgage payments to the seller. The former owner then writes out his own check and makes payment to the holder of the mortgage. Unless this is done with the mortgagee's consent, however, both buyer and seller could be in for a future financial shock. If done to avoid a legally enforceable due-on-sale clause, for example, and the lender finds out that the property has changed hands, the entire mortgage could become due in one whack. Have your lawyer examine the mortgage documents (all mortgages are matters of public record and copies can be obtained from the local courthouse) to determine whether or not buying the property subject to the mortgage, or even assuming the mortgage, for that matter, requires the lender's consent.

In all too many cases, buyers have negotiated deals for houses where they understood the mortgage to be clearly assumable, only to discover later that the mortgagee requires a 2 percent loan assumption fee, say, and wants to raise the mortgage interest rate by anywhere from 5 to 8 percentage points. The economic consequences of such an occurrence can be devastating.

To avoid a large hike in interest rates with nonassumable mortgages, not a few buyers are acquiring their properties using land contracts or long-term lease-options to hide the fact that the property has changed hands. If you think it's worth the risk, all we can say is, *caveat emptor.*

Not all mortgages are worth assuming. If the mortgage is well "seasoned," a large portion of the monthly mortgage payment will go toward paying off the loan principal, reducing the share of the payment that can be deducted at tax time as interest. If the debt has reached the stage where as much of the payment is going toward the principal as toward interest, you could be just as well off with a new first mortgage, even at the higher interest rate.

Consumers are willing to pay more for a house with a fixed-rate assumable mortgage than for the same house with a significantly lower purchase price without an assumable mortgage. Many are "buying mortgages" instead of houses today. As a prospective purchaser, though, you should be aware that most sellers know the attraction of a large assumable mortgage and will sometimes jack up the price of their home unrealistically because they have that low-interest lure to dangle and are willing to carry a second mortgage. If you don't know the real-estate market, hire a professional appraiser to make an evaluation of any property on which you are ready to make a purchase offer.

You should also ask the seller or his broker to obtain an estoppel letter from the lender spelling out the terms and conditions under which the mortgage can be assumed and showing the remaining term, the monthly payment, the remaining balance, and what funds have been escrowed for payment of insurance and taxes. You also need to know about the assumption fee and any other up-front costs that might be involved in taking over the mortgage.

Just because due-on-sale clauses have been held to be legally enforceable doesn't mean that you necessarily will have to pay full-market-rate interest with an otherwise "nonassumable" mortgage. The Federal National Mortgage Association, whose $60 billion portfolio of residential mortgages (many of them on properties whose owners have never even heard of Fannie Mae) is largely made up of low-interest loans, knows that a nonassumable mortgage can kill a sale and leave the corporation stuck with that low-yield mortgage for who knows how many years to come. Any credit-worthy buyer of a home on which Fannie Mae owns the existing loan is eligible for FNMA discount-rate resale financing. By trading in an existing FNMA loan (whether FHA-insured, VA-guaranteed, or conventionally financed) for a new conventional mortgage reflecting the home's current market value, buyer-borrowers can obtain up to 95 percent financing.

The interest rate on the resale finance mortgage is determined on a case-by-case basis, reflecting the unpaid balance, interest rate, remaining term, and other features of the old loan, and the amount and term of the new mortgage. In most cases, the resulting monthly payments will be lower than those for a new market-rate first mortgage or the combined payments on the existing loan and a new market-rate second mortgage. The new loan rate may vary from one FNMA-approved lender to another. Loan origination fees may also vary from lender to lender, but will in no case exceed 3 percent of the loan amount. The maximum amount of a new mortgage for a single-family home under the program is $98,500, except in Alaska and Hawaii, where it is 50 percent higher.

To find out if Fannie Mae owns the existing mortgage, ask the homeowner to contact the lender collecting the mortgage payments. In most instances, the lender collecting the monthly payments on the original FNMA mortgage will be able to provide the new financing.

Here's an example, supplied by Fannie Mae, on how the loans work: The Thorntons plan to buy a house that is selling for $94,750, and they've checked different ways of financing its purchase. When they asked about getting a new 30-year loan, the lender quoted them a rate of 15 percent; their monthly P/I payments, after putting 5 percent ($4,750) down, would be $1,138. Since the existing $41,600 VA-guaranteed loan on the house is assumable, they looked into taking over the payments on that mortgage and getting a $48,400 second mortgage at 18 percent for 10 years. The payments on the existing loan are $338 a month and payments on the new second mortgage would be $872, for a total of $1,210. Since the existing loan is owned by Fannie Mae, they had one other option: an FNMA resale finance mortgage. They could get a $90,000 resale loan at 12.875 percent, with monthly payments of $987—that's $151 a month less than a new first mortgage and $223 a month less than assuming the old loan and getting a new second mortgage.

Even if Fannie Mae does not own the mortgage, the savings and loan or other lender holding the mortgage on the property may offer a similar plan just to get those old low-interest loans off the books. The new, larger loan on the same property is commonly referred to as a "blended mortgage." As with the Fannie Mae resale finance loans, it is issued at a compromise rate rather than at current market levels. Both assumable and nonassumable mortgages qualify for this "preferred-rate" treatment.

WHAT IF YOU CAN'T PAY YOUR MORTGAGE?

A job layoff. Huge medical bills. A big jump in property taxes. Marital incompatibility. Unless you're financially prepared, any of these eventualities could scuttle your budget and put you behind in your mortgage payments. And once behind, with housing costs as crushing as they are today, it can be deucedly difficult to dig out from under and avoid foreclosure. What can you do, if anything, to ensure that you won't one day find yourself among those unfortunates whose homes are being auctioned off from the courthouse steps?

Fannie Mae and other interested agencies, including the Mortgage Bankers Association, have analyzed hundreds of thousands of residential mortgage loans and come up with some revealing conclusions:

- The higher the loan-to-value ratio, the greater the chance of the homeowner's defaulting.
- Larger loans tend not to foreclose.
- If the homeowner is going to become delinquent in his mortgage payments, it usually will happen during his first two years of ownership.

These "axioms" notwithstanding, marital discord is the No. 1 factor in foreclosures. If there's a bust-up, the wife generally gets the property, and then finds she can't keep up the payments. However, we wouldn't suggest that you *not* buy a house if married. Nor would we recommend that everyone make a large down payment (the protective equity represented by the down payment protects the lender mostly, it being easier for buyers with less at stake to walk away from a home). If you're facing a crisis, the best protection against foreclosure is an early warning to the lender. Notify the lender promptly if for some reason you won't be able to meet the next mortgage payment, or will be able to make only a partial payment. Don't let your financial difficulty come as a surprise to him.

You have a moral, if not legal, obligation to advise your lender or lenders of any change in your life-style that could threaten the continuance and promptness of your mortgage payments. Putting the lender on the alert becomes even more essential when the seller is participating in the financing. Institutional lenders are geared to expect a certain percentage of delinquent accounts. Your lender, though, may be a retiree dependent on that monthly income. Or he may be trading up as a homeowner and using the payments to meet *his* new and bigger mortgage payments.

Grace periods allowing you to delay payment if a personal emergency arises vary from lender to lender. The specifics will be in the mortgage contract. If payments are more than 30 days in arrears with most S&Ls, the mortgage is held to be in default. Some lenders will crack the whip after only a two-week delay. (Under the terms of most mortgage contracts, the lender must notify the mortgagor in writing that he or she is in default and that if the default is not "cured" within a specified period of time the lender will commence foreclosure proceedings.) Besides being damaging to your credit rating, often there will be a late-payment fee (usually limited by state law to no more than 5 percent of the delayed payment). Other contracts may provide for a one-quarter-of-1-percentage-point increase in the mortgage rate if a payment is not met within 15 days of the due date.

Don't expect a seller-lender to be as patient or as flexible if you fall behind in your payments as a bank or thrift might be. But if your payment history has been good, and the crisis appears to be of a temporary nature, few sellers, and even fewer institutional lenders, are likely to deny you a breather of sorts until you can get back on your feet again financially. In any case, the seller would be foolish to foreclose unless he's going to be better off *after* the often costly and time-consuming legal process (it can take a year or more to complete foreclosure proceedings) than he was before he sold the property. If he's holding a second mortgage, the most likely situation, and there are insufficient proceeds from the foreclosure sale, he will lose money.

When mortgagor and mortgagee get together early enough, they generally can work out something. At the end of 1981, 5.3 percent of all residential mortgages—53 per 1,000— were a month or more in arrears. But fewer than six mortgages per 1,000 were as much as three months delinquent, the usual trigger for initiating foreclosure action. Few loans even 90 days overdue ever result in foreclosures, however.

Delinquency rates are highest on no- or low-down-payment government-backed loans—and FHA and the VA tend to be softhearted when mortgagors insured by them are threatened with foreclosure due to circumstances beyond their control. Both agencies require local lenders to forbear until at least three full monthly payments have been missed. With FHA loans, seriously delinquent borrowers can apply to have their loan assigned to HUD. Not all loans are accepted, but under "reassignment," payments are suspended or reduced until the mortgagor can resume his obligations. Then payments are readjusted to eventually make up for the missed installments. If you're having difficulty meeting the payments with an FHA or VA mortgage, go to the appropriate office and discuss the matter with a financial counselor.

There are any number of ways that the mortgage contract can be reworked to stave off the agony of foreclosure. The borrower might negotiate with the holder of the mortgage for a period of forbearance, with the missed payments tacked on at the end of the loan term. A series of graduated payments, with or without negative amortization, possibly could get the mortgagor through the crisis period. If there's enough equity in the property, and the borrower's future financial prospects are good, a second or third mortgage could give the delinquent borrower the cash needed to consolidate his debts and meet the payments on his mortgage until he can get his financial house in order.

Refinancing the problem loan is another solution. It can be an expensive one though. If there are prepayment penalties on the existing loan and a bunch of closing costs on the new one, the borrower could find himself struggling for years to make up for a short-term setback.

Work your problem out with the holder of the mortgage. An independent "debt consolidator" could take you to the cleaners. There also are a lot of "mortgage manipulators" lurking in the woods who would be happy to help you out of your financial troubles—*in exchange for the deed to your house.* Beware of these gyp artists who steal homes. If you no longer can afford the house and *know* you're headed down the tubes, chances are you'll salvage a good deal more of your equity in the property if you enlist the services of a real-estate broker and sell the house quickly, on the open market, before the sheriff gets his hands on it.

SECONDARY FINANCING

The quickest and easiest resales today are made where there's a freely assumable mortgage and the seller is willing to take back a second mortgage to reduce the amount of cash needed by the buyer to close the deal. If it weren't for seller-financed "seconds," the existing-housing market would be in far worse straits than it is in today.

Purchase-money seconds are not to be confused with "home equity loans." Those too are second mortgages. But they're personal loans—borrowings by homeowners from commercial sources on the difference between the market value of their property and the amount owed on the mortgage—and have nothing to do with buying a home. That money generally is used for home improvements, college for the kids, a car, or debt consolidation.

Not too many years ago, the taking out of a second mortgage of any kind was viewed as an act of financial desperation, and all too frequently represented a pit stop on the road to foreclosure. Seller-held seconds, however, are not only a highly popular but a respected means of financing the purchase of a home in the 1980s.

To see how secondary financing works, lets's say you've found *the* house and the seller is holding out for $100,000. There's an assumable 9 percent mortgage on the property, with a remaining balance of $50,000 and another 24 years to go on the loan. You can come up with only $20,000 cash though, leaving you $30,000 short of meeting the seller's cash-over price and assuming that lovely 9 percent mortgage. You broach the subject of a second mortgage to the seller and you subsequently negotiate an agreement, approved by your lawyer, under which the seller will extend a $30,000 note to you, the buyer, at 14 percent simple interest, with the loan principal payable in full at the end of seven years (you tried for ten). The 14 percent rate is what you'd have to pay a lender on a conventional mortgage loan, but at least 3 percentage points below the market rate on second mortgages at the thrifts.

Out of this deal, the seller will get $20,000 cash at the closing, $350 per month interest for seven years, and a lump-sum payment of $30,000 at the end of seven years—for a total of $79,400. Your monthly loan costs will total $752.32—$350 per month to the seller, and $402.32 to the holder of the first mortgage. At the end of seven years, you will have to pay off that $30,000 second mortgage, either out of accumulated savings or by refinancing.

All in all, it's a very good deal for both you and the seller. Had you financed your $100,000 purchase with a 30-year conventional loan, your monthly mortgage payment, after $20,000 down, would have been $947.90, at 14 percent. That's nearly $200 more per month than you're now paying—and would have meant stretching yourself too far financially. You also avoided many, though not all, of the settlement costs involved in refinancing a first mortgage.

While the seller-held second in the above example is subordinate, or junior, in priority to the existing first mortgage, the seller runs little risk of ever having to take a loss on his loan. With a 20 percent cash down payment, you aren't likely to walk away from the home; if you encounter financial difficulty, there should be ample protective equity in the property to guard against any loss through foreclosure. Furthermore, inflation will increase the market value of the property, not as fast as in the "roaring '70s" perhaps, but sufficient to ensure the loan quality. For the seller, the loan should represent a safe, profitable, and trouble-free investment. His security is the home he is selling.

But let's take a worst-case scenario. If that's a working couple scraping to buy that home, and the wife walks out on the husband, leaving him to shoulder the payments alone, he easily could become delinquent in his payments. A divorce is the most frequent event leading to the loss of a home and our couple appear to be headed toward the courts. Most financial counselors would advise those owners to unload the house at once to avoid getting deeper into debt. If the husband defaults several months running, and it comes down to a foreclosure, the holder of the first mortgage would be paid off in full from the proceeds of the foreclosure sale before the holder of the second mortgage would receive any funds. Any remaining money after the second mortgagee is paid off would go to the foreclosed couple.

The lender's risk is a little higher with a second mortgage than it is with a first mortgage, which is why lending institutions charge a higher rate of interest on second mortgages than they do on first-mortgage loans. But most lenders would not have been reluctant to grant a second mortgage to our hypothetical buyer of that $100,000 property had he not been able to make his deal with the seller. He might not have been able to qualify for an $80,000 first-mortgage loan, but with that assumable first mortgage in place, a $30,000 second mortgage would not have been held to be beyond his means.

Institutional lenders who couldn't (by regulation) or wouldn't grant purchase-money seconds in the past are finding it more profitable, under deregulation, to issue seconds than firsts today and, in some instances, have all but abandoned their first-mortgage business. And no wonder. If they can get 14 or 15 percent interest on a long-term conventional or adjustable mortgage loan, they can, unless limited by state usury laws, get 17 or 18 percent on a short-term second-mortgage loan. If you can make a reasonable down payment and are credit-worthy, shop around among the institutional lenders if the seller has an assumable mortgage but is unwilling to defer part of his sale proceeds by taking back a second mortgage.

When the second-mortgage money comes from an "outside" source, and the cash will be turned over to the seller of the property, it's known as a "hard-money" mortgage. When the mortgage is held by the seller, with no cash changing hands, it's known as a "soft-money" mortgage. In going to an outside source for second-mortgage money, stick with the larger institutional lenders rather than patronize one of the small-scale second-mortgage companies. Like smooth-talking car salesmen piling on the options, some of these outfits can unconscionably boost the interest rate you'd be paying without your really being aware of it. Check on fees and points charged by lenders when comparison shopping for a second mortgage. Some major lenders will lend up to 90 percent of the appraised value of the home, condominium, or town house, less the amount of the seller's existing low-interest-rate assumable first mortgage.

The terms on second mortgages are fully negotiable, whether dealing with the seller or an institutional lender. The one thing to avoid here is a short-fuse mortgage, unless the mortgage is guaranteed renewable or you clearly can see yourself in a position to pay off that balloon when the loan matures in from one to three years. Smart buyers hold out for five- to ten-year mortgages.

Essentially, there are three ways to structure purchase-money second mortgages:

• **Nonamortized loan.** Payments are interest only, for from one to ten years, with a lump-sum principal balloon payment due and payable at the end of the loan period.

• **Partially amortized loan.** Principal-and-interest payments are based on a 20-, 25-, or 30-year amortization schedule, but with a balloon payment, covering the unpaid balance, due and payable at the end of five to ten years.

• **Fully amortized loan.** Principal-and-interest payments are calculated to pay off the loan in full during its term, whether that's five years or twenty-five years.

One of the most innovative approaches to second-mortgage financing that we've come across is the repayable second-mortgage buy-down. In this instance, there was no mortgage to assume and the young couple were having difficulty getting bank financing to purchase the $70,000 town house they had decided would make a fine first home for them. With their combined income though, local lenders wouldn't qualify them for better than 80 percent financing at 12 percent on the $70,000 property. Unfortunately, the interest rate was then at 15 percent—requiring a monthly P/I payment of $708. That was $132 more per month than the $576 they could qualify for at the 12 percent rate.

The seller and the broker liked the young couple and found a way to save the sale. Using the house as collateral, the seller agreed to a second mortgage that would run for three years. He would contribute a monthly payment of $132 to subsidize their monthly payment, bringing it down to the $576 the lender found acceptable. At the end of three years, the young couple would have to pay him a lump sum of $4,752 ($132 x 36 months) plus interest at 15 percent. When the seller's repayable "sleepy second" comes due, they likely will have to refinance the first mortgage—hopefully at a rate lower than 15 percent—or possibly get a hard-money second on their appreciation in the property. They see no problem with this. Both are young professionals moving ahead in their careers.

There are times when even a third mortgage may be required to close a deal. When looking for houses with assumable mortgages, most home shoppers look for *large* assumable mortgages, representing the biggest portion of the purchase price. But there are many properties that have appreciated to the extent that even a fairly new mortgage may represent no more than a third of the asking price. In which case, the seller might not be willing to take back a large second mortgage. He may require a large amount of cash out of the sale to get into his new home. Here, you may have to turn to an institutional lender for a sizable, medium-term second mortgage, and to the seller for a smaller, short-term third, to put the financing together.

Again, seconds and thirds don't necessarily mean that you are overextending yourself financially. Often, they're a more practicable solution than taking on long-term financing from a single lender. When it comes time to pay off or refinance a loan, there may also be an advantage in having more than one loan. The greater part of the financing could then be left undisturbed. The last thing most buyers want to do is disturb that low-interest assumable first. The more mortgage remaining, the more useful it could be to them in a resale.

Lenders willing, you could cover the contract price with your two or three loans—and avoid having to make a down payment. We can't, however, recommend structuring financing where the total of your monthly payments is going to be more than you can reasonably afford. If you *can* afford the payments, and the seller isn't uncomfortable with the lack of protective equity, he just might be fool enough to accept an "overfinance." That's a California-style creative financing scheme where the buyer assumes the seller's existing mortgage, obtains the largest hard-money second he can from a lending institution, a soft-money third from the seller—and effectively finances a $100,000 purchase, say, for $110,000. With the deal, the seller returns up to $10,000 cash to the buyer, out of his proceeds from the hard-money second-mortgage loan.

After the California real-estate market turned weak in 1981, the Department of Real Estate there noted a marked increase in the number of problem cases involving "cash-to-buyer" transactions. Buyers all too frequently were simply walking away from the property with the cash, without having made any payments on the new mortgages. Sellers, their junior mortgages worthless, and without the funds to protect their equity by meeting the buyer's obligations, are on the losing end when the overfinanced property is foreclosed.

Another common but questionable practice is the so-called "backdoor" second mortgage. Buyers aren't supposed to borrow money to make up the down payment when the first mortgage is coming from a savings and loan. Many do, though, getting a good chunk of cash from a friend or relative. And then, recorded weeks after the settlement is complete, they issue an interest-bearing second mortgage against the property to whoever assisted them with the financing.

BALLOON MORTGAGES

Prior to the Great Depression, virtually all mortgages were "balloon" mortgages. There was no scheduled reduction of loan principal (payments more often than not represented interest only), and the balance of the mortgage—the balloon—became due and payable at one fell swoop at the end of an all-too-short loan period. It was the inability to get these short-term loans renewed that sent so many families to the wall in the early '30s.

Today, the balloon-payment provision is a routine feature of seller-held mortgages, particularly in the West and Midwest— and there is growing concern that many of those balloons are going to burst in the borrower's face.

Will home buyers be financially able to meet their obligations two, three, or five years from now? Are we ignoring the lessons that led to the introduction of the standard, fully amortizing mortgage? Or is there something new and different about balloon mortgages that is making the balloon payment one of the most common features of 1980s home financing?

Most seller-financing arrangements are temporary. The buyer generally is required to obtain new financing from an outside source, such as a bank or thrift, after only a few years. Typically, a seller might agree to take back a second mortgage, but he wants the mortgage due and payable in three years. Say the purchase price of the property is $85,000, and there's a $30,000 balloon note (the second mortgage) calling for monthly payments of $350 at 14 percent simple interest. When that second mortgage matures in three years, the buyer will have to come up with the $30,000 in a lump-sum final payment, there having been no reduction of the loan principal. Not even a partially amortized loan, with the loan calculated as though it had 30 years to run, would have done much to deflate the balloon. After 36 monthly payments of $355.47, the balance of the loan, at $29,757, would still be within a whisper of the original $30,000.

"If you are in the unlikely position of wanting to make three years pass very quickly," to quote Anthony M. Frank, a California banker, "take out a three-year second mortgage." The thought of having to meet a $30,000 balloon payment in a few short years doesn't faze most buyers when well-located houses are appreciating in value 10 to 15 percent a year. By the time that $30,000 short-term note matures, the market value of that $85,000 purchase easily could be $115,000, and refinancing—or resale, if the buyer wants to cash-out—shouldn't be a problem. But what if interest rates keep rising and/or housing prices fall?

If a balloon mortgage, or a mortgage that includes the balloon-payment feature, is not guaranteed renewable by the lender there is *always* the risk that the borrower might not be able to pay off the mortgage debt when the balloon comes due. If the buyer can't find new financing, or if the then-prevailing market rate is considerably higher than the original interest rate on the loan, he may be forced to sell the property or to default on the loan.

These risks would tend to be offset by a steady increase in the borrower's income, such as can be expected from an upwardly mobile borrower. The borrower's equity is also likely to increase significantly as the market value of the property increases with inflation, further reducing the risks of short-term financing.

Nevertheless, balloon mortgages are almost always a gamble. As a borrower, you are betting that high interest rates will drop to more affordable levels within a few years and property values will continue to appreciate. The best way to improve those odds, of course, is to stretch out the term of the balloon note. A three-year balloon note is cutting it close for the buyer. Where the lender is under no obligation to refinance the loan, smart borrowers insist on at least a five-year term, with no prepayment penalties.

The real-estate broker may have suggested that the seller might be willing to take back a two- or three-year second mortgage to help you get into the house. In your purchase offer, specify that the seller is to take back a five-year second mortgage. Don't be surprised if the seller accepts the longer term. Or, make the seller guarantee, in writing, to extend the shorter mortgage, subject to renegotiation, if other financing is not available when the balloon comes due. Don't be shy about haggling with the seller. If he's that close to making the sale, he's likely to be willing to make a few concessions.

A safety valve being used increasingly with short-fuse mortgages is a progressively higher interest rate. The interest rate is fixed for the first two or three years, but then rises 1 percentage point per year until the loan is paid. The increased interest compensates the seller for the payment delay—and encourages the buyer to refinance as soon as possible. At the same time, it doesn't put the property in jeopardy if refinancing at a reasonable interest rate is not possible for a few years.

In seller financing, the most common balloon loan is the gap-filling second mortgage. Think of it as a temporary filling. You essentially are buying time to build up enough equity in the house to refinance or recast the first mortgage with a commercial lender. Taking out a larger first mortgage will give you the cash to meet the second-mortgage debt. If that first mortgage is at a low interest rate, you might prefer not to disturb it though. Your best bet then would be to find a hard-money second to pay off the existing loan. To avoid finding yourself back in the same soup, with another balloon payment down the road, you might take out a fully amortizing 10- or 15-year second mortgage.

Balloon payments are not only a feature of seller financing but of many of the new flexible mortgages offered by the lending institutions as well. Wherever they occur, they're dangerous only if you don't know how you'll meet the balloon payment. Unless the loan is renewable, you'd be smart to plan ahead at least six months for that final lump-sum payment. If interest rates are still high, or higher, you may have to settle for a more expensive way to go, but it's better than losing your equity. The final solution, of course, would be to sell the house.

If you expect a job transfer within a few years, or are otherwise planning only a short residency, a balloon note might not give you any more cause for concern than a common cold. Sell before the balloon comes due and you would simply pay off the loan from the proceeds of the sale of the property. A seven-year balloon note would give many families a comfortable enough time span so that an opportunity to sell or refinance will occur before the balloon falls due.

Under deregulation of the banking industry, institutional lenders are also showing renewed interest in balloon mortgages. To the banks and thrifts, they're like adjustable-rate mortgages, only better. When the balloon comes due, whether in two years or ten, and the borrower asks for an extension of the loan, the lender can "renegotiate" the interest rate without having to tie it to one of those money-market indexes. That is, *if* he chooses to extend the mortgage. Most lenders will renew the loan, but without that option to deny the renewal, the loan would be classified as an adjustable-rate mortgage, and thus subject to limits on interest-rate increases.

Since October 1981, when the Federal Home Loan Bank Board amended its rules, federally chartered thrifts have virtually had carte blanche when it comes to writing balloon mortgages. Previously, the borrower couldn't obtain a balloon mortgage with a term longer than five years from the thrifts. He also had to make a cash down payment of at least 40 percent. Now, the borrower can obtain a nonamortized or a partially amortizing balloon mortgage covering up to 95 percent of the value of the property securing the loan. And while we generally think of balloon payments in connection with short-term loans, the FHLBB, to give lenders maximum flexibility, is permitting thrifts to make balloon-payment loans that, at the lender's discretion, can run for up to 40 years. The lender, however, as noted, is under no obligation to refinance the loan when the balloon comes due at the end of each loan period.

REFINANCING WITHOUT PAIN

To get old low-interest-rate loans off their books, many institutional lenders are now offering easy below-market-rate refinancing. But what happens when you are facing a refinance-or-foreclosure situation with a balloon mortgage that's about to burst? Or what happens when you seek to take advantage of a drop in interest rates and refinance a *high*-rate, long-term mortgage loan?

Most seller-held loans are short term and must be refinanced at some point. If the seller can't be persuaded to continue in the role of lender, the buyer has to seek financing from a conventional source. Unless mortgage interest rates have plunged, or the property has appreciated significantly, a lot of mortgagors, already overextended, may not qualify for financing from a bank or thrift when that note comes due. They may have to pay a very high rate at a finance company. Or they may not be able to get the money at all. The seller will then foreclose, and their two, three, or five years of payments will have been for nothing.

To guard against losing it all, include in your written agreement with the seller a proviso that he will extend the mortgage (perhaps subject to renegotiaton) if other financing is not available when the balloon comes due. The agreement should also allow you to pay off the loan early, without a prepayment penalty. You can then take advantage of longer-term financing with another lender when money-market conditions turn favorable. Keep in mind that mortgage rates dropped 5 percentage points from April to July 1980 and then climbed back up again almost as quickly.

Suppose you had bought your house in April 1979, assuming a $25,000 vintage-1974 mortgage at 9.5 percent, and the seller had taken back a second mortgage for $30,000 at 13 percent simple interest, with a balloon payment due in three years. The monthly payments on the two loans totaled $535. If you refinanced in July 1980, when mortgage rates dipped to 11.5 percent, you could have replaced the two loans with a single 30-year $55,000 mortgage at virtually the same monthly payment—and removed the threat of that Damoclean $30,000 balloon note.

The whole point in getting a second mortgage is to buy time until you can arrange for an affordable new first mortgage. Had you waited until April 1982 to refinance that second mortgage when it came due, you would probably have had to pay 18 percent interest on a 10-year amortizing loan at a savings and loan. With the underlying mortgage at 9.5 percent and the new second mortgage at 18 percent, you'd be paying $661 per month in mortgage payments. An interest-only second mortgage with a five-year balloon would have held the payments to $585, but you'd only be postponing until 1987 the due date on the $25,000.

Refinancing is not free. Unless you're dealing with the lender who originated the loan, you're going to be treated just like any other applicant for a first-mortgage loan, and will be faced with the whole slate of closing costs—from a credit check and property appraisal to a title search and recording fee. To refinance a long-term, fixed-rate mortgage costs about 3 percent of the total amount being refinanced, or about $1,800 on a $60,000 loan. It's generally cheaper to refinance a second mortgage than it is to refinance a first mortgage. But shop around. A lender of last resort, such as a second-mortgage company, could really sock it to you in points, assorted fees, mortgage insurance, and other tacked-on charges. Read the documents *before* you sign!

Refinancing out of necessity, to pay off a balloon note, is one thing. Refinancing to take advantage of lower interest rates is another. If there are prepayment penalties involved, plus normal closing costs and legal fees, it might not pay you to refinance unless you intend to continue living at the same address for another four or five years or more. With a $60,000 mortgage at 16 percent, you're paying $807 per month on a 30-year loan. If interest rates drop to 13 percent, and you refinance the $60,000 for another 30 years, you'd be paying $664 per month. That's a saving of $143 per month, $1,716 per year. Or it would be, without a prepayment penalty. Prepayment penalties vary from state to state, and none are allowed with FHA-insured or VA-guaranteed loans, but there are situations where you could be required to pay up to six months' interest for the "privilege" of prepaying a first-mortgage loan. Six months' interest on that $60,000 loan at $807 per month would be nearly $5,000! You'd have to come up with a wad of cash at the closing and it could take four or five years to get even on the loan. You might be better off taking the money you'd have to hand over in refinancing charges and investing it instead.

Lenders have the welcome mat out for mortgagors who wish to refinance old low-rate loans for larger mortgages at higher interest rates. This is the situation that usually applies when the homeowner wants to turn some of his built-up equity in the property into ready cash. On the other hand, if you are in the position of applying for a *lower* interest rate on an existing mortgage loan, the lender is not going to be quite so gracious. There's usually a balance point though, and rather than lose the mortgage to another lender, many lenders will not only refinance the loan but will give you a break on closing costs, sometimes waiving the title search, survey, and other such items the second time around. S&Ls typically refinance loans held by them for about 1.5 to 2 percent of the face value of the new loan. Don't expect the lender to waive a prepayment penalty if the loan is subject to one. Lenders generally do this only when the loan is being rewritten at a higher rate. The whole purpose of the prepayment penalty is to discourage frequent refinancing by mortgagors every time the interest rate dips. If you must pay a prepayment penalty, remember that it's tax deductible.

There's one special situation where refinancing could benefit you as a buyer when arranging for the original financing.

Say there's an assumable VA-guaranteed mortgage on the property, but the remaining loan balance is only $25,000, or roughly one-third of the $72,000 purchase price. The seller doesn't want to take back a second mortgage and you're having problems obtaining reasonable financing to fill the gap. The seller, whose income and credit are better than yours, offers to go to the original lender and refinance the existing loan on the basis of the current market value of the property. Say he succeeds in obtaining a new blended-rate, 30-year, VA-guaranteed mortgage for $60,000. You would assume the loan, the seller would keep the $35,000 loan proceeds (the $25,000 loan would be paid off), and you would only have to come up with a $12,000 down payment. You would reimburse the seller, of course, for the costs of the refinancing. Chances are that this would be a significantly less expensive solution than your taking out either a new first or a second mortgage. Since a VA loan is involved here, there are no prepayment penalties, and the VA makes refinancing relatively easy.

WRAPAROUND MORTGAGES

The wraparound, or "all-inclusive," mortgage can be used only where there is an assumable first mortgage. In most states, the wraparound is held to be a second mortgage, which means there could be a conflict with some state usury ceilings. But where it can be made to work, it's the basis of one of the most popular methods of creative financing, benefiting both buyer and seller.

With a wraparound mortgage (WAM for short), the seller keeps his existing mortgage and continues to pay on it. The buyer gets a larger, secondary mortgage from the seller, usually at a favorable interest rate, that "wraps around" the first mortgage. The buyer-borrower makes a monthly, all-inclusive payment to the seller. The seller, in turn, handles the payment to the holder of the first mortgage and pockets the balance of the amount received from the buyer.

To illustrate how a typical wraparound works, let's say the

house you want to buy costs $110,000 and has a $50,000 assumable mortgage at 9 percent, with 25 years to go on the loan. For you to take advantage of that low-interest-rate mortgage, you've got to come up with $60,000. The most cash you can raise toward a down payment is $20,000, which means you need another $40,000. You might seek a $40,000 second mortgage from one of the local lending institutions, but you have serious doubts that you'd be found qualified for the loan. The seller *might* grant you a second mortgage, but he's talking short term and high rates. At the urging of the broker, and after consulting with his lawyer, the seller agrees to give you a 25-year $90,000 wraparound mortgage at 12 percent, which is 3.5 percentage points below the going market rate at the time for conventional mortgage loans.

Had you been required to finance the $90,000 conventionally, your monthly mortgage payment, on a 30-year loan at 15.5 percent, would have been $1,174.07. With the $90,000 WAM at 12 percent, you're paying only $947.91. Not too bad. The seller, though, does even better. He's making 3 percent on the underlying mortgage, plus 12 percent on the $40,000 "at risk." His "real" rate of return on that $40,000 soft-money second, therefore, is closer to 16.5 percent.

For the seller of the property to do as well by granting you a simple second mortgage for $40,000, he would have had to charge you that same 16.5 percent interest. At that rate, your monthly mortgage payment would have been $961.62—$402.32 on the underlying 9 percent mortgage plus $559.30 on the 25-year second mortgage. A bank-financed second mortgage would probably have been at 18.5 percent interest, and would have brought your total monthly payment to $1,105.71.

(For purposes of simplification, we have not made an allowance for the reduction of principal on the wrapped mortgage. After five years of payments, the remaining balance on a 30-year $50,000 loan at 9 percent would be $47,940. Whether the buyer or the seller receives the benefit of the $2,060 equity buildup would depend on the language of the purchase contract.)

It's easy to see why sellers become converts to seller financing when they're shown the math on a WAM. Suppose that underlying mortgage had been $60,000 at 8 percent, and you had made a 20 percent down payment. The seller-lender's effective annual yield on the $28,000 at risk here would have been almost 21 percent! To break that down for you:

contract price	$110,000
down payment	22,000
wraparound	88,000
assumable mortgage	60,000
seller's "at risk"	28,000
monthly payment on 25-year $88,000 wraparound at 12%	926.85
monthly payment on $60,000 underlying mortgage at 8%	440.26
monthly return to seller on $28,000 at risk	486.59
	× 12
annual return to seller	5,839.08
yield	20.85%

WAMs work only when there's an appreciable spread between current market interest rates and those available five to ten years earlier, the situation we have today. As a rule of thumb, the larger the existing mortgage and the lower the interest rate on that mortgage, the better the potential for a WAM. The seller usually can afford to accept an interest rate on the wrap that is several percentage points below prevailing market rates, while still preserving a very attractive yield on the amount he has at risk. This would be an area of negotiation for the buyer to exploit. In most cases, the WAM gives the seller his maximum yield in seller financing. It's better for a seller than a second mortgage, yet the buyer gets "easy financing," usually at a lower rate than is obtainable elsewhere. Most WAMs carry terms to coincide with the number of years remaining on the underlying loan.

In a few states, the seller may be obliged to give the buyer an even lower rate to keep under a usury ceiling. Most states have raised their ceilings on second-mortgage loans, however. And the Federal Home Loan Bank Board has moved to redefine wraparounds as having the "effect" of first liens, which would sidestep state usury law restrictions.

As a buyer-borrower, it is essential that you have your lawyer confirm that the existing loan on the property you are proposing to buy *is* assumable. The last thing you want to do is close, move into the house, and then have the original lender call that underlying low-interest-rate loan. Both you and the seller would be up the proverbial creek. To close the deal, the seller normally gives the buyer the deed to the property and the buyer simultaneously gives the seller a promissory note that reflects the wrapped debt. The title change *may* come later in some states. But whether it comes now or later, insist on a title search (get the seller to pay for it). There's always the risk that the seller doesn't have a clear title to give.

You may be very punctual with your monthly payments to the seller, but how can you be sure that he's keeping up those payments on the first mortgage? What if he lives out of state now and instead of making those payments decides to pocket *all* the cash? To relieve yourself of that worry, you could arrange to make your payments to the trust department of the lending instituion holding the first mortgage and have a trust officer forward the seller's share of the monthly payment to him.

It's in the seller's own interest, of course, to make sure the first-mortgage payments are kept current. Indeed, he's now in a better position to forestall foreclosure should the buyer default than he would be if the buyer had assumed the first mortgage and obtained a second mortgage from him. In that situation, *he* wouldn't know whether the payments were being made on the underlying mortgage or not, since the buyer would be making two separate payments, instead of the one monthly payment.

Sellers aren't the only sources of WAMs. Banks and S&Ls also see the profits in assuming low-interest-rate mortgages and putting up new funds, whether they're the original lender or not. Even though the interest on the wrap portion of the new loan is a couple of percentage points below the prevailing first-mortgage rate, they usually can score a few bonus points.

Suppose you are negotiating to buy a house on which there is an assumable $48,000 mortgage at 8.5 percent. The asking price on the property is $135,000 and the buyer wants all cash. That means you've got to come up with $87,000. You can manage $40,000, leaving $47,000 to be financed. You could probably get that from a second-mortgage company, but it would cost you an arm and a leg at current second-mortgage rates. You'd probably have to face a balloon payment within five years, too.

At the recommendation of the real-estate agent, you go to a local savings and loan (in this case, not the original lender) and discuss the possibilities of obtaining a wraparound mortgage on the property. Following some lengthy sessions with the loan officer, the S&L agrees to assume the old mortgage and issue you a new 25-year $95,000 mortgage at 13 percent interest, which is 2.5 percentage points below the going rate on first-mortgage loans. The S&L will be earning almost 18 percent on the $47,000 at risk. But do you really care? You're paying nearly $170 less per month than you would be paying had you been required to finance the entire $95,000 (for 30 years) at 15.5 percent. The only one hurting here is the original lender. That 8.5 percent mortgage could be on his books for another 25 years. The new lender collects one monthly payment, keeping the amount due on the new loan and forwarding the payment due on the old below-market loan to the original lender.

Even where the loan is not assumable, many S&Ls, including federally chartered thrifts, are now offering WAMs for new buyers of resale homes on which the S&L holds the existing mortgage. To get that old low-interest loan off its books, the S&L will replace it with a new, larger loan carrying a blended rate that generally starts at 2 to 3 percentage points below the regular market rate. For example, after a 20 percent down payment on a property priced at $80,000, with a $35,000 nonassumable mortgage issued at 9 percent, the buyer-borrower might qualify for a 13 percent WAM. The S&L would have to come up with only $29,000 in new money—on which it would earn better than 16 percent annually.

LEASE-OPTIONS

A real-estate agent isn't likely to suggest to the would-be home buyer that a lease coupled with an option to buy later could hold the solution to both a down-payment problem and high interest rates. The agent receives only a small commission up front (6 or 7 percent of the annual rent) from the seller on this type of deferred-purchase arrangement. He has to wait until that option is exercised, if it is to be exercised, before he can collect the balance of his commission on the sale. Most lease-options that are fairly priced *are* exercised—and naïve realty agents are passing up a tried-and-true sales device that is particularly well suited to tight money markets.

Despite this lack of enthusiasm on the part of agents who don't understand lease-options, enlightened buyers and sellers, in California and Florida in particular, have been making good use of both short- and long-term lease-options. A short-term lease-option typically runs for from one to two years. The prospective buyer moves into the house or apartment as a tenant and pays monthly rent to the lessor until he either exercises the option to buy or allows the option to expire and walks away with no further obligation. Generally, the lessee is required to put up a couple of thousand dollars for the "consideration for the purchase option." If he exercises the option, the money goes toward the down payment. Often, all or part of the rent he pays is also credited toward the down payment. If the lessee doesn't exercise the purchase option, he forfeits the option money as well as the rent payments he has made. The option money is not reported as income by the property owner until the option is either exercised or allowed to expire. If the option expires unexercised, the money is treated as ordinary income. If it is exercised, with the money credited toward the purchase price, the money becomes part of the seller's capital gain.

The lease-option arrangement not only gives the home buyer time to accumulate a good down payment, it lets him take advantage of any near-term drop in interest rates. There are no tax breaks for the lessee, however, until he becomes a homeowner. Rent payments are not deductible. The lessor, as beneficial and legal owner of the property, continues to pay the property taxes and insurance coverage until the option is exercised.

There's no rule of thumb on option money. One owner might ask for $1, another might ask for $10,000. Developers trying to move unsold condominium units with lease-options often don't require any money at all up front. Instead, they set the rent at somewhat above the market in return for the option to buy, and typically credit 50 percent of the rent paid toward the purchase price when the option is exercised. In a "private" arrangement, the lessor may be tempted to ask for a larger consideration for the option, to more or less guarantee the eventual sale. But then, too much up-front cash will discourage prospective tenant-buyers. If the option calls for more than one or two thousand dollars, the lessee, to protect himself financially, should insist that the contract include a clause that would allow him to assign the lease-option to another person should he decide not to buy, for whatever reason, while the option is still in effect.

Anyone renting with an option to buy needs a detailed agreement, drawn up by an attorney experienced in these procedures, setting out the exact terms under which the option is being granted. A few lines in the lease stating the monthly rent, the purchase price, and what portion of the rent is to be credited toward the purchase price are not sufficient. It needs to cover the ground that purchase contracts do. Who is responsible for taxes and insurance along the way? Who is responsible for making any needed repairs? Is the property being sold "as is"? Under what arrangements, if any, can the option be extended? The prospective buyer should insist on most of the precautionary measures that an institutional lender would require in granting a mortgage loan, including a title search, survey, and probably a termite inspection.

Unless the prospective buyer is 100 percent certain that he can find mortgage financing if and when he exercises the option, he might have to kiss off that option money if he doesn't have the financing prearranged before he becomes a tenant. His best source for that needed financing, of course, is the seller. If there's an assumable mortgage and the seller-lessor has agreed in advance to take back a second mortgage, this should be noted in the leasing agreement.

For a practical illustration of the lease-option, we'll look in on the Diegelmans. When Jack Diegelman, a pharmacologist fresh from the graduate program at Rutgers University, landed a well-paying job with a major Philadelphia-based pharmaceutical manufacturer, he and his wife, Francie, went house-hunting. Francie, a registered nurse, had more or less been the provider since their marriage two years earlier. Now, with better than $40,000 in combined income, they saw no reason to settle for another apartment and were looking for a house in the Philadelphia suburbs.

This was the summer of 1981, and mortgage interest rates were up around 18 percent. At that interest rate, and with no savings to speak of to put toward a down payment, Jack and Francie kept striking out on financing with the institutional lenders. Jack had been doing some homework though and was becoming aware of various arrangements possible with creative financing.

The Diegelmans hadn't planned to locate as far out from Philadelphia as Paoli, but Jack had been intrigued by a classified ad for a house there. The ad read: "Year lease at $600 per month. Option to buy at today's price any time within a year. $2,000 moves you in!" The Diegelmans visited the house and liked it very much. It was located near enough to the Paoli railroad station so that the 20-mile commute to Jack's job, if he chose not to drive, wouldn't be a problem.

Asking price for the house was $72,000. Under the lease-option, the motivated owner, who had been trying to sell the property conventionally for four months, was willing to give the Diegelmans full credit toward the purchase price for the rent paid if they would accept a contract price of $75,000. Jack and Francie agreed to that. The owner was reluctant to continue any financial participation after the option was exercised. As a concession, however, he would agree in the contract to extend the lease for another six months if the Diegelmans could not find mortgage financing at 15 percent or less within 12 months.

The Diegelmans were required to put up the first and last months' rent plus the $2,000 consideration for the option. If they close on the house at the end of 12 months, they will have accumulated $9,200 toward the purchase price. To establish priority and secure their title rights, the Diegelmans, at the recommendation of their lawyer, took the precaution of recording a "memorandum of purchase option." Should another party seek to purchase the property before the Diegelmans exercise their option, a title search would disclose the seller's binding contract with the Diegelmans.

A common housing dilemma today when you are trading up is: Do you sell the old house first, or do you acquire the new home and then sell the old one? A lease-option can be useful here. If you can move into the new house under a lease-option, it will give you time to get your money out of the old house in a slow market. As a renter, you would exercise your option as soon as you sell the old house and can produce the cash required to close the sale on the new one. An option also allows you to try out the house and neighborhood before you really commit yourself. If, on the other hand, you have made your financing arrangements on the new home, a lease-option on the house you are leaving, if still unsold, could cover the mortgage payments and other continuing expenses on it until you can effect a sale. Where property values are appreciating at a good rate, you may want to base the purchase price on the projected value of the property or include an escalation clause in the contract.

Do not confuse a lease-*purchase* agreement with a lease-option. Under a lease-purchase agreement, you are legally committed to buy the property at the agreed-upon sales price. The closing is merely delayed, usually for 12 months. If you back out of the deal, the seller can take action against you for breach of contract. The lease-purchase, like the lease-option, is frequently used to give the buyer time to save up for the down payment or wait for a predicted drop in mortgage rates. It's also used by investors as a tax shelter where property values are rising at a good clip. As an investor, you might buy a property, or take an option on it, and almost immediately resell it ("flip" the contract) under a lease-purchase agreement. By delaying the closing for 12 months, your profit on the sale would be treated as a long-term capital gain.

A lease-purchase agreement could also be used by an owner who is within two years of his 55th birthday and wants to sell now. If he has lived in the house for the preceding three years, and the lease-purchase agreement calls for the closing within two years, but not before he will have reached age 55, he can exclude from taxation up to $125,000 of his profit on the sale. Homeowners should keep in mind that this is a once-in-a-lifetime exclusion.

It should be taken only when the owner doesn't anticipate being in a position to take an even larger accumulated profit on some future sale.

Up to this point, we've been discussing short-term contracts. There's also the long-term lease-option. It's a particular favorite of Robert J. Bruss, who writes the nationally syndicated "Real Estate Mailbag" and "Real Estate Law and You" newspaper features. An attorney, Bruss advocates the use of 30-year lease-options to circumvent enforcement of the due-on-sale clause in nonassumable mortgages. If the seller-landlord and the buyer-tenant specify in the contract that they are entering into an installment sale for tax purposes, the IRS recognizes it as a sale from the day the "rent" payments begin.

The long-term lease-option is used only where there is an existing low-interest-rate mortgage on the property and the seller agrees to help finance the buyer's purchase. It's much like a wraparound mortgage, since the seller keeps up the payments on the underlying mortgage out of the monthly rent money he receives. For tax purposes, the rent is treated as interest and payment toward principal. The buyer can claim a deduction for those "interest" payments, and also for property taxes. He pays property taxes and for hazard insurance through the seller.

Just as under a land contract, there is no immediate transfer of title. The contract usually states that the tenant-buyer may obtain the deed anytime by converting his unpaid installment-sale balance into a mortgage secured by the property.

The promissory note that the buyer-tenant signs is secured by the lease-option. Nothing is recorded except possibly a purchase-option memorandum. Hazard insurance is maintained in the seller's name and there is little likelihood of the original lender's learning that the property has effectively been sold, unless the buyer moves to assume the underlying mortgage.

Most mortgage documents now state that a lease of more than three years with a purchase option is the equivalent of a transfer of title and makes the mortgage callable under the due-on-sale clause. According to Bruss, however, lenders are unsure of their legal rights vis-à-vis long-term lease-options and have not challenged such transactions in the courts. To protect both parties, the lease-option agreement should be drawn up by an attorney who is practicing real-estate law and not just some hack who is drawing up simple wills and handling "no-fault" divorces.

LAND LEASES

A consumer-attitude study conducted in early 1981 by the Building Industry Association of trend-setting Orange County, California, asked the question: How likely would you be to consider a lease option in which you would only lease the lot but own the house? Only 7 percent of the respondents answered "Very likely," while 62 percent answered "Not at all likely"—even though the question was posed so that the 1,558 home shoppers interviewed knew that purchasing their home on a leased-lot basis would lower the down payment by 20 percent and their monthly payments by 10 percent.

Despite the beneficial trade-offs in such deals, the thought of owning only the house and not the underlying land, for many, obviously goes against the American Dream. But many others are benefiting from the rediscovery of this cost-cutting scheme that dates back to colonial days. Not that it's been dormant all that while. Land leases are well known in Hawaii and Maryland. They're becoming increasingly popular also in Florida, Colorado, Nevada, and, Orange Countians to the contrary, California.

Land leases, or ground rents, are the norm in Britain and are common in Canada. In this country, they go back to 1632, when Lord Baltimore leased a vast tract of land near Chesapeake Bay from King Charles I of England. The rent: two Indian arrows annually plus one-fifth of all the gold and silver found on the property. Leasing out parcels to settlers, Lord Baltimore established Maryland Colony as this continent's first subdivision. Ground rents have remained a tradition in Maryland and more than half the homes in Baltimore's inner city are on leased land, which explains the popular name for such arrangements: "Baltimore land leases."

Leaseholds often are used with the purchase of commercial real estate. Most of the hotels on Miami Beach, for example, are built on leased land. But now leased-land deals designed for the residential buyer are turning up all over the country. The professional builders' journal, *Housing*, gave impetus to an incipient trend when it devoted eight pages to lease programs in its February 1981 issue. Builders and developers weren't too thrilled initially with the idea of tying up capital in a large land inventory, but they're finding leasing one answer to the consumer affordability problem—and a better alternative than not selling homes. Land leases are also turning up in many private arrangements between buyer and seller. Quite simply, as *Housing* noted, the reduced down payment and lower monthly carrying costs available via lease deals allow buyers to purchase a home they could not afford through a conventional purchase at current mortgage rates.

The leasing program introduced by Ken Levitt, an Orlando, Florida, builder is typical of the land-lease plans offered by developers. As applied to his Rollingwood Homes subdivision, the plan (in September 1981, with the mortgage rate at 17 percent) works like this: For the owner who buys a $90,000 house and lot, the monthly mortgage payment, after 20 percent down, would be $1,026; for the owner who leases his lot (valued at $20,000, for this example), $898, including $100 per month for ground rent. The buyer saves $4,000 in reduced down-payment costs plus another $128 per month in lower carrying costs. While the land lease is written for 40 years, Levitt doesn't expect buyers to pay ground rent anywhere near that long. The homeowner can opt to buy the land at any time. Scheduled price increases encourage owners to exercise their option to buy the land early. In five years, the $20,000 lot would cost the Rollingwood homeowner $33,000.

For another example, in California, where lot prices are high enough to cause nosebleeds, a $129,000 home in the Charter Crest project of Charter Development Company, of Tustin, would normally require $25,800 down and a $103,200 mortgage. With the land-lease option, Charter deducts a $40,000 lot cost—and charges $89,000 for the structure. This makes the buyer eligible for 90 percent financing rather than 80 percent, reducing the required down payment to $8,900. Lease payments for the land are $267 per month (8 percent of the lot value on an annual basis). The monthly ground rent remains constant for the first 15 years, and then goes up by 50 percent every five years for the remaining 55 years on the lease. Charter Crest home buyers, however, may exercise their option to purchase the underlying land at any time after the first year of the lease term. The "reversion" price at the time the option is exercised is determined by adding a 7 percent compound escalator each year to the original value placed on the land.

Not all land-lease deals offer the homeowner the chance to buy his lot. Most do though, and that is the most significant difference between today's land leases and earlier versions. Baltimore land leases used to run for 99 years and were renewable, but a law enacted in Maryland several years ago now gives lessees the right to purchase after 20 years. Generally, a right-to-purchase option today comes anywhere from the end of the first year to 20 years from the signing of the contract. Often there is an option to buy for an agreed price or renew, at five, ten, or twenty-year intervals.

Some developers have been offering land-lease plans that give the home buyer the option of deferring up to 75 percent of each monthly land payment for the first two years, making it still easier for would-be buyers to become homeowners. It should be noted here, however, that the only break many California buyers get with land-lease deals is a more affordable down payment. Because of high land costs, the total monthly house payments with land leasing there can exceed the costs of a straight purchase.

With a privately arranged land lease, the seller of the property is in effect providing part of the financing. Since he retains an interest in the property, the seller, in essence, is taking back a second mortgage, without the restrictions of a second mortgage—and often without the need to gain approval by the holder of an underlying first mortgage.

The cost of leasing is typically fixed at from one-half of 1 percent to 1 percent of the land value each month, or from 6 to 12 percent a year. On a (non-California) $75,000 home, that comes to from about $75 to $150 per month. Depending on the arrangement, part of the ground rent may be credited toward the eventual purchase of the land.

If you're working out a land-lease deal with a seller and structure the plan to comply with Section 1055 of the Internal Revenue Code, which applies to ground rents, your payments can be claimed as tax-deductible interest payments. If you don't observe the Code to the letter, those payments are simply rent and, as such, are nondeductible. To be deductible, 1) the land lease must be "redeemable," which means that it must include an option to buy at a "determinable" price; 2) the term of the lease must be more than 15 years, including renewal periods; and 3) the lease must be freely assignable should you decide to resell the property.

Cut-Rate Loans ∎

Housing subsidies, which grew to a torrent under Lyndon Johnson's Great Society, have been reduced to a trickle under President Reagan. To take but one example of the HUD-administered "buy-down" programs stemming from the Johnson years, Section 235 of the National Housing Act provided homeownership assistance for more than half a million low- and moderate-income families in the 1970s. It was terminated March 31, 1982.

There were dollar limits on Section 235 mortgage loans and property prices, but the home buyer made only a 3 percent down payment and was required to contribute only 20 percent of his adjusted gross income to monthly mortgage payments. HUD subsidies, which effectively reduced Section 235 mortgage interest rates to as low as 4 percent, took care of the rest.

The White House's budget-balancing efforts have led to the elimination or severe scaling down of most other non-self-supporting federal housing programs as well. But while the "free lunch" may be over, there still are a number of sources of below-market-rate home financing open to individuals and families of low to moderate income in both urban and rural areas. There are even some cut-rate loan programs under which there are *no* income limits.

Subsidized housing programs applicable to a given area might get a mention in the local press when first announced, but they rarely are front-paged or advertised. It's up to the would-be home buyer, if he's aggressively seeking ways to make homeownership affordable, to check with the nearest HUD field office, housing and community development agencies of local government, and the community affairs department of his state government for information on any current low-cost home-loan programs for which he might be eligible. He might also check with his employer, since many major corporations not only provide mortgage subsidies for relocated personnel, but finance homes for new employees at below-market rates as well.

Obtaining financing for older homes in the city has often proved difficult. It's not unusual today, however, to find lending institutions shutting their doors to qualified buyers seeking loans for suburban purchases at the prevailing market rate, while at the same time rolling out the red carpet for barely qualified buyers applying for cut-rate loans under an urban housing or community development program. Even though you have been turned down by a number of loan officers for conventional financing, you could be in line for a good deal on housing if you can find your way to a lender participating in a program aimed at attracting new blood to older neighborhoods and averting further deterioration.

If you still can't quite cut it financially, look into urban homesteading. There you might qualify to buy a house for as little as one dollar.

FARMERS HOME ADMINISTRATION LOANS

You don't have to be a farmer to get a Farmers Home Administration loan. An agency within the U.S. Department of Agriculture, the Farmers Home Administration (FmHA) gets it name from its original mission as a farm-loan agency. However, as the makeup of the rural population shifted, the work of Farmers Home has changed. Now farm families make up only 15 percent of rural population, and FmHA has become a rural and small-town community development institution, serving a much wider variety of purposes than its name implies.

Most loan authorities conferred on FmHA are intended to serve rural people and communities of greatest need who cannot get credit from private lenders at affordable rates and terms. Many of the loans bear interest rates well below prevailing market levels. Farm-loan authorities emphasize assistance to the family-size farm or ranch operated for purposes of making a family living. Most home-loan programs are for persons or families of low to moderate income. An objective in many programs is to enable a borrower family to improve its circumstances enough to eventually "graduate" to private credit.

FmHA Section 502 homeownership loans may be used to buy, build, improve, repair, or rehabilitate rural homes and to provide water and waste-disposal facilities for the homes. Eligibility for FmHA-financed single-family housing is based on "adjusted" family income, with low-interest loans available to "low"- and "very-low"-income applicants. Adjusted income is the sum of the income of all adults in the household, minus 5 percent of this sum, and less an additional $300 for each minor child in the household.

Ceilings on adjusted income classified as "low," "moderate," or "above-moderate" are determined from time to time by the government. The current maximum adjusted income for qualifying as a moderate-income family is $15,600 ($18,500 in Hawaii and $23,400 in Alaska). "Rural areas" include open country and places with population of 10,000 or less that are rural in character and not closely associated with urban areas. Some towns with population between 10,000 and 20,000 may qualify if located outside Standard Metropolitan Statistical Areas (SMSA), and depending upon local mortgage credit conditions.

Housing financed under FmHA programs must be modest in size, design, and cost but of adequate quality under government-observed Minimum Property Standards. FmHA will not ordinarily make loans on houses that contain more than 1,300 square feet. The dwelling must be used as a principal residence, and building plans for new construction must be approved by FmHA officials. An existing house is inspected before a loan is made. Access to safe drinking water, waste-disposal facilities, and good roads is essential. Application for a single-family housing loan is made at the FmHA county office serving the county where the property is located.

FmHA can lend for up to 100 percent of the value of the

property as appraised by FmHA. There is no down-payment requirement. Interest rates are based on the cost of money to the government. Maximum loan term is 33 years. Low-income families may qualify for interest credits (reduction of interest to as low as 1 percent) to make the housing payments fall within their means. FmHA will compute the amount of allowable interest credit based on an FmHA formula.

FmHA also guarantees up to 90 percent repayment of housing loans made by private lenders to borrowers of above-moderate income. In this case, the interest rate is negotiated between the borrower and the commercial lender, and a small down payment is required. Applications for guaranteed loans are made at the office of the lender, who then contacts FmHA for approval of a loan guaranty. FmHA charges a one-time fee of 1 percent of the amount of the loan being guaranteed.

The agency also makes home-improvement loans to families who cannot secure credit from regular commercial lenders. A condition of a Section 502 home-improvement loan is that the house be up to federally recognized Minimum Property Standards when the repairs are completed. This may influence the amount of work that must be done and the amount of money that must be borrowed. Repayment terms of up to 25 years may be scheduled for repair loans of no more than $7,000. Interest rates are based on each family's adjusted income. Other home-improvement loans are repayable in 33 years or less. These loans are made at the regular interest rate, or with interest credits, depending upon family size and income.

The basic FmHA farm-loan programs are for ownership and operation of family-size farms and ranches. They are also designed to help young people finance their entry into farming. Loans are made for land, building, equipment, supplies, and other expenses necessary to farming operations. The local FmHA county committee, made up of three persons appointed by the FmHA state director, and who know local farming and credit conditions, determines eligibility for farmer loans. Before acting on an application, the committee members may ask the applicant to meet with them, or they may visit the farm.

Interest rates for direct farm loans vary according to the cost of money to the government. Reduced rates are available to limited-resource borrowers. Interest rates for guaranteed loans are negotiated between the borrower and the lender. The maximum term is 40 years. Each loan must be adequately secured by real estate, but FmHA may lend up to 100 percent of the value of the security property. There is no down-payment requirement. Borrowers who receive direct loans from FmHA are required to "graduate" to private credit sources as soon as they are able.

Inquiry about applying for an FmHA loan may be made at any of the agency's 1,750 county or district offices. FmHA office locations are listed in the "U.S. Government" section of telephone directories under "Department of Agriculture." Applications from eligible U.S. military service veterans are given preference in order of consideration, but veterans and nonveterans must meet the same eligibility and credit requirements.

FmHA funds occasionally may be limited in some areas. However, FmHA periodically reviews the income of its borrowers and requires those whose income has risen to the point where they can get conventional financing to do so. In this way, FmHA maintains and recycles its funds.

REHABILITATION LOAN PROGRAMS

The Bureau of the Census estimates that by the mid-1980s, there will be more money spent annually on the rehabilitation of run-down, but basically sound, houses than on constructing new residences. Buying cheap and then fixing up is a time-honored way for the young, ambitious, and handy to afford a first home. The wholesale swing toward improvement and rehabilitation of the nation's existing housing stock, however, goes beyond the expediency of an affordable home-buying alternative. It's our most visible evidence that we, as a nation, are becoming conservationists at heart and shucking the image of being a "throwaway" society.

The Bicentennial celebration had something to do with it, focusing attention on the value of restoring historic neighborhoods. So did the continuing craze for collectibles that took root in the

1970s. But the tyranny of the gasoline pump and the pain of commuting to city jobs are also important factors in the revitalization movement, which is nowhere more evident than in once-decaying urban areas with expanding downtown white-collar employment bases. The children of families who left the cities for the suburbs following World War II are now returning and could make the rejuvenation of our cities the great growth industry of the 1980s.

If you're looking for ways to ease your entry into homeownership, you can find below-market "fixer-uppers" and "workman's specials" in almost any neighborhood, urban or suburban. With the shortage of decent rental apartments severe in many major cities and getting worse, there's also a strong trend toward buying sound, well-located, larger houses and remodeling them to provide an income apartment or two, in addition to generous living quarters for the owner. But the real housing bargains are to be found in decaying neighborhoods with good potential for intensive renovation.

Rather than being planned, the revitalization of most urban neighborhoods begins with one or two middle-class pioneers, sensitive to housing bargains but short on funds, moving into a rundown but once-attractive neighborhood, and then pouring a whole lot of "sweat equity" into their properties. Their interest in the neighborhood encourages remaining owner-occupants to engage in repair and maintenance of their own properties—and may trigger community action, including special funding via one or more local lenders. Before long, housing values are appreciating and the neighborhood is attracting other young first-time home buyers willing to work hard to give the area an ambience of its own.

In a number of major cities, particularly on the East Coast, there are blocks after blocks of narrow, attached brownstones or row houses in poor neighborhoods that have been wracked by arson and largely abandoned. One or two old-house enthusiasts moving in and rehabilitating properties that may represent little more than four walls isn't going to spark a revival of the neighborhood. There has to be a dedication to creating a community. For a bargain hunter in the city, the neighborhood should not have degenerated beyond the point where two or three key renovations won't encourage other owners to upgrade their properties.

Many houses built 50 or more years ago have a lot of hidden values. Strip away the layers of paint and paper applied over the years by a parade of owners and you'll often find decorative touches of earlier days—from carved woodwork to pressed-tin-plate ceilings—that are well worth preserving. The wall and floor thicknesses and heavy beaming of many of these old houses can also provide a degree of soundproofing that is all but impossible in modern urban construction.

Put condition over style. Your first consideration should be a solid foundation, straight walls, and sound roof beams. Don't be swayed by a Federal mantelpiece, Victorian gingerbread, or wide-planked floors. Retain the services of a house inspector to confirm that the structure is worth preserving in the first place. Many renovators discover too late that they would have been better off tearing down the old structure and building anew.

Don't make a decision to buy in the city without having visited the property under less than ideal conditions. A fresh snowfall or a quiet summer Sunday could conceal any number of potential neighborhood nuisances. Is the house on the route the fire engines usually take? Is there a noisy or noisome factory nearby? Is the crime problem likely to be any worse here than elsewhere in the city? What are the honest chances of the neighborhood becoming a viable community again? Balance the risks against the rewards.

Young first-time buyers are in the vanguard of urban revitalization. Typical buyers are single professionals or childless two-career couples still well below their income potential. Like almost all home buyers today, they're looking to participate in the tax and equity benefits of homeownership. As urbanites, they're also seeking easier access to the hubs of commercial, social, and cultural life.

Revitalization, however, is not without its critics. The cry has been raised that the influx of middle-class buyers into urban areas is, to some extent, pushing out the poor. The process even has a name: gentrification. But studies by HUD and the National Association of Housing and Redevelopment Officials have found that displacement, as the reciprocal of revitalization, accounts for less than 4 percent of all moves by low-income urban families.

Indeed, most of the federal, state, and local programs aimed at encouraging revitalization reserve low-interest mortgages and renovation loans to inner-city areas and buyers with low or modest incomes—or to investors who are renovating buildings to be rented or sold at cost to disadvantaged families (and earning a nice tax deduction for doing so). The majority of moderate-income owners buy and improve their properties with funds borrowed conventionally from banks and savings institutions, but there are opportunities to reduce the monthly carrying costs here too.

In consideration of the need for adequate housing for low- and moderate-income families, Congress has authorized FHA to insure lenders against loss on mortgage loans to finance the purchase, rehabilitation, or construction of housing in older, declining, but still viable urban areas where conditions are such that normal requirements for mortgage insurance cannot be met. The terms of the loans vary according to the HUD/FHA program under which the mortgage is insured.

The program most useful to the readers of this book would likely be Section 203(k) of the National Housing Act: Rehabilitation Mortgage Insurance. This program is tailor-made for moderate-income buyers interested in rehabilitating run-down one-to-four-family properties in neighborhoods that are turning around. The program permits buyers to finance both the purchase price and the estimated cost of the planned improvements with a single FHA-backed mortgage. Loan limit on a single-family dwelling, with a down payment averaging 4 percent, and a term of up to 30 years, is $67,500, as under the basic Section 203(b) HUD/FHA home-mortgage insurance program (see page 74). Although the interest rate on the loan may be close to prevailing market levels for first-mortgage loans, the financing for the renovation is obtained at an interest rate considerably lower than the buyer-borrower would have to pay with a conventional home-improvement loan.

Another rehab program under the National Housing Act, the

Section 312 Direct Rehabilitation Loan Program, grants low-interest loans to finance rehabilitation in designated areas and prevent unnecessary demolition of basically sound structures. Loans, with maturities of up to 20 years, may not exceed $27,000 per dwelling unit. The applicant must be unable to secure necessary financing from other sources on comparable terms and conditions, and must evidence the capacity to repay the loan. Priority is given to low- and moderate-income applicants.

Urban Renewal Mortgage Insurance, Section 220 of the Housing Act, provides for insured loans on liberal terms to assist in the rehabilitation of existing dwellings in urban renewal, code enforcement, or natural-disaster areas receiving federal aid. This program enables sponsors—both private and public—to obtain financing in localities not favored by private lenders, but occupant and nonoccupant mortgagors may also apply. The program covers the purchase or rehabilitation of both single-family and multi-family dwellings.

For a less restrictive program, there's the Rehabilitation Mortgage Program launched in 1979 by Fannie Mae to provide long-term financing in urban areas for the rehabilitation of one-to-four-family houses. Under the program, FNMA buys conventional first-mortgage loans made to borrowers whose credit has been previously approved by the corporation. The loans must be within normally applicable limits on mortgage amounts and loan-to-value ratios. However, the loan amounts are based on the estimated values of the mortgaged properties as though already rehabilitated, rather than on their value in their present condition.

By basing the loan on the estimated value of the property after rehabilitation, the loan made available to the borrower is large enough (when added to the required down payment) for the home buyer to finance the acquisition of the property and the proposed rehabilitation work. This single loan, like the FHA-insured Section 203(k) loans, enables the home buyer to avoid the expense and trouble of obtaining separate loans first for acquisition and later for the improvement work. Also, these loans are made at interest rates customary for long-term first mortgages instead of at the higher rates usually charged for short-term, second-mortgage rehab loans. The portion of the loan that exceeds the amount needed for acquiring the property "as is" is deposited in an interest-bearing escrow account (administered by the lender) that may be used only for completing the rehabilitation work in accordance with previously approved plans. Interest on the escrow account is payable to the borrower.

For the purchase and rehabilitation of a single-family home, the maximum amount that can be borrowed under the FNMA program is $93,750, with a 10 percent down payment, or up to $75,000 with a 5 percent down payment. The loan limits are higher in Hawaii and Alaska. In all cases, mortgage insurance is required where the mortgage exceeds 80 percent of the "as completed" value of the property as established by an appraiser and based on the assumption that all work will be completed (within one year) in accordance with the plans accompanying the mortgage application.

Under a program approved by Congress during Jimmy Carter's last full month in office, state, county, city, and small-town governments have the authority to sell tax-exempt revenue bonds (within prescribed limits) to raise funds and provide home fix-up loans through commercial lenders at below-market rates. With the federal exemption on the bonds, the loans can be granted for 2 to 3 percentage points under the going rate on first-mortgage loans. Rehab loans of up to $15,000 can be offered under the program. Any limitations on the market value of the property undergoing repair or on the income of the owner would be established by the area administrator.

Tax-exempt bond programs (covered in greater detail under "Discount Mortgage Programs") have been running hot and cold due to the fluctuations of the bond market. But ask around. If your city or county has made a commitment to preserving and improving worn-down neighborhoods, there just may be some money lying around for a home buyer dedicated to the same end.

URBAN HOMESTEADING

Between 1911 and 1925, when the pioneering spirit was still calling families to free land in the West, more than half a million homesteads were established, many of them in states that had only recently been admitted to the Union. Industrious families staked out the 160-acre tracts allotted to them, built homes, cultivated the land, and developed farms through sheer dawn-to-dusk effort. Some of that spirit is still alive in the land, only now it's manifesting itself in the inner cities, the new territory for young pioneers.

In scores of cities, both large and small, it's possible to buy a vacant house for as little as $1, provided the buyer agrees to fix up the structure to meet local standards and occupy it for a specified period of time. Low-interest rehabilitation loans are frequently earmarked for such projects, which are aimed at revitalizing declining neighborhoods. While most of the properties offered are dilapidated, they are essentially sound.

Urban homesteading has been gathering momentum since 1975, when a HUD demonstration program began an evaluation of the concept in cities like Chicago and Boston, as well as in a number of smaller communities, including Islip, New York, and Decatur, Georgia, a town of 22,000 population. The program is now a regular operating program, with more than 95 participating localities.

The national program was designed to revitalize declining urban areas and reduce the inventory of HUD-held properties by transferring vacant single-family properties to new home owners for rehabilitation. Suitable properties held by the Veterans Administration, Farmers Home Administration, or local governments have also been used in this program.

The properties, usually acquired by the federal agencies through foreclosure or abandonment, are transferred at no cost to local governments that have developed HUD-approved homesteading programs within designated neighborhoods. The local governments "sell" the properties for a token sum (as low as $1) to individuals or families who have been equitably selected by each participating locality. The buyer-homesteader must occupy the property as a principal residence (making any needed repairs to meet minimum health and safety standards before occupancy) for at least three years. Within 18 months of occupying the property, he must bring it up to local building-code standards.

The rehabilitation may be carried out by a contractor or by the homesteader. During the process, the homesteader must permit inspections to be made of the property and of the rehabilitation work performed, for code approvals. At the end of three years, when all these requirements have been met, the homesteader receives full title to the property.

HUD makes funds for rehab loans available through the participating local government. Interest on these loans to homesteaders is generally 3 percent, for terms of up to 20 years. Loan limit on single-family dwellings is $27,000.

Homesteaders are usually selected by public lottery. Typically, the Urban Homesteading Program hopeful pre-qualifies with the community development division of the participating city and goes on its mailing list to receive an application approximately two weeks before each scheduled drawing. From then on, his chances depend on how many housing units are being made available under the program that day and how many other eligible individuals or families have mailed in applications. The drawings may be for a particular house or for one of a number of dwellings within the area(s) designated for homesteading.

Properties made available under homesteading programs range from sprawling old manses to skinny row houses. Many of the homes picked up for the programs have been abandoned by absentee landlords who got caught between a rock (rent control) and a hard place (soaring property taxes). Without sufficient income from the property to make it pay its way, such properties are often allowed to fall into disrepair, tax bills eventually go unpaid, and squatters may take over the building. This ultimately leads to foreclosure, abandonment, or the property being condemned.

The city most housing officials visit when they want to see at first hand just how effective urban revitalization can be is Baltimore, Maryland. It's hard to find a neighborhood there without some rehabilitation in progress. As part of its larger revitalization program, under which thousands of vacant homes have been recycled by the city and rented to the poor or sold below cost to middle-class families, more than 500 homesteads have been awarded. Baltimore's first homesteading venture was confined to a single block, but that block has become a model for revitalization programs across the country.

Hard hit by race riots in the 1960s, the 600 block of Baltimore's Stirling Street had decayed into a slum. The dilapidated row houses that filled the block were scheduled to be torn down in the 1970s and replaced by new public housing—until, under President Nixon, urban-renewal funds were suspended. It was only then that city housing authorities accepted that it might not be a bad idea to try to preserve those old row houses. Built back in the 1830s as working-class quarters, there was a lot of history in the two-and-a-half-story, red-brick buildings.

The homesteading program launched by Baltimore's city housing department in 1974 focused on the 600 block of Stirling Street. Ultimately, 42 homesteads were awarded and the new owners, who had paid $1 for their properties, organized themselves as the Stirling Street Neighbors. Rehabilitation loans of up to $37,500 per dwelling (at a sliding scale of interest: from 1 to 7 percent, depending on the applicant's income and family size) were made available under the City Housing Assistance Program.

By concentrating the homesteaders, the restoration became a neighborhood effort. Homesteaders could see one another at work and be reassured that all the hammering, scraping, and painting would redound to the benefit of every resident of the block. The Stirling Street program proved so successful that the Baltimore city fathers extended homesteading to more than a dozen other declining neighborhoods. They've also learned that if you can save the *one* abandoned house, you usually can save the block.

St. Louis, Missouri, is another city that has made a strong commitment to inner-city rehabilitation. Under a variety of programs combining federal loans and city loans, some 15,000 houses have been reclaimed in the Gateway city since 1977. Homesteaders who agree to fix them up and live in them have been able to buy abandoned houses there for anywhere from $100 to $10,000.

HUD isn't the only source of homes for homesteaders. In more than 40 cities, Neighborhood Housing Services, a nonprofit offshoot of the Washington-based Urban Reinvestment Task Force, brings together citizens' groups, government agencies, local officials, and lenders in a coalition aimed at preventing the spread of urban decay by helping existing homeowners rehabilitate their homes and making money available at low interest rates for homesteaders.

Once the fever to rehabilitate strikes a city, the competition for homesteads and rehabilitation loans accelerates. But, surprisingly, the supply of money to be had at bargain prices may even then exceed the demand. A full year after a recent $3 million loan program was announced for the purchase and renovation of homes in a run-down neighborhood of Milwaukee, Wisconsin—30-year mortgage money at 6.75 percent, with only 5 percent down— there was still $1 million on the books.

DISCOUNT MORTGAGE PROGRAMS

In October 1981, three months before the arrival of their first child, the combined annual income of Larry and Norma Barnett was more than $42,000. When Norma left her job on the advice of her obstetrician that month, their income dropped to less than $27,000. The Barnetts were apartment renters in Margate, Florida, a Broward County community, and knew that their lease, which would be up shortly after the baby's expected date of arrival, would not be renewed, since the development in which they lived had an adults-only policy.

The Barnetts went looking for a place to buy, but with mortgage rates still close to their 1981 highs, they were running into financing problems. At Larry's present income, and with no guarantee that Norma would become a wage earner again in the near future, loan officer after loan officer was stamping "Unqualified" across the face of the family's mortgage application.

But then in January 1982, which was when Joseph Curtis Barnett arrived, a real-estate agent suggested to Larry that they might qualify for a below-market mortgage under the county

Housing Finance Authority's new bond program. Under the program, funded by the sale of $25 million in tax-exempt mortgage-purchase bonds, families earning less than $30,680, and who had not owned a home during the preceding three years, could apply for loans to purchase houses priced at up to $63,270. Interest rate on the loans was 13.5 percent, 3.5 percentage points below the then prevailing rate on conventional loans.

The Barnetts applied at one of the eight lending institutions participating in the program and, soon after, got a loan commitment for the purchase of a small town house, costing $62,500, in the Margate area. They closed the deal by putting $12,500 down, and are financing $50,000.

A unique feature of their loan, with first-year payments calculated as though the loan had 30 years to run, is that the loan will be paid off in a little more than 16 years. The interest rate doesn't change, but monthly P/I payments escalate 3 percent annually for the first nine years of the loan, and then remain level until the loan is repaid. All of the annual increase goes toward reducing the loan principal.

The Barnetts' monthly payments started at $572.71. By the beginning of the 10th year, they will be paying $747.25 per month on the mortgage. Under the plan, they will pay nearly $130,000 less in interest than a buyer who pays 17 percent for 30 years on a conventional $50,000 loan. The mortgage, called a "growing equity mortgage," was designed by Merrill Lynch, the brokerage-house giant and bond underwriter for Broward County's Housing Finance Authority. The reason the funds were available at the discount rate is that the county funded the program with tax-exempt housing bonds issued under an authority granted by the U.S. Congress in December 1980.

The idea behind tax-exempt revenue bonds for financing single-family housing is simple. State, county, and local governments, through their housing finance agencies, raise funds by selling tax-exempt housing bonds to investors. The proceeds are then funneled through S&Ls and other lending institutions to provide cut-rate mortgages to qualified area home buyers. Bonds whose interest is nontaxable carry a significantly lower rate than bonds whose interest is taxable, which translates to a discount rate for the mortgages against which the bonds are issued.

Four out of five states and roughly 250 local governments have issued single-family mortgage revenue bonds since 1978, when the first of these securities was floated. In 1980, nearly $13 billion of tax-exempt housing revenue bonds were issued. Under the Mortgage Bond Subsidy Act of 1980, however, new restrictions were introduced, and tax-exempt bonds for single-family housing were virtually in limbo throughout most of 1981. Even so, the federal government is moving to terminate the program by the end of 1983.

The program, which costs the Treasury up to $30 million per year in terms of forgone tax revenues for every billion dollars of revenue bonds issued, has been severely criticized for being far too generous. The law sets no limit on the income of home buyers using bond-sale proceeds. This is left to local housing finance authorities. We've seen the income limit set at anywhere from 90 percent to 120 percent of the median income of area families. The law, however, does specify that a property acquired under the program can't sell for more than 90 percent of the average sales price for new or existing homes in the area.

In some states, such as Connecticut and California, this has permitted area families using discount mortgages to purchase houses costing as much as $130,000. In Chicago, with only 20 percent of a recent $55 million in bond-raised mortgage funds reserved for purchases in low- and moderate-income neighborhoods, the income ceiling was set at $40,000, for the purchase of new or existing homes costing up to $82,000. (That Broward County limit of $63,270 would have been considerably higher, too, had not the Treasury Department lumped single-family houses and condos, including thousands of lower-priced retirement units, together.)

Even with the discounts, the funds raised through the selling of tax-exempt bonds don't get snapped up as fast as you might think. Check for state and local area programs that might be beneficial to you. If your income is in the moderate range and you aren't already a homeowner, you've probably got as good a shot at such funds as other applicants. Especially now that, except in very economically depressed areas, all the dollars must go to first-time home buyers (defined as anyone who has not owned a home in the past three years). It was largely the misuse of these funds by speculators and homeowners trading up that led to the revisions in 1980 and the move to close down the program.

Whether or not the program survives remains to be seen. Proponents can make a strong case for the additional building and related manufacturing activity that is directly attributable to the availability of "seed money" in the form of discount mortgages—with an eventual return to the Treasury that is far greater under the otherwise self-supporting program than the revenue forgone on the tax-exempt bonds.

State-sponsored homeownership programs, such as the New Jersey Neighborhood Loan Program, which makes sound, reasonably priced houses available to qualified low-to-moderate-income buyers at reduced interest rates, may not be continued if the government closes the tap on tax-exempt housing bonds. Community programs, such as the Washington, D.C., Home Purchase Assistance Program, which provides qualified buyers with no-interest loans and a portion of their down payment, could also be in trouble. Whether "needy" home buyers get any kind of a break or not is pretty much going to be in the hands of state and local governments.

Instead of being run from Washington, as a huge, federally directed program, funding will be continued, although at a considerably reduced rate, under no-strings-attached Community Development Block Grants. With federal allocations for housing folded into the block-grant funding mechanism, it will be up to state and local governments to determine how the money is to be used. Depending on their sense of priorities, you may or may not find you have a friend at City Hall when you look for some house-buying assistance.

All else failing, you might consider a move to Alaska. A state-backed lending program launched there in November 1980 offers mortgages at rates as low as 6 percent to low-income residents, 9 percent to veterans, and 10 percent to all others. There is no income ceiling on the 10 percent loans. A 5 percent down payment is required in each case and the limit on loans for single-family homes is $147,000.

While the program administered by the Alaska Housing Finance Corporation is based on tax-exempt-bond sales, revenue from Alaska's ever-growing oil wealth subsidizes the difference between bond costs and the loan costs to borrowers. Under the program's low-income guidelines, eligible borrowers can borrow up to $76,000 at 6 percent. In Alaska, to qualify for a low-income loan, a single buyer can't earn more than $26,650 a year, a couple can't make more than $27,650.

HELP FOR BLUE-CHIP TRANSFEREES

Young managers on their way up the corporate ladder are subject to their employer's relocation whims. As part of their program for developing future senior managers, the larger national corporations relocate their more promising personnel every three to four years on average. But where the young manager used to jump at a transfer, it being a sign that he was on the corporate fast track, he may go into shock at the prospect of a move today.

A move from the Midwest, say, to the Big Apple, or just about anywhere in California, easily could double the transferred employee's housing costs. If a homeowner weighs the long-term benefits of the career move against a bargain-rate mortgage and the comparatively low property taxes he pays on a comfortable home acquired pre-1979, he just might opt to stay in place.

The doubling of mortgage interest rates in three years—from 1978 to 1981—had a dramatic impact on corporate relocation practices, with many firms cutting back drastically on personnel moves. It made for recruitment problems as well. Potential middle-management executives were avoiding moves to locations where the costs of homeownership could destroy them financially. But management is finding ways to induce valued employees to move and to recruit new executives.

In order to cope with the scarcity of seasoned employees, corporations not only are picking up the employee's relocation costs but are offering creative—and expensive—mortgage-assistance plans. Where 10 years ago it might have cost an employer $3,500 in up-front relocation costs to transfer an employee within the U.S., the average cost of moving a family of four 1,000 miles today is in excess of $34,000. That can cover everything from an initial trip to meet the new boss and make a quick tour of available housing to picking up the difference between the monthly payments on the employee's old and new mortgages for up to five years.

If you are contemplating a job change and have demonstrated management potential, one of the first questions posed to the interviewer or recruiter should be about the company's "relocation plan." If you are going to be required by your new employer to make a number of moves for career reasons during your "seasoning years," a generous relocation plan can loom just as important as salary and benefits. If you'll be moving to a new city, don't hesitate to ask what assistance you might expect in acquiring a home. While most mortgage-assistance plans apply to corporate transferees, a growing number of companies are offering home financing to newly recruited employees at below-market rates.

A few blue-chip corporations have their own in-house relocation divisions, but most of the Fortune 500 rely on the services of one or more of the many companies that are part of the multibillion-dollar real-estate relocation business. These specialists handle the sale of the home the transferee is leaving, help him to find a new home and the financing for it, and may even assist his spouse to find employment at the new location. The employer picks up the tab for the relocation firm's services and in many cases guarantees the employee a fair market price for his old home and frees funds for the purchase of the new property.

The price for the old property may be established by the relocation company, but the employee generally has the option of finding a buyer for it himself, if he thinks he can do better. There's rarely any quibbling though when the price is arrived at by averaging two independent appraisals, the growing practice today. With a guaranteed price for his old home, and his employer paying the broker's fee on the eventual sale, the transferee in a must-sell, must-buy situation can then just walk away from the house. Any headaches encountered in selling the property are his employer's.

All house-hunting, closing, and moving costs are also absorbed by the transferee's employer. But with the move, the transferee could also face punishingly higher mortgage payments, even though he may find a satisfactory house priced no higher than the one he is leaving. The interest rate he'll be paying on the new mortgage could make a stunning difference. So the move won't represent a financial sacrifice on the employee's part, three out of five blue-chip corporations have adopted the practice of paying a mortgage-interest differential (MID). This is intended to cover the difference between what the transferee was paying on his old mortgage and what he would be paying on his new one without a subsidy.

For example, the transferee might be leaving a home with an $80,000 mortgage on which he was paying 9 percent, or $643.70 per month. Say his new house costs about the same as the old one, but the interest rate on the new mortgage is 15 percent. On a 30-year $80,000 loan, that's $1,011.56 per month, for a difference of $367.86. With a MID, the employer typically would reimburse the employee to the tune of $4,414.32 per year (though some corporations limit the differential to 5 percentage points), for anywhere from three to five years.

Unfortunately, the Internal Revenue Service treats MIDs as income, and the employer may or may not compensate the employee for the additional tax bite. If you're on the brink of a move, find out what your present or future employer's policy is in this situation. If you're being transferred or recruited, you're generally in a strong negotiating position. You not only should expect an increase in salary but you should not be placed at a financial disadvantage because of the move. Junior and middle-management executives who *will* move today tend to get the royal treatment. You should hold out for the same.

As mentioned in our coverage of builder buy-downs, corporations are also turning to buy-downs, the costs of which can be deducted from corporate income taxes, to reduce the transferee's monthly mortgage payments on a new home. In Southern California's booming Santa Clara Valley, a number of the highly competitive electronics firms located there have resorted to equity participation plans to entice new employees from less costly living areas. Equity participation? That's our old friend SAM, the shared-appreciation mortgage, where you have a "partner" (in this case, your employer) who puts up the down payment and/or contributes a portion of the monthly mortgage payment, and you cut him in for a share of the profit when the property is resold at some future date.

Large insurance companies, which used to be a popular source of home mortgages, are becoming active again as mortgage bankers, if only to write cut-rate loans for their relocated executives. You might even find yourself working for a corporation that holds mortgages for employees who can't qualify for conventional financing. The trend to hold second mortgages to assist employees in buying homes is also growing. All of this assistance is generally made available at below-market rates.

Even if you're not executive material, you'd do well to buy where transferees generally buy, if you want to assure yourself of an easy resale when it comes time for *you* to relocate. A transferee has probably been relocated several times, and expects to be transferred again within a few years. He buys with an eye to resale value, in an area where the market in homes is brisk. Most junior and middle-management executives aren't ready to settle into their dream house. They buy what is best described as a mid-range house in a suburban area where middle-level executives typically live.

Acquiring Land as a First Step

Legend has it that sharpers once sold off the entire floor of Death Valley for homesites. We wouldn't put it beyond them. Hundreds of thousands of families have fallen victim over the years to unscrupulous land salesmen and hold deeds to property suited only for scorpions or alligators. While most such junk land is bought by the gullible for "investment purposes" or to "lock in a site in the Sunbelt" for their retirement years, the lesson to be learned here is that one should *never, never* buy property on which one has not set foot.

Whether you're looking for a developed suburban lot or raw land in the country, the decision to buy the homesite should be based not only on a thorough, firsthand inspection of the property but also on an appraisal by a skilled professional who can tell you what the property is *really* worth and how much it's going to cost you to meet local code requirements. With raw land especially, development expenses easily could double the cost of the site. And restrictions in either kind of locale might effectively prohibit building there at all.

Say you're looking for a piece of land on which to build a log house or a dome home from a precut kit, or on which to erect a posh multisectional factory-built. Even if all the construction

225

work is performed by professionals, most existing surburban codes would deny you a construction permit (although the situation is improving in the case of factory-builts). You might also acquire a site and then learn that you can't even have a house built for you conventionally, stick by stick by a contractor, because the town fathers have placed a moratorium on water and/or sewer-system hookups.

You need to have your eyes wide open when buying land today. If buying through a broker, don't expect him to clue you in on all the pitfalls of a parcel that you might be close to buying. In a rural area, as a member of the fraternal order of good ol' boys, he could be in cahoots with the seller—or just anxious to make a sale and pocket a commission. Brokers generally collect 10 percent of the purchase price from the seller on land sales. But you know who pays the seller.

You don't necessarily have to go through a broker to buy land, of course. You can investigate the "lots-for-sale" listings in the classified section of a newspaper serving the area where you would like to build. Or you could drive around prospective neighborhoods and look for lot-for-sale signs. Shop carefully, and compare both price and value. If you spot an unmarked lot in a desirable location, you might query a neighbor residing on either side of the property as to its availability. Although it may not be listed for sale, the owners may be interested in selling it. Talk to local farmers who may be willing to sell you a small parcel of land on which you can build your home.

Most raw land is bought from and financed by the seller. Do not hesitate to negotiate. Sellers often will come down as much as 20 percent from the asking price if they're anxious to sell. In a buyer's market, press your advantage. But do bring in an appraiser to tell you what the property is worth. He'll examine all the factors and could keep you from making a bad investment. If you're going to have to sink a well for your water supply and install a septic system, you'll want confirmation that abundant potable water is within a reasonable depth from the surface and that the land can pass the percolation test required with a septic system. In the absence of preliminary testing, any purchase offer should be made conditional, with certain contingencies which, if not met, will void the sale.

The price of land varies greatly depending on location. You don't always save, however, by settling for a rural or semirural rather than a suburban location. Where a building code might permit four standard, 75-by-100-foot subdivision lots to the acre in a built-up area, a county ordinance might require you to purchase a minimum of two acreas of land in the country. Also, that suburban lot, typically priced at $2 per square foot (or $15,000 for the property), is likely to be a finished lot, with sewer, water, and electric lines ready for hookup.

Two acres of raw land in the country at 10¢ per square foot, say, would cost you $8,712 (there are 43,560 square feet in an acre). But then you might have to pay to have the land at least partially cleared and graded, a road paved, and additionally meet the expense of bringing in electricity, putting down a well, and installing a septic tank and leaching field.

We're a long way from running out of land—nearly 85 percent of America is taken up by farms, forests, and pasturelands or is owned by the government—but restrictive zoning practices and the scarcity of what real-estate professionals refer to as "buildable" land have contributed to the land-price explosion. The best housing sites were built on long ago and much of the increase in housing prices can be attributed to the rising cost of buildable land, which has outstripped the cost of building itself. Land and the cost of developing it have risen sevenfold since 1950, to the point where anyone buying a house in suburbia today spends an average of 25 percent of his total housing investment on the land alone. In 1950, land accounted for only about 11 percent of the builders' cost.

According to a recent study by the Homer Hoyt Institute, of Washington, D.C., average lot costs per square foot for single-family housing range from between $1.60 and $2.45 for such growing cities as Houston, Dallas, Salt Lake City, Denver, and Fort Lauderdale, to between $2.50 and $4.50 for much of California, and better than $10 for Honolulu. Today, in Hawaii, land accounts for nearly half of the average sales price of a new home! On the other hand, in Maine, the Dakotas, Tennessee, North Carolina, Mississippi, and Delaware, land costs represent only about 15 or 16 percent of the cost of the house. Although prices in many areas seem dreadfully inflated, "reasonable" buys still do exist. In an area where the *average* lot price is $25,000, there will be many more same-size lots selling for $20,000 or less than for $30,000 or more. As has been said by nearly everyone who has ever written on real estate, the three things that determine the worth of property are location, location, location.

While land speculators did exceedingly well in some areas of the country during the 1970s, we cannot recommend buying land today as an investment. Don't buy unless you plan to build—and soon. Land needs to increase in value by at least 20 percent a year for you to break even on your investment. And in 1981, with the construction of new housing at a near standstill, the value of land for residential developments, according to an index maintained by the Homer Hoyt Institute, suffered its sharpest decline since 1925. Land developers who develop lots for sale to builders are sitting on a *huge* inventory of unsold lots.

For many young families, though, acquiring land is the key to the housing problem, especially if they plan to do all or part of the building themselves. Once you own a piece of buildable land, it's often all the equity you need to swing a mortgage commitment and a construction loan. These days, anyone with a paid-for site is halfway home.

Subdividers can make it easy to purchase a lot in a remote community that is still in the planning stages (and may forever remain there). You've seen the ads: $495 down and $50 a month (for who knows how many years). Even with a choice building site, buying vacant land with an installment land contract generally is not a good idea. You will not own the land—and normally do not get the right to build on it—until the final payment is made. Under most installment agreements, if you miss a payment or two, the seller can foreclose, keep all the money you've already paid, and peddle the land to someone else.

Avoid such problems by having the seller take back a purchase-money mortgage, at a mutually acceptable rate of interest. The contract should allow you to start building your house before you own the lot free and clear. Or arrange for a "homesite mort-gage" with a bank or other lending institution. That way, you would have a deed to the property. If you miss a mortgage pay-ment or two, you still retain ownership until a court orders fore-closure. This could take six months or more, by which time you may be able to "cure" the default or sell the property.

With good, reasonably accessible land, you should be able to get financing for up to 75 percent of the value for even an unde-veloped homesite, for terms of up to five years, if a good credit risk. The loan could be calculated as though it would be amor-tized over ten years, leaving you with a balloon payment to be met at the end of five. This means you could acquire a $12,000 parcel with a down payment of $3,000. The payments on a $9,000 fully amortized five-year homesite mortgage, at 16 percent, say, would amount to $218.87 per month. If the 10-year schedule is applied, the monthly payment would be reduced to $150.77, and you would have a lump-sum payment of $6,019 to meet at the end of the fifth year.

With undeveloped land, lenders are much more likely to listen to someone who plans to build in the very near future than some-one who wants to buy land as an investment. Some banks will even require that a part of the land loan go into improving the site, with an access road, site clearance, or whatever. And even before the land is paid for, you may be able to mortgage-out—that is, borrow enough from the same lender to build your house and pay off the land loan too.

If you're buying land in a rural area and meet the income con-ditions, you may be able to get below-market financing for both the land and your home through the Farmers Home Administra-tion. If you don't qualify for a direct FmHA loan, you might look into FHA and VA mortgage-guaranty programs that cover both land acquisition and construction. These agencies also guarantee financing to acquire manufactured housing and the land on which it will be permanently located, usually as a package deal. Interest rates will run a little higher than on conventional existing housing though.

Financing Sweat Equity

One answer to the high cost of buying a house is to build it or finish it yourself. Invest your own energy—sweat equity, a fine old American tradition—instead of money and you can roll back housing prices. Eliminate most labor costs and contractor profits and you can save as much as 35 percent of what the completed house would cost if you paid others to do all the work.

We're not suggesting that you go the full route, being both contractor and carpenter with a custom design—not with the terrific range of houses that can be purchased today in kit form, either partially panelized (with preassembled wall sections and roof trusses) or with all the key lumber precut and numbered to correspond to its exact location in the plan. With most construction problems worked out in advance, your house goes from foundation to roof quickly and comparatively easily. Weather problems and pilferage are virtually eliminated, as most kit houses can be "dried in"—with walls, roof, and lockable doors and windows in place—in far less time than it takes with conventional stick-built construction.

As detailed in *The Complete Kit House Catalog,* * an earlier

* *The Complete Kit House Catalog.* Frank Coffee, 1979. Wallaby Books, 1230 Avenue of the Americas, New York, N.Y. 10020; $6.95.

work by the author, there are packaged houses for every budget, and in just about every size and style imaginable—from log houses, chalets, and traditionals to contemporaries, domes, and solar homes. If you don't wish to tackle the "heavy" work, you could have the shell erected by a builder or the manufacturer of the kit. With the shell completed by others, the project isn't nearly so formidable to the novice, and it's an increasingly popular builder-homeowner arrangement, with the homeowner completing the interior in his own good time.

Approach some bankers as a prospective owner of a house that you propose to build yourself though, and you may find that their attention wanders a lot. However, bankers are in business to lend money. If you have a good credit rating and can prove to the lender that there is little risk involved in lending you money, a financing plan often can be worked out. While long-term mortgages on unbuilt houses are rare—a pile of precut lumber is not the best collateral—lenders are seeing more and more demand for financing for this type of construction and are coming into the market to provide it.

The more complete your plans are, the better your chances for obtaining financing. When you sit down with the lender, you should be able to present him with a full set of construction plans, a complete materials list with prices, a list of the subcontractors needed (most building codes require that electrical, plumbing, and heating system installations be handled by licensed professionals) and estimates from each, zoning and legal clearances, and a financial dossier attesting to your credit-worthiness and sense of responsibility. You'll probably need two types of loan: a short-term construction loan (also referred to as "interim financing") and a conventional long-term mortgage (or "permanent financing") on the completed house.

Commercial banks are the common source of construction financing. Interest rates on these esentially unsecured loans are several points higher than on long-term mortgages; as a rule, the construction-loan rate is pegged 2 or 3 points above the prime rate. With a kit house, the owner-builder typically would apply for sufficient funds (beyond what he can provide from his own resources) to buy the kit and the required additional building materials, and to pay for any needed outside labor during construction and into the finishing phases. The term of the loan might range from six months to a year or longer. At the end of its term, he would be expected to obtain permanent financing and pay off the short-term note held by the construction lender.

It's easier to secure the short-term construction loan if you *first* arrange for permanent financing. You do this by presenting your detailed plans for the project to a savings bank, savings and loan, or other lending institution that is writing residential mortgages, and applying for a "conditional mortgage," which is a commitment for a permanent mortgage once the construction work has been completed to the satisfaction of the lender and any other contingencies it designates are met. The written commitment can then be used in applying for the construction loan.

It's also possible to obtain permanent financing on a construction-loan basis, with the money advanced to the borrower in installments, as needed. The lender generally requires that you use your own money first, either to buy the land or pay for the initial stages of construction. The lender then advances enough money to meet your costs as various phases of construction are completed. Until the final payment has been received, you pay interest only on the amount of money that has been advanced to you. You don't begin paying off the mortgage until the house has been completed.

To apply for a standard construction loan, you must own your property free and clear. For loan approval, you may also be required to employ the services of a licensed general contractor, who would be committed by contract to build the house. This makes it somewhat more difficult for the owner to do very much of his own work. Since the contractor will be responsible for satisfactory completion of the work, the amount of the loan must reflect the cost of having the contractor do *all* the work. Most owners work out an arrangement with the contractor, however, to compensate them for the portion of the work they are able to do themselves.

With a construction loan, the bank will likely charge a fee for processing the loan and to cover inspection of the project at various stages of construction. This would be in addition to the going interest rate on the loan. As an alternative, if you have enough cash at your disposal to pay for the basic kit, you might look for a direct personal loan from a bank or credit union to finish it off. Once the house is completed, you could apply for permanent financing to pay off your short-term note(s). Personal loans command a higher rate of interest than mortgage loans, but then you can save on those construction-loan fees, which could more than offset the interest differential. You also have the same advantages here as when building with cash: you can take advantage of cash discounts, ranging from 2 to 10 percent, given by contractors and suppliers.

If these methods of financing fall short of your needs, most kithouse manufacturers stand ready to suggest other approaches, which may or may not include a temporary credit arrangement to get you over the hump. Most of these companies have had a lot of experience helping other owner-builders. Very likely they or their representatives will have some acquaintance with lenders in the general area in which you plan to build and will work closely with the lender of your choice. Some will even provide you with a list of lending institutions that have financed other kit-builders.

There are many factors to be considered here, of course, and the type of loan or mortgage for which you may qualify will depend on everything from the size and cost of the project to how much of the work you plan to do yourself. The type and terms of financing available will also vary in different regions of the country. If you pour a fair amount of sweat equity into your house, however, chances are it will be worth considerably more than the total cost of the project, and a mortgage loan, enabling the initial financing to be repaid when the "essentials" of the house are completed, should be no problem. The fact that many of the houses built from kits are more energy efficient than conventional stick-built houses makes them easy to resell and is becoming an important plus with lenders.

Sweat equity, as a cost-cutter, isn't limited to houses that you rehabilitate or build yourself. There are a number of major builders putting up homes today who offer the buyer the opportunity to do some of the finishing work himself and save a bundle of money. On selected "bonus room" plans offered by Pulte Home

Corporation, buyers can save up to $10,000 on the purchase price by finishing a number of areas left unfinished by the builder. Pittsburgh's Ryan Homes is selling shell homes that buyers can finish at 15 percent savings by installing drywall and interior doors, and doing the painting themselves. Capp Homes, in the West, and Ridge Homes, in the East, are two other names to know. They have been specializing in custom-built, finish-it-yourself homes for years.

If you have the energy, but not the income to qualify for the financing needed, to build a home on your own, you might want to look into Farmers Home Administration mutual self-help housing loans. A group of families who wish to work together to build their own homes may receive financing and technical assistance through the FmHA self-help housing program. Any group of six or more low-income families may qualify providing they cannot individually afford to build modest houses by customary methods.

FmHA or a technical-assistance organization helps the groups to get organized, holds preconstruction meetings that include basic instruction in construction, and hires a construction supervisor, if necessary. The group must agree to work together, attending preconstruction meetings and keeping to assigned work schedules, until all the homes are completed. The FmHA county supervisor determines eligibility and works out repayment terms with each applicant.

VACATION-HOME FINANCING

Don't expect help from FmHA or the other federal agencies if you're looking to finance a vacation—or second—home. Whether you're putting a weekend hideaway together from a kit or hoping to purchase that cottage at the beach, you're going to have to come up with a good deal more of the financing, proportionally, from your own resources, than you would when financing a principal residence.

Financing the purchase of a vacation home is a lot like financing any other home, with a few important differences: the interest rate on a vacation-home mortgage generally is from 1 to 3 percentage points higher than rates quoted for primary homes, the down payment typically ranges from 30 to 50 percent, and the term of the loan may be only 10 or 15 years. In short, you aren't supposed to buy a second home unless you can afford one. Many financial experts would advise that you not buy vacation property unless you are at least prepared to pay cash.

If you buy in the boondocks, you may *have* to pay cash. It's a lot easier to find financing for properties in leisure communities developed by commercial builders, and where resale is likely to be easy, than it is to finance a remote mountain cabin near a trout stream, say. It's also easier to finance properties that can be used year around, rather than for just the one season.

Many families who can't otherwise afford one acquire a second home by renting it out and making it pay its own way for at least a few years—while also building up a solid investment. If you want the full business tax benefits from renting out your vacation home, however, IRS says you cannot make personal use of it more than 14 days per year, or 10 percent of the number of days it is rented, whichever is greater. If you exceed the limit, your business deductions (other than for interest and real-estate taxes, which are always deductible as itemized personal deductions) are limited to an amount that does not exceed the gross rental income.

Under tax law changes made in 1981, the appeal of putting a vacation home to work has been sweetened. Any properties acquired after January 1, 1981, may be depreciated over 15 years. That means, if you qualify for unlimited deductions for renting out your vacation property, you can take an annual deduction for 6.66 percent of the structure's (land cannot be depreciated) market value on the date of its "conversion" to rental use.

Let's say you are depreciating a vacation home that cost $50,000 and that the value placed on the land is $10,000. If you are entitled to take the full deduction for depreciation, you would be able to claim $2,664 per year—6.66 percent of the $40,000 net value. You would also be able to take deductions, as business expenses, for maintenance and repairs, utilities, insurance, management fees, and travel expenses necessary to inspect and prepare the property—even if a "tax loss" results. Manufactured housing acquired as a vacation home after January 1, 1981, and earning itself out, can be depreciated over just 10 years.

You might even find a good buy in a condominium in a resort area that could carry itself until you're in a financial position to afford greater use of the property. In both sun and snow country, it's possible to buy into projects where the management, for a fee, will endeavor to find short- or long-term renters for your unit during periods when you have not reserved it for your personal use. Be careful here, though. Condo bylaws increasingly are barring short-term subleasing.

Glossary

Abstract of Title—A short legal history tracing chronological ownership of the property and noting the existence of any liens or encumbrances of public record bearing on the title.

Acceleration Clause—A common provision of a mortgage stipulating that the outstanding principal balance of the loan becomes immediately due and payable in the event of default or failure by the mortgagor to comply with certain other conditions set forth in the note or mortgage.

Agreement of Sale—A written agreement, signed by the buyer and the seller, setting forth the terms and conditions of the real-estate transaction; a contract.

Amortization—The gradual reduction of the outstanding principal amount of the loan at the time of each payment of interest. With a fixed monthly payment, the portion that goes to pay off the principal increases as the portion required to pay the interest on the principal decreases.

Appraisal—An expert opinion of the current market value of a property supported by a presentation and analysis of relevant data. Also, the process by which this estimate is obtained.

Appraised Value—What the property should sell for in the marketplace, as estimated by a professional appraiser.

Appreciation—An increase in value.

Asking Price—The price, usually flexible, that the owner puts on the property when it is listed with a real-estate broker. A "firm price" would not be subject to bargaining.

Assumption of Mortgage—Taking title to property on which there is an existing mortgage and becoming personally liable for the remaining payments on the loan.

237

Balloon Payment—The larger, final payment that becomes due as a lump sum at the end of the term of a loan that is not fully amortized.

Binder—A receipt for money—or the sum of money itself—paid by the buyer to secure the right to purchase an indicated property on agreed terms.

Blended Mortgage—A new, larger loan issued by the lender at a compromise rate rather than at current market levels to get an old low-yield loan off its books.

Broker—The licensed real-estate professional who assists buyers and sellers of property and earns a commission on such sales.

Building Code—Local ordinance or law regulating the location, design, and construction of buildings. There's usually a structural code plus separate codes covering electrical, plumbing, and heating installations.

Certificate of Eligibility—A certificate issued by the Veterans Administration confirming the loan applicant's entitlement to GI loan benefits.

Chain of Title—The documented history of the conveyances and encumbrances relating to a parcel of real property.

Closing—The formal meeting at which the buyer and seller of a property—or their representatives—conclude the transaction. The closing, also known as the settlement, includes delivery of the deed and mortgage documents, the signing of the note, and disbursement of funds necessary to the sale.

Closing Costs—Sometimes called settlement costs, these costs are in addition to the purchase price of the property. They normally include a loan origination fee, title search and insurance costs, attorney's fees, and transfer-of-ownership charges.

Cloud on Title—An outstanding claim or encumbrance against the title that, even if not valid, could tend to reduce the property's value.

Condominium—A form of ownership of real property—or the unit itself—under which the purchaser receives a marketable title to an individual dwelling unit in a multi-unit complex and an undivided interest in the common areas and facilities that serve the project.

Contract for Deed—A contract for the purchase of real estate under which the buyer takes possession of property on which the seller continues to hold the deed until all or an agreed-upon number of installments have been paid. Known also as a land contract, installment land contract, or a conditional sales contract.

Contract Rate—The interest rate stated in the mortgage contract.

Conventional Mortgage—A mortgage loan that is neither insured by

FHA nor guaranteed by the VA, although it may be privately insured.

Conveyance—The document by which ownership of real property is transferred from one person to another. Contracts and deeds are two forms of conveyances.

Cooperative—A form of ownership under which an apartment building or a group of buildings is owned by the residents and operated for their benefit by their elected board of directors. The resident occupies his dwelling unit under a proprietary lease and owns shares of stock in the corporation. Unlike with a condominium, the resident (tenant shareholder) does not hold a marketable title to his own unit.

Co-signer—A person, in addition to the mortgagor, who signs the promissory note for the loan and assumes equal liability for it.

Counteroffer—A new offer as to price, terms, and conditions, made by the seller or the prospective buyer in reply to a prior, unacceptable offer or response.

Debt Instrument—The promissory note or bond pledging the property as security for the loan and signed by the borrower.

Deed—The legal, written document by which ownership of property is transferred from seller to buyer.

Deed of Trust—The document used in some states in place of a mortgage. For the greater protection of the lender, a third-party trustee holds title to the property as collateral security for payment of the note. The trustee has the power to sell the property and pay the debt to the lender in the event the borrower defaults on the loan.

Default—Failure by the borrower to meet a mortgage payment when due.

Down Payment—The cash difference between the contract price for the property being purchased and the amount covered by the mortgage(s).

Due-on-Sale—A clause included in many mortgage contracts that enables the lender to call the loan (make the balance of the debt immediately payable in full) when the property is sold, thereby denying assumption of the mortgage by a new owner without the lender's permission.

Earnest Money—A sum of money given to the seller or his broker by the potential buyer as a deposit to show that he is serious about buying the property. If the deal goes through, the money is applied against the down payment. If the sale fails, the money may be forfeited, unless contingencies under which the money can be returned are spelled out in the purchase offer.

Effective Rate—The actual rate of return or yield to the lender, reflecting both ordinary interest and the initial fees and charges, including points paid to increase the yield on the loan. Generally, the effective rate is calculated by amortizing the fees and charges over 10 years.

Equity—The difference between what you owe on your home and its current fair market value. What you paid when you bought the property is irrelevant.

Equity Buildup—The owner's increasing equity in an amortized loan through the repayment of the principal. As amortization decreases the debt, the owner's equity in the loan increases.

Escrow—In law, to put a deed or other written agreement in the care of a third party until certain conditions are fulfilled. The deed, for example, is held in escrow until all conditions of the sale, including any prepayments, have been met.

Escrow Payment—The portion of a mortgagor's monthly payment held in trust and accumulated by the lender to pay for property taxes and hazard insurance as they become due. In some states, escrow payments are referred to as impounds.

Estoppel Letter—An instrument provided by the lender when a mortgage is being assigned to another. It spells out the terms and conditions under which the mortgage may be assumed and shows the remaining term, the monthly payment, the remaining balance of the indebtedness, and what funds have been escrowed for payment of insurance and taxes.

Fannie Mae—Nickname for the Federal National Mortgage Association (FNMA), a quasi-governmental corporation created by Congress to guarantee primary lenders a market for their residential mortgages (especially those insured by FHA or guaranteed by the VA) if they choose to sell them, thus making it possible for the lender to replenish his funds for further lending.

Fee Simple—Ownership with unrestricted rights of disposition; the maximum interest a buyer can acquire in real property.

FHA Mortgage—A mortgage issued by a private lender and insured by the Federal Housing Administration, a division of the Department of Housing and Urban Development. By insuring the mortgage holder against loss on the loan, HUD/FHA induces the lender to advance a larger sum to the home buyer than he would normally with conventional financing.

FHLBB—Federal Home Loan Bank Board, the government agency that supervises and regulates the federally chartered savings institutions.

First Mortgage—A loan that creates a primary lien against real property and takes precedence over a junior, or second, mortgage.

FmHA—Farmers Home Administration, a government agency. It gets its name from its original mission as a farm-loan agency, but more broadly today serves rural residents who are unable to obtain loans elsewhere.

Foreclosure—The process under which the lender, in order to satisfy the debt at least partially, deprives the mortgagor of the right to redeem a mortgage on which payments are in serious default.

Freddie Mac—Popular name for the Federal Home Loan Mortgage Corporation (FHLMC), a private corporation authorized by Congress to provide a backup market for conventional mortgage loans. It gets the bulk of the mortgage-resale business of the savings institutions.

GI Loan—Colloquial term given to a mortgage loan made by a lending institution to a qualified veteran and guaranteed by the Veterans Administration under Title 38, United States Code (formerly the Servicemen's Readjustment Act of 1944, as amended).

Ginnie Mae—Popular name for the Government National Mortgage Association (GNMA), which, as a government-owned corporation within HUD, supplies mortgage credit that supports the government's housing objectives. Also, the name for the mortgage-backed securities that originate with FHA-approved mortgagees and are guaranteed as to timely payment of principal and interest by GNMA.

Ground Lease—Contract for the possession and use of land, usually with an option to buy at an agreed price or renew at designated intervals.

Ground Rent—Payment for the possession and use of land in accordance with the terms of a ground lease.

Guaranteed Mortgage—A loan on which the VA, FHA, or FmHA insures the lender against loss should the borrower default.

Hazard Insurance—Insurance to protect against property damage by fire, windstorm, or other natural hazard. To protect their investments, institutional lenders require mortgagors to carry such insurance, with the lender named as an additional assured.

HUD—The Department of Housing and Urban Development, a Cabinet-level agency that is responsible for the implementation and administration of government housing and urban development programs.

Insured Mortgage—A mortgage issued by a bank, savings and loan, or other private lender on which the lender is insured against loss by the VA, FHA, or FmHA.

Joint Tenancy—Ownership of property by two or more persons, with the understanding (confirmed in the deed) that in the event of the death of one owner, the other(s) automatically acquires his or her share of the property under the right of survivorship.

Junior Mortgage—An additional mortgage or lien placed on property already mortgaged, making it subordinate, if claims are presented, to a prior (senior) mortgage.

Late Charge—A charge levied against the borrower when a scheduled payment is not met on time. The formula for assessing late charges is stated in the original debt instrument.

Leasehold—Property, especially land, which is held under conditions that do not carry with them the rights of ownership.

Lessee—A person holding rights to occupy and use specified property under the terms of a lease; tenant.

Lessor—A person who owns property and gives to another (tenant, or lessee) the rights to occupy and use the property for a specified time and consideration; landlord.

Leverage—The effective use of borrowed money, investing the least amount of capital possible in order that it may bring the maximum percentage of return.

Lien—A legal claim recorded against the property of another as security for the repayment of a just debt.

Life Estate—A right to use and occupy property that terminates upon the death of the holder.

Listing—An authorization for the sale of property given to a broker by the owner of the property. An exclusive listing is limited to one broker; a multiple listing is open to more than one real-estate firm.

Loan-to-Value Ratio—The percentage of the appraised value of the property reflected in the amount of the mortgage loan. The higher the loan-to-value ratio, the lower the cash down payment required.

Marketable Title—A title to property that a court would hold to be free of any serious encumbrances or clouds.

Market Value—The highest price that a buyer is freely willing to pay under normal conditions on the open market and the lowest price that a seller, willing but not compelled to sell, will accept.

Maturity—The terminating or due date of a loan.

Money Market—The institutions that put investors' money to work and supply money and credit to borrowers. With interest rates based on the availability of and demand for money, the market fluctuates like any commodity market.

Mortgage—A pledge of real property as security for the payment of a debt, given by the borrower to the lender and recorded in the County Recorder's Office.

Mortgage Commitment—The written notice from the bank or other lender stating that it will advance mortgage funds to the applicant and indicating the amount and terms of the loan. Commitments can be either "firm" or "conditional."

Mortgagee—The bank, savings and loan association, or other lender which loans money to the mortgagor to finance the purchase of real property.

Mortgagor—The homeowner who receives and is obligated to repay a mortgage loan secured by property he has purchased.

Open-end Mortgage—A mortgage that permits the borrower, once the loan principal has been sufficiently paid down, to borrow additional funds, usually up to the original amount, without putting up any other security.

Option—A contract agreement granting a right to purchase property at a future date at a specified price and terms.

Origination Fee—This is sometimes called the initial service fee, and is the institutional lender's time-and-effort charge for establishing and processing a new mortgage loan.

Points—A charge assessed by a lender as a loan origination fee or to sidestep the low interest ceiling permitted on government-backed loans and increase the yield on the investment. Each point is 1 percent of the face amount of the loan.

Prepayment Penalty—A consideration paid to the lender for the privilege of paying all or part of a debt ahead of schedule.

Private Mortgage Insurance (PMI)—Insurance written by a private company and paid for by the mortgagor against loss to the lender occasioned by a mortgage default. It's generally a requirement of a conventional loan when the down payment represents 20 percent or less of the purchase price of the property.

Promissory Note—The written promise to pay, signed by the mortgagor and secured by the mortgage or deed of trust.

Purchase-Money Mortgage—A first or second mortgage granted directly by the seller, as lender, to the buyer of the seller's property.

Purchase Offer—An offer in writing to purchase a property for a specified amount provided certain contingencies, such as the prospective buyer's finding financing at an affordable rate and terms, can be met. A purchase offer is considered a contract when signed by buyer and seller.

Real Property—Land and improvements, including anything of a "permanent" nature, such as houses and trees. Anything else is personal property.

Realtor—A trademarked word used to designate a real-estate broker or an associate who is a member of the National Association of Realtors.

Refinancing—The repayment or restructuring of mortgage indebtedness from the proceeds of a new loan using the same property as security.

Secondary Financing—An additional loan or loans that are subordinate to a first mortgage or first deed of trust.

Secondary Mortgage Market—The resale market for existing loans, which includes pension funds, life insurance companies, and other private investors. Loans that enter the secondary market may go directly from the primary lender to private investors or through one of several government-created secondary-market organizations designed to provide additional liquidity to the mortgage market.

Survey—The determination by a registered land surveyor of the exact boundaries and location of a particular piece of property.

Sweat Equity—Labor or services performed by the purchaser that directly increase the value of real property.

Tenancy in Common—In law, ownership of real property by two or more persons, each of whom is considered as being possessed of a separate, undivided interest. The owners usually are not related and retain the right to resell or will their portion of the property.

Tenant—A person who pays rent under a lease agreement to occupy real property with the consent of the owner.

Title—The document evidencing a person's right to possession of property, normally in the form of a deed including a legal description of the land and the buildings or improvements on it.

Title Insurance—Special insurance that protects lenders against loss of their interest in property due to unforeseen challenges to the title. An owner can protect his interest by purchasing separate coverage.

Title Search—An examination of public records, generally by a title company or an attorney, to verify that the purchaser is acquiring property from the legal owner and that the property has no claims against it.

Usury—Charging more than the legal rate of interest for the use of money. Usury ceilings are established under state law and may vary not only from state to state but depending on the type of loan to which applied.

VA Mortgage—A mortgage issued by a private lender to an eligible veteran of the armed services, with repayment guaranteed in part by the Veterans Administration.

Index

245